The Politics of American Feminism

Gender Conflict in Contemporary Society

James T. Bennett

UNIVERSITY PRESS OF AMERICA,® INC.
Lanham • Boulder • New York • Toronto • Plymouth, UK

Copyright © 2007 by
University Press of America,® Inc.
4501 Forbes Boulevard
Suite 200
Lanham, Maryland 20706
UPA Acquisitions Department (301) 459-3366

Estover Road
Plymouth PL6 7PY
United Kingdom

All rights reserved
Printed in the United States of America
British Library Cataloging in Publication Information Available

Library of Congress Control Number: 2007929720
ISBN-13: 978-0-7618-3783-1 (paperback : alk. paper)
ISBN-10: 0-7618-3783-3 (paperback : alk. paper)

∞™ The paper used in this publication meets the minimum
requirements of American National Standard for Information
Sciences—Permanence of Paper for Printed Library Materials,
ANSI Z39.48—1984

Contents

Acknowledgements   v

1   The Politics of American Feminism   1
2   Boys Will Be (Damned for Being) Boys   21
3   Bad Characters   48
4   Rewriting His-Story, from God to Hillary Rodham Clinton   79
5   Pulling Out Our Tongues: The Assault on Language   103
6   Stealing Our Wallets (and Making Us Apologize for It)   125
7   Guilty Pleasures—or Guilty of Pleasure?
     Balls, Guns, and the Recreational Tyranny of the Male   144

Acknowledgements

I am grateful to many for their assistance with and support of the research and editing of this book. The research would not have been possible without the generous financial support of the Sunmark Foundation and help from the Locke Institute. Research assistance was provided by William Abbott, Anthony Evans, and Brian R. Rooney. I also owe profuse thanks to my editor, Bill Kauffman, for I am indebted to him for significant contributions to this study.

James T. Bennett
George Mason University
Fairfax, Virginia

Chapter One

The Politics of American Feminism

Valerie Solanas, founder and only member of SCUM (Society for Cutting Up Men) and the woman who achieved a brief fame for shooting but not killing Andy Warhol, wrote in her *SCUM Manifesto* (1967): "The male, because of his obsession to compensate for not being female combined with his inability to relate and to feel compassion, has made of the world a shitpile."[1]

Say this for Valerie Solanas: she didn't mince words.

Solanas, who if not for her lousy aim with a gun would have been a convicted murderer, has become, of late, a sort of cult-figure heroine to twenty-first century feminists, even to the point of having a film made about her. She saw men for what they are, and she acted in accordance with her hyperfeminist principles, shooting a man. (Though Andy Warhol was not exactly a testosterone-reeking brute.)

One needn't engage in the self-pitying victimhood-mongering of the Men's Rights movement to see that the American male has become the scapegoat for a multitude of social ills. He is, or so the partisans of Women's Studies departments and their shills in the media and allies in the bureaucracy would have us believe, violent, ignorant, tyrannical, misogynistic, greedy, and a rotten lover. He writes women out of history texts; he manipulates the English language so as to make women invisible (it's his-story, isn't it?); he beats and rapes with impunity, and even if he's technically not guilty of rape or abuse, he's guilty of it in his black heart; he keeps women out of the boardroom and has ingeniously devised an economy wherein a woman earns only 59 cents for every dollar a man makes even though they are performing the same jobs; he has somehow arranged it with the patriarchal dictator known as God that women have the unpleasant task of bearing those nuisances known as children; come on, he won't even watch the WNBA!

Valerie Solanas's response to this male-created mess was to shoot a man. But poor Andy Warhol was only one man, and a strange man at that, and besides, the gun is so . . . masculine. Her sisters in ideology had, and have, a better weapon to use against their enemy, the male of the human species: the State. And from daycare centers to public schools to college textbooks to playing fields to corporate boardrooms, the propaganda campaign against men is succeeding in ways that Valerie Solanas never dreamed of.

Nor did the early feminists—or at least some of them.

Elizabeth Cady Stanton told the New York State legislature in 1854, "We ask no better laws than those you have made for yourselves. We need no other protection than that which your present laws secure to you."[2] The demands of Stanton and the other signatories of the historic 1848 conference on women's rights at Seneca Falls, New York, were largely within the classical liberal tradition. They demanded—or, rather, they faulted men for refusing to permit—the vote for women, clarification of the rights of married women, property rights for females, education for women, jury service for women, and so on.

William O'Neill, author of a classic text on the history of women in America, has written that the earliest American feminists tended to advance their case "largely on the Declaration of Independence and the republican and egalitarian principles advanced since 1776"[3]—principles advanced, one cautiously points out, by men, indeed conceived by men and enshrined, at considerable cost in treasure and even life, by men.

Twenty-first century feminists mouth no such libertarian or equalitarian sentiments. Instead, as the individualist Wendy McElroy has complained, contemporary feminism "has created an orthodoxy, which presents women as victims of patriarchy who must be protected from making wrong choices. Feminism has gone from sexual liberation to sexual correctness, from the politics of equality to the politics of revenge."[4]

In the words of the liberal political scientist Benjamin Barber, feminism as it erupted in the 1960s taught that "marriage was hell, sex was political, coitus was killing, married women were prostitutes, babies were traps, intercourse was rape, love was slavery, families were prisons, and men were enemies."[5]

We are living with the fallout today.

This book is a survey of the social and political manifestations of the antimale movement. Without slipping into lurid melodrama, it is not an overstatement to say that men find ourselves under attack. Our history, our tongue, our Gods, our sports, our guns, our wallets, our character, our sons—men are taking a beating from tendentious scholars, insensate bureaucrats and educrats, and feminists who lust after state power. That lust is real, and it is dangerous. For the transformation of our culture is not to be voluntary. The gutsy and invaluable Christina Hoff Sommers quotes feminist Sandra Lee Bartky (from

Femininity and Domination): "A thorough overhaul of desire is clearly on the feminist agenda: the fantasy that we are overwhelmed by Rhett Butler should be traded in for one in which we seize state power and reeducate him."[6]

This is the language of Lenin, of Stalin, of Hitler, of Mao, of Pol Pot. It is the language of powerlust, of the total state, of tyranny. Those who fantasize on it, whether male or female, are to be pitied—and feared.

The feminist re-educators desire nothing less than the eradication of human nature.

In *Thinking About Women: Sociological Perspectives on Sex and Gender* (Fourth Edition), one of the most popular feminist textbooks used in college Women's Studies courses, author Margaret L. Andersen defines feminism not as certain nineteenth-century feminists would have defined it—that is, as the belief that men and women ought to enjoy equal legal rights—but rather in this way: "Feminism begins with the premise that women's and men's positions in society are the result of social, not natural or biological, factors."[7]

Motherhood is thus, to the feminist, a social, not a biological, construct. The fact—the natural fact, to most of us—that women, not men, conceive children, carry them in their wombs for nine months, give birth, and then nurture them in their infancy and beyond, is a source of preternatural vexation to the feminist. Children are a curse, a burden, an albatross to be flung, if not into the ocean then into the nearest government-subsidized daycare center.

To this way of thinking, there is no behavior naturally associated with maleness or femaleness; rather, we have only "socially learned behaviors and expectations."[8] Boys play with trucks and footballs because we teach them to, not because they are naturally inclined. Girls like pretty colors because we drill such tastes into their brains and for no other reason. As we shall see, this is utter nonsense, a know-nothing negation of everything we have learned about childhood development, but then facts never are allowed to get in the way of an ideologue with an agenda.

The reader of Andersen slogs through 400 pages of turgid prose, learning much about hermaphrodites, Indian hijras (neutered members of a "third sex"), the disease of homophobia, Karl Marx and the social construction of knowledge, and the ways in which American women are oppressed by having names and nicknames that ends in vowels. (Unlike, say, Tommy, Bobby, Billy, Joey, Jimmy, Sammy....)

The harried reader will search in vain for evidence that competing views exist: critics of feminism get scarcely a page, and they are reduced to the straw men of the religious right, who "support prayer in the public schools, preferred tax status for Christian schools, and other policies that would ensure women's subordination to male authority."[9] Just how tax credits for Christian schools would perpetuate the patriarchy is a bit fuzzy, but Andersen does not dwell on the subject. For feminists prefer to deal with critics in that time-honored way of all smug bullies: by ignoring them for as long as possible before caricaturing or mocking them as beneath notice.

Feminists have raised the cult of victimhood to Mount Everest-like heights whilst demonizing men and marginalizing children in a fashion that can only be called rabid. Women, as feminist theologian Mary Daly has written, are "the victims of a planetary caste system whose very existence has been made invisible to us."[10] You can't find a victim much more hopeless and wretched than that: not only is the oppression of women "planetary" in nature, its superstructure is "invisible"! The only response, it might seem, would be to build a spaceship and fly to Venus. Alas, the aerospace engineers are almost all men. Not because men have any kind of aptitude for the work, mind you, but because women who wish to study aerospace engineering have all sorts of obstacles to overcome—for instance. . . . well, um, maybe these obstacles, too, are both planetary and invisible.

Even the nitwit celebrity culture is infected by these attitudes—or should I say especially the nitwit celebrity culture is infected. When pretty boy actor Brad Pitt split from his wife, pretty girl actress Jennifer Aniston, allegedly because Aniston did not want to bear children and Pitt wished her to, the divorce was elevated to a kind of cause célèbre among some of the dimmer members of the sisterhood.

Gossip columnist Liz Smith, writing about "a lunch of free-thinking, feminist-minded, high and mighty females" (whenever someone calls herself "free-thinking," you know she's not) who were exercised over a cartoon in the *New York Times* teasing the estimable Ms. Aniston, quoted one "steamed" chatterer: "This is red-state mentality—women should stay home barefoot and pregnant! Brad is the wounded one. Such junk! Is the *Times* so intimidated by the Bush administration that it lets itself become a party to such anti-feminist propaganda? Is this the twenty-first century, or are we still in the Middle Ages?"[11]

All that just because two mannequins severed the ties that bind?

The peevish lunch lady's real gripe, of course, is with human nature, and in particular that inescapable fact of Mother Nature: women bear children. And the vast majority of women delight in the fact, for it enriches their lives, deepens and extends their family, gives meaning, even, to everyday existence.

But not feminists. Not all go as far as Denise Riley, who argued in *I am That Name* (1988) that "woman" is not a biological category, a fact of nature, but rather a mere "cultural-linguistic convention."[12] There is no such thing as a woman, in this view. (Though men, you may be sure, remain the devil in disguise.) But Riley is a lot closer to the mainstream of contemporary feminism than is the typical American woman.

In *"Feminism Is Not the Story of My Life": How Today's Feminist Elite Has Lost Touch with the Real Concerns of Women*, the late and highly respected historian Elizabeth Fox-Genovese takes up "the problem of why so many women who fiercely value independence refused to identify with feminism."[13] Only about one-third of American women call themselves feminists; less than 20 percent of college women say that they are "definitely" feminist.[14] Why the reluctance to embrace the f-word?

Fox-Genovese's answer, after conducting numerous interviews, was that "they had a sneaking suspicion that feminists do not think that their lives are important."[15]

Indeed, the Denise Rileys would deny that these women even have lives. They are cultural-linguistic inventions, phantoms wearing dresses and bearing children, and the sooner such pathetic women disappear the better off the planet will be.

Several years ago, a pregnant female reporter remarked, "You know, last week I attended the NOW convention and, out of hundreds of sessions, only one focused on children—and it was on lesbian mothers."[16] In its ignoring of mothers *qua* mothers and of children, in its obsession with abortion, its hostility to men, feminism has placed itself in opposition not only to all men and most women but even to Mother Nature.

When Ellen Willis, resident harridan at the *Village Voice*, rejoiced that "the family is a dying beast,"[17] she was (wishfully) speaking for what has become the dominant tendency within Women's Studies departments at the nation's colleges and universities. So it was no wonder that one student at Eastern Washington University complained in 2005 that precious few of her sister students wished to join a feminist organization. "When someone says feminist," she lamented to the *Spokane Spokesman-Review*, "you immediately think of a short-haired lesbian, someone who is out for women's rights to the point that men have no rights. It's a word that isn't greatly respected in some places."[18] And whose fault is that?

It was the National Organization for Women that demanded 24-hour daycare centers and that filed an *amicus curiae* brief in favor of women being subject to the military draft. Government care of children, government conscription of adults: what fitting bookends these policies would be. NOW feminists demand "equality" but in fact promote policies that penalize traditional families or women who prefer to raise their children rather than sit in an office under a fluorescent light from 9 to 5 each day.

Wendy McElroy, while noting that "the abolitionist feminists, who were largely Quaker, believed that the individual must be free to find salvation and perfect the soul," laments that "later feminists wished to take choice out of morality issues. Among the many implications of this key difference was the post-war feminist tendency to look toward the state for purity rather than toward the individual."[19]

Before touring the *outré* precincts of radical feminism and the mainstreams into which this anti-male ideology has been sluiced, let us first consider the political history of American feminism and its proudest achievement, suffrage. The story is about as far from the sanitized, Susan B. Anthony-exalted, Lives-of-the-Saints version fed to our children in public schools as can be imagined.

In William L. O'Neill's standard *Feminism in America: A History*, the author argues that the emphasis of nineteenth- and early twentieth-century feminists on suffrage was a serious, even crippling mistake. For "when the vote was gained it made little difference to the feminine condition. A few women were elected to office, political campaigning became more refined, and the sex lives of candidates were more rigorously policed. The ballot did not materially help women to advance their most urgent causes; even worse, it did not help women to better themselves or improve their status."[20] Yes, women have bettered themselves economically, but "[n]o one has been able to demonstrate that feminism was directly responsible for the tangible gains that were secured."[21]

Contemporary observers, their eyes not bedewed by sentimental stories of brave suffragettes risking abuse at the hands of brutish louts, concurred. Colorado federal judge Moses Hallett remarked at the time that his state's granting of the vote to women had changed little: "the presence of women at the polls has only augmented the total votes; it has worked no radical changes. It has produced no special reforms, and it has had no particularly purifying effect on politics."[22] O'Neill points out that when in 1911 the state legalized racetrack betting, all four distaff members of the legislature voted yes. Good for them—but where was that purifying alembic of female virtue?

Yet even the newly sainted suffragists and feminists whose every doing and saying is lauded in today's elementary school textbooks were, quite often, unpleasant viragoes or even deranged political dominatrices. Victoria Woodhull, the prophetess of free love (and, as is more often emphasized in schoolbooks for preteens, woman suffrage), was no earnest campaigner for the measly vote but rather, as William L. O'Neill writes, "an incredibly dangerous woman by virtue of her peculiar temperament and bizarre views. She not only supported every drastic prescription for society's ills, from spiritualism to Marxism, but represented another outcropping of that vein of free love which underlay Victorian monogamy."[23]

Woodhull is today presented to American schoolchildren as the equal of Washington and Jefferson. Or even as their superior, for Victoria owned no slaves. That her "intense partisanship and unrestrained invective had given many people good reason to hate her"[24] is glossed over. Her critics have become invisible, and if by some longshot they are given a sentence in the textbooks, it is as caricatured members of prudish organizations like the American Purity Alliance.

But then the simplistic and propagandistic depiction of suffragists and American feminists ignores a lot of unpleasant and messy little secrets. Their racism, for one. For instance, suffragist Mary A. Stewart primly lectured the U.S. Senate Judiciary Committee in 1880, "The negroes are a race inferior, you must admit, to your daughters, and yet that race has the ballot."[25] You will search Women's Studies textbooks in vain for this and countless similar quotes. History, it seems, is more fun to clean up than a home.

H.L. Mencken, the brilliantly witty voice of classical liberalism, was not impressed by the fruits of the nineteenth Amendment. He wrote in 1922: "Years ago I predicted that these suffragettes, tired out by victory, would turn out to be idiots. They are now hard at work proving it. Half of them devote themselves to advocating reforms, chiefly of a sexual character, so utterly preposterous that even male politicians and newspaper editors laugh at them; the other half succumb absurdly to the blandishments of the old-time male politicians, and so enroll themselves in the great political parties. A woman who joins one of these parties simply becomes an imitation man, which is to say, a donkey. Thereafter she is nothing but an obscure cog in an ancient and creaking machine, the sole intelligible purpose of which is to maintain a horde of scoundrels in public office."[26]

One might chalk that amusing verdict up, or down, to Mencken's well-advertised (if largely surface) misogyny. He was trying to be funny, and he was picking on the ladies. But Mencken's view was widely shared even by friends of woman suffrage. Writing in the reform journal *Forum* in 1936, John Gordon Ross pointed to the enduring corruption in city governments that had not been mitigated by female suffrage; nor had bureaucracies been made more human, less impersonal. If women had not been made into imitation men, as Mencken jibed, "rather their new responsibilities have brought out only the undesirable traits women have always had, that is, fussiness, primness, bossiness, and the tendency to make unnecessary enemies.... They had not come up with any useful new political ideas. As voters they tended to be excessively moralistic and intolerant."[27]

Which is to say that Emma Goldman, who opposed woman suffrage because she thought that women were busybodies who would use the state to tell other people how to act in their private lives, had been right.[28] Women politicians were ciphers who had not made things better, and too many women voters and politicos were in fact busybodies who sought to tell strangers what to drink, what to smoke, and what to think.

What is most alarming, in retrospect, about the gathering tide of feminism is the way in which these women adulated, idealized, even—dare we say it?—fantasized over the throbbing muscle of The State. Suffragist Elizabeth Boynton Harbert wrote in 1878, "The new truth, electrifying, glorifying American womanhood today, is the discovery that the State is but the larger family."29

No one pined for the firm hand of the State more than the truly egregious Alice Paul.

Paul—"an absolute fanatic," in the words of one historian sympathetic to feminism, who was "incapable of recognizing any merits in those who resisted her"30—is today lionized as the founder and for decades the indefatigable engine propelling the Woman's Party.

She formed the Woman's Party, nee the Congressional Union, in 1913, after she had been booted from the National American Woman Suffrage Association. Marked by fierce, humorless dogmatism, Paul's Woman's Party singlemindedly pursued the ratification of an Equal Rights Amendment to the U.S. Constitution. William O'Neill writes that "the Woman's party became a feminist equivalent of the Socialist Labor party, doctrinally frozen, sealed off from reality, forever anticipating historical changes that would make the old ways relevant again."31

Those "old ways" were, ideologically, perhaps even more noxious than the atrophied doctrines of the Socialist Labor Party. For Alice Paul believed that "the State [should] assume entire responsibility for the maintenance and education of children."32

Yes, entire responsibility. Not even the Bolsheviks went that far. Paul, who despised men and children with a wrath positively terrifying in its comprehensiveness, hated the fact that women were designed biologically to bear and nurture children. She thought that breasts, uteruses, and suchlike organs and appendages crippled women, retarded them economically, physically, and emotionally. Since not much could be done about these irrefrangible facts of physiology in those pre-transsexual days, Paul called on the State—which she worshipped with all the cringing lust of a masochist for a dominatrix—to take children from parents and raise them in impersonal institutions where such atavisms as mother-love and familial affection would be drained from them.

To Alice Paul, *Brave New World*, *1984*, and *Fahrenheit 451* were not dystopian horror stories—they were anti-family utopias that gave a hopeful glimpse of a world beyond motherhood, beyond breast-feeding, beyond marriage. They represented the negation of motherhood; they represented, to Alice Paul, heaven on earth.

Paul may have been an extreme example of the man-hating feminist ideologue, but she was typical in being unmarried, childless, and hostile to those women who in their blindness and misfortune had chanced on a penis and not fled from the demon in horror.

Perhaps the most prophetic, most quoted, most influential, and most deeply disturbed of early twentieth-century feminists was Charlotte Perkins Gilman.

Gilman, who has been twisted into an admirably moderate and thoughtful intellectual by the regnant political correctness, in fact despised the family. All families, yes, but also her own family, for as the college freshpersons who are assigned Gilman are never told by their instructors, she "resolved [the conflict between family and career] by divorcing an entirely satisfactory husband and giving up an agreeable child."[33] She simply left them, with as little emotion as one might return a rental car to the Hertz lot. They were in her way; they were an inconvenience—children and even husbands do have a way of obtruding themselves into one's daily life—and so she dumped them for her books and her fame.

We might consider Gilman an object of pity. Her own father had deserted his family in her infancy, and "[h]er mother deliberately withheld any show of affection to her children . . . in order to make them emotionally self-sufficient."[34] Charlotte re-enacted this tragedy, dumping her painter husband Charles Walter Stetson and giving him their daughter to raise.

So perhaps it is not so very strange that Charlotte Perkins Gilman titled her influential, even prescient, volume with the name of that institution she most feared and loathed: *The Home* (1903).

Gilman forces the game reader to first wade through an epigraph in the form of a long poem in which "Home" metamorphoses from a sleepy, torpid lair of oppression into an enchanting land of possibilities. "The World! The World is crying! Hear its needs!"[35] exclaims Gilman in high poetic mode. *The Home*, you see, becomes palatable to Gilman when it is redefined to be coterminous with the boundaries of the very Earth itself:

"Home was the World—the World was Home to me!"

This discovery gives the author license to interfere in the affairs of every single person residing from the Arctic to the Amazon. After all, home is the world! Chung Hee, pick up those socks! Liesel, take out the garbage! Vladimir, knock off that racket!

Similarly, Woman was no longer a pair of suckling breasts and a house cleaner:

> So when the great word "Mother!" rang once more,
> I saw at last its meaning and its place;
> Not the blind passion of the brooding past,
> But Mother—the World's Mother—come at last,

> To love as she had never loved before—
> To feed and guard and teach the human race.[36]

Gilman had failed in her role as mother to the child she had borne. She had in fact abandoned her family, ran out on them as if they were so many dust bunnies whose care was beneath a woman of her intellect and aspiration. But the failed mother of a real if heartbroken family was to receive a promotion: to Mother of the World! She would "feed and guard and teach the human race," and her students—that is, the benighted members of that race, male and female—had best learn the lessons well. Mrs. Gilman was not an indulgent teacher.

In her influential tome *The Home*, Gilman proposed to reform, to purify, to redeem this venerable institution by stripping it of all its functions. She asks "Why is it more sacred to make a coat at home than to buy it of a tailor, to kill a cow at home than to buy it of a butcher, to cook a pie at home than to buy it of a baker, or to teach a child at home than to have it taught by a teacher"? The cult of the home is the reason why, she answers, and so she proposes that Americans—that all humans everywhere in the world, for recall that her home is the world—stop doing things for themselves and start relying on experts. These experts should be certified and credentialed, for parents are ignorant clods, incapable of feeding their children proper food, teaching them math, or swaddling them in warm and comfortable clothing. The home should be stripped of all functions and serve only as "a place to rest."[37]

Gilman envisions "the pouring streams of social progress"[38] washing over the home, flooding it and dumping its refuse—that is, mothers and fathers and children—onto higher ground. Once liberated from the home, these guinea pigs, er, citizens, can be subjected to the "progressive socialization of humanity."[39] This will take place in the institutions which the modern state has constructed: first among them the schoolhouse, which "represents a larger love, a higher function,"[40] than the old-fashioned home.

After all, "parents idealise their children; and the children . . . idealise the parents."[41] The filial relationship is not based on a cold, hard, assessment of the strengths and weaknesses of Mom and Pop and Junior and Sissy. Raised in such an atmosphere of love and affection—at least in homes not rent by the likes of Ms. Gilman—children grow up with what latter-day psychologists like to call "self-esteem." This is dangerous, in Gilman's eyes: children's talents are overrated by their parents; presumably the offspring of ethnic parents and slum-dwellers and other rabble may grow up not knowing their places. Thus the child must be transferred from the loving environment of the home into the impersonal confines of the public school before any more damage is done.

Lest we think that the state can wait until the child is of kindergarten age before getting him or her in its solicitous grasp, Gilman rejoices that the "larger love, the broader knowledge, of doctor, nurse, and teacher are penetrating the innermost fortress of home"[42] to bring wisdom even to infants. "A newborn baby leads a far happier, healthier, more peaceful existence in the hands of the good trained nurse, than it does"[43] in the care of its mother, argues Gilman without bothering to adduce a shred of evidence for this extraordinary claim. She estimates that it ought to be cared for by this nurse for five years — at which point the child is transferred to the school.

A "mother's love" and a "mother's care" Gilman ridicules; mothers must "conside[r] their enormous responsibilities as a class"[44] and place their babies in vast child-care centers — kennels for children, really — where experts, trained and certified, will ensure they receive proper nutrition, the correct measure of discipline, appropriate education — everything but love. But then Gilman, who could not love even the child she bore, knew love to be a slippery and unreliable commodity, hardly fit for the forward-thinking progressive of the early twentieth century.

Gilman had opinions on everything, and those opinions always and in every case called for more power for the collective, less for the individual and the family. People must be fed in communal eateries, for those who rely on Mom's Home Cooking end up with dyspepsia, bad teeth, and ailments of the bowel susceptible to no known cure. Food must be purchased by "trained buyers," for "the private purchase and preparation of food"[45] means that food is cooked by "unlearned amateurs"[46] (which is to say mothers) and eaten by families within private homes rather than prepared by "scientific"[47] cooks and consumed in vast communal kitchens. Eighty-one years early, the calendar in Ms. Gilman's kitchen read 1984.

It goes without saying that the state — the holy mother the state — will play an outsized role in the provision of these services. Gilman's model is the armed forces, wherein men act together for a common goal (that it is the mass killing of others she decorously fails to note) and sacrifice their lives "to the public service without hesitation."[48] If valorous soldiers can give up their lives, surely men and women can give up their children. After all, "neither self nor family must stand for a moment against the public service."[49]

"The mother, by virtue of being a mother, is supposed to know just what is right for her children,"[50] she scoffs. One doubts that abandonment was "right" for Gilman's family, so she may have a point in some instances, but Gilman's larger argument is that parents must be stripped of the power to direct the upbringing of their children. Rather, the tykes are to be turned over to professional social workers, trained teachers in progressive schools, and the courts and bureaucracy of the *Brave New World*. After all, that "the care and education of children have developed at all is due to the intelligent efforts of doctors, nurses, teachers, and such few parents as chose to exercise their human brains instead of their brute instincts."[51]

Gilman is not without her misogynistic side. She disparages the female contribution to cooking and credits men for having "gradually improved the vessels, utensils, and materials of the home food supply."[52] The woman, after all, is not a "trained expert,"[53] and Gilman believes that only trained experts should perform any function more complicated than tying one's shoes.

Women are also cowards, she writes, weak and helpless creatures reduced to quavering idiots by the sight of a mouse. "This home-bred cowardice," she states, is weakening her sex every bit as much as "black mothers must alter the complexion of a race."[54] (Gilman, like so many of the feminists of her age, was a pretty frank and appalling racist.)

Curiously, she denigrates "the aesthetic sense of woman," which "has never interfered with her acceptance of ugliness, if ugliness were the fashion."[55] The great paintings, architecture, furniture, and embroideries of the world were made by men, she points out, while women cherish all manner of hackneyed prose and gewgaws. Yet we should not be surprised by Gilman's contempt for common women; after all, the home has been largely their dominion, and there is no entity she execrates quite so loudly as the home.

And as for mothers? Gilman lets her rip: "Who, in the name of all common sense, raises our huge and growing crop of idiots, imbeciles, cripples, defectives, and degenerates, the vicious and the criminal; as well as all the vast mass of slow-minded, prejudiced, ordinary people who clog the wheels of progress? Are the mothers to be credited with all that is good and the fathers with all that is bad?"[56]

This is the voice of a proto-Nazi, a eugenicist, a despiser of the "weak," a worshipper of the state triumphant. This is the voice of the heroine of feminism: the woman who ranks with Susan B. Anthony as the most revered American feminist of the early twentieth century. (Say this, though, for Gilman: when she remarks, "The figure of the man is far and away more beautiful than that of the woman,"[57] she is setting herself apart from the, ah, typical sexual proclivities of her feminist sisters.)

"Children are at last emerging from the very lowest grade of private ownership [that is, they are "owned" by their parents] into the safe, broad level of common citizenship. That which no million separate families could give their millions of separate children, the state can give, and does,"[58] writes Gilman in a chilling passage. She was no seer; she could not have anticipated the horrors of "common citizenship" that would ravage Russia, China, Germany, Cambodia, and other nations in which the feminist dream of state child-rearing would be practiced. But her kinderphobia, her detestation of the role of the parent, her execration of home, find echo and expansion in the writings of feminists in the century since Charlotte Perkins Gilman shared her horrific visions with the unenlightened.

Our present-day Gilmans, like the original article, fall to their knees when that strapping hulk known as The State walks into the room. Professor of Social Justice and Democracy (huh?) Judy Rebick of Canada's Ryerson University complains that while "everyone accepts that the state has a responsibility" for five-year-olds (no, they don't, Ms. Ryerson), "everyone" is more reluctant to turn infants over to the state, since a good chunk of "everyone" retains the outdated belief "that women should care for small children."

Those who take issue with this maven of social justice operate under a delusion, for "it is folly to think we can turn the clock back."[59] Just why we should trust Professor Rebick to keep time for all of us is a matter she does not address.

Ultimately, the quarrel of the Rebicks is with biology: with God or nature or evolution, take your pick. The child is conceived within the woman, gestates for nine months within the woman, is borne in painful labor by the woman, wishes to suckle at the woman's breast, and no matter how many *Brave New World*-ish Child Care Centres are created, the child still desires its mommy. No amount of social engineering can change that.

Although communism has been thrown on the ash heap of his-story, many a feminist has crawled out of the husk of its remains and resumed the fight, albeit under a different banner. For instance, in 2005 Gudrun Schyman, the leader of Sweden's confessedly communist Left Party, launched a new feminist party whose central issue—whose only issue, really—is "gender equality." Among her partners in this enterprise is Maria-Pia Boethius, author of the 2002 polemic "The Anti-Patriarchal Manifesto," essential night-time reading for the scrupulously sexual egalitarian Swede.

As a communist member of the Swedish Parliament, Schyman was perhaps best known for her proposal that the state should subsidize the cost of tampons and sanitary napkins for women. She also urged that men be taxed, *qua* men, to pay for domestic violence programs. (In the compliant mass media, Schyman's crazed anti-male platform was translated into "equal pay and ending violence against women.")[60]

That a communist slides so easily into the chairpersynship of a radical women's party ought not to surprise us: the basic philosophy undergirding each movement is that the State ought to remold, ruthlessly if necessary, basic economic, familial, and private associations. Somewhat hearteningly, 27 percent of Swedish women said they would consider voting for Schyman's party—which means that 73 percent would not.[61] Even in the land of rigorous gender equality, women still insist on paying for their own tampons. Perhaps all is not lost after all.

If female American politicians have yet to take up the cause of state-subsidized tampons, neither have they behaved on a higher moral plane from male legislators. Political scientist Sue Thomas, in *How Women Legislate*, sought to "discover what difference, if any, women's presence has made to the political process or to legislation."[62]

Focusing on female state legislators, Thomas found that whereas women in the early 1970s "held themselves apart from the process and operated on its margins," by the late 1980s they had "joined in the fray and adapted to ongoing norms and procedures."[63] They met with lobbyists, they made bargains, they traded votes, they trolled for PAC money—in other words, they behaved like male legislators. Which is not a matter of great pride.

Yet if they lowered themselves into the nitty-gritty of politics just like the men, they did not vote like them. Women legislators "were consistently more liberal than their male counterparts, more attitudinally supportive of women's issues and social welfare issues."[64] They also tended to gravitate to "women's committees," whence tax money was spent without much regard to how much money was coming in, as opposed to revenue committees, or "men's committees."

Political scientists have found that a similar male-female disjunction exists in the U.S. House of Representatives. And as the feminist t-shirt (never wet) tells us, a woman's place is in the House, as well as the Senate. That women might be better off avoiding the House, Senate, and political power altogether seems never to enter the discussion. If politics is a dirty business, why should women wish to muck themselves up in it? Mightn't they instead seek to reduce the influence of politics on our everyday lives? Mightn't they become, politically, a kind of libertarian lobby that would cleanse and purify our country by vastly shrinking the role that dirty politicians play in American life? Sure. Dream on.

Christine L. Day, Charles D. Hadley, and Megan Duffy Brown of the University of New Orleans, writing in *Social Science Quarterly* on "Gender, Feminism, and Partisanship Among Women's PAC Contributors," noted that in numerous surveys, "women politicians and activists were found quite consistently more liberal than their male counterparts on a wide variety of issues ranging from social welfare and government regulation to defense, crime and punishment, and women's rights."[65] Interestingly, the gender gap is far wider between female and male elites than between females and males in the rank and file; indeed, some studies have found that women are less likely to support legalized abortion than men.

Day, Hadley, and Brown speculate that the greater presence of women within "redistributive occupations" such as nursing, child care, social work, of the elderly may account for the gender gap. A cynic might say that since women disproportionately benefit from an interventionist state they are simply voting their purses, though feminist philosophers such as Carol Gilligan argue that female morality places an emphasis on caring and cooperation (not to mention coercion), while male morality is focused on liberty and justice.

In the wake of the campaign-finance reforms of the 1970s, for-women-only political action committees (PACs) arose from the fetid swamp of politics. They bore names like EMILY's List (Early Money Is Like Yeast—it makes the dough rise) and WISH List (Women In the Senate and House). Though EMILY was Democratic and WISH Republican, both PACs placed legalized abortion at the cynosure of their concerns. They were prochoice, and insistently so, and before the Equal Rights Amendment was tossed onto the slagheap of history, they milked that, too, for all it was worth. Which was a considerable penny: from 1977 to 1982, the years when the ERA made its last and dying stand, NOW expanded its annual budget from $700,000 to $8.3 million and its list of members from 55,000 to 210,000.[66]

Alice Paul's dream of inserting an Equal Rights Amendment into the U.S. Constitution was almost realized—the less sensitive would say "aborted"—in the 1970s. After numerous false starts, both houses of Congress easily approved the ERA and sent it to the states for ratification in 1972. The proposed amendment read, "Equality of rights under the law shall not be denied or abridged by the United States or any state on account of sex."

Thirty-five of the necessary 38 states ratified the ERA until, in the bitter words of Betty Friedan, "it bogged down in hysterical claims that the amendment would eliminate privacy in bathrooms, encourage homosexual marriage, put women in the trenches and deprive housewives of their husbands' support."[67]

These hysterical claims, we now see with the benefit of three decades' hindsight, were spot-on, with the possible exception of unisex public bathrooms. (Though these are common in colleges and are coming to a city hall near you.) And who, really, other than the upper-middle-class academic feminists whose knowledge of the country in which they live extends no further than the no-smoking sign on the faculty lounge wall, was surprised when the Pauline Equal Rights Amendment met with serious opposition in Middle America?

NOW, NARAL (the National Abortion Rights Action League), and other battleships of establishment feminism have also exploited the issue of abortion—or what we are now supposed to call "choice," since the A-word has been banished to linguistic Coventry by Democratic pollsters.

People of goodwill can and do disagree on the extent to which abortion should be legal. Most Americans take a middle ground between prohibition and subsidization. The absolutist character of the two major parties' abortion platforms does not capture the views of their adherents; as Susan Page noted in *USA Today*, "Six in 10 Democrats would outlaw abortion in some cases; nearly seven in 10 Republicans would allow abortion in some cases."[68]

These nuanced views go out the window when feminists enter the room. Abortion, to the more fervid among them, is no longer a disagreeable option for desperate women, or even a valid if morally complicated method of birth control—no, it is a secular sacrament, an act to be celebrated. Jennifer Baumgardner, who describes herself as a "professional feminist"—hey, it beats working—sells t-shirts which read "I had an abortion."

She wears the shirt with pride, without shame or remorse. Women don the shirt "to destigmatize"[69] abortion, in the estimation of Jane Bovard of Fargo, North Dakota, who is president of something called the National Coalition of Abortion Providers. Bovard cheerfully reports wearing the t-shirt when her staff recesses for happy hour at a local establishment. If this sounds gruesome to you then you must hate women and want to keep them all barefoot, pregnant, and servile. You Red Stater, you!

Betty Friedan asked in 1981, "Who is really for abortion? That is like being for mastectomy. I, myself, am for life. I am for the choice to have children, which those who would ban access to safe, legal, medical abortion endanger."[70] Friedan's equivocation, her uneasiness with the idea of being "for abortion," seems prissy and old-fashioned to today's vanguard feminists, for whom an abortion is no more disturbing than the removal of a decayed tooth.

We have reached a nadir, it seems, in which, according to the Canadian feminist Janice Kennedy writing in the *Ottawa Citizen*, a "predictable, doctrinaire, and, worst of all, intransigent. . . . Official Feminism can not accept that there might be feminists who have difficulty with an unrestricted prochoice position, or admit that abortion might have about it an element of sadness or failure, let alone tragedy."[71] Feminists are willing to accept the vacuity of the redoubtable Mary Daly, whom we shall meet in more rollicking depth later, and who in 1972 told a Catholic (or catholic, with a small-c, as she would insist) audience that "One hundred percent of the bishops who oppose the repeal of anti-abortion laws are men and one hundred percent of the people who have abortions are women."[72]

Ooh—penetrating analysis!

Until 2005, when yet another unexpected defeat of a by-the-book prochoice presidential candidate caused party panjandrums to reassess their position, the Democratic National Committee refused even to link to Democrats for Life, an organization that includes Democratic members of Congress. In the 1992 Democratic convention, popular Pennsylvania Governor Bob Casey was denied a platform to speak—a choice example of feminists' contempt for even the most elementary level of a free exchange of ideas.

"The dominant viewpoint of mainstream feminism is political liberalism (in the modern sense of that term) with a strong socialist influence"[73] writes Wendy McElroy, but that mainstream has drifted leftward even as the country has, at least in some ways, moved to the right. Liberalism, whatever one may think of it, never singled out men as the enemy of civilization, and even among socialists, there were traditions of free speech and equality of the sexes. The idea of a war between men and women would have struck most liberals or socialists of the twentieth century as ridiculous.

But times do change. The war, which is sometimes waged explicitly and sometimes insidiously, is here. And it is being fought in a one-sided manner. Philosopher and critic of feminism Christina Hoff Sommers writes, "Real-life men have no war offices, no situation rooms, no battle plans against women. There is no radical militant wing of a masculinist movement. To the extent one can speak at all of a gender war, it is the New Feminists themselves who are waging it."[74]

In 1838, the abolitionist feminist Sarah Grimke declared, "I ask no favors for my sex. I surrender not our claim to equality. All I ask of our brethren is that they will take their feet off our necks, and permit us to stand upright on the ground which God has designed us to occupy."[75]

Good for you, Sarah Grimke. But where are your descendants? Our feet have been off your necks for some time now. Yet as we shall see, the modern American male has Birkenstock marks on his neck, his rear end in a sling, his reputation in tatters, his good name in the mud, and his private parts in a wringer. The American Male has become the prime target in a war on liberty, justice, and human nature.

NOTES

1. Mary Daly, *Outercourse: The Bedazzling Voyage* (San Francisco: HarperSanFrancisco, 1992), 344. Perhaps applying Solanasian principles in multicultural fashion, the anti-Russian rebels in Chechnya have used, almost exclusively, female suicide-terrrorists. Chechen women carried the bombs that exploded two Russian airliners in midflight in the summer of 2004. These Black Widows, as they are called, constituted about half of the terrorist squad that assaulted a Moscow theater two years earlier. Palestinian terrorists have also been, increasingly, drawn from the veiled sex. Muslim radicals may not want them to drive cars, but women make powerful symbols as suicide bombers. See Ben Macintyre, "Women Are Deadlier Than the Male in the Propaganda War," *The* (London) *Times*, September 11, 2004, 26.

2. Christina Hoff Sommers, *Who Stole Feminism? How Women Have Betrayed Women* (New York: Simon & Schuster, 1994), 22.

3. William L. O'Neill, *Feminism in America: A History*, Second Revised Edition (New Brunswick, NJ: Transaction, 1989), 14.

4. Wendy McElroy, *Sexual Correctness: The Gender-Feminist Attack on Women* (Jefferson, NC: McFarland & Co., 2001), 3.

5. Jonathan Yardley, "Different But Equal: The 3rd State of the Women's Revolution," *Washington Post*, July 4, 1983, B1.

6. Sommers, *Who Stole Feminism?*, 257.

7. Margaret L. Andersen, *Thinking About Women: Sociological Perspectives on Sex and Gender*, Fourth Edition (Boston: Allyn and Bacon, 1997), 8.

8. Andersen, *Thinking About Women*, 20.

9. Andersen, *Thinking About Women*, 241.

10. Mary Daly, *Beyond God the Father: Toward a Philosophy of Women's Liberation* (Boston: Beacon, 1985/1973), 132.

11. Liz Smith, "Unveiling Details on 'The Dress,'" *Newsday*, January 21, 2005, A13.

12. Barbara Taylor, New Internationalist, <www.newint.org/issue247/old.htm> (Sept. 1993).

13. Elizabeth Fox-Genovese, *"Feminism Is Not the Story of My Life": How Today's Feminist Elite Has Lost Touch with the Real Concerns of Women* (New York: Doubleday, 1996), 2.

14. Fox-Genovese, *"Feminism Is Not the Story of My Life"*, 32.

15. Fox-Genovese, *"Feminism Is Not the Story of My Life"*, 2.

16. Fox-Genovese, *"Feminism Is Not the Story of My Life"*, 1.

17. Fox-Genovese, *"Feminism Is Not the Story of My Life"*, 30.

18. Jamie Tobias Neely, "'Feminist' Retreat: For Mostly Image Reasons, College-Age Women Haven't Embraced the 'F' Word Like Their Older Counterparts," *Spokane Spokesman-Review*, March 6, 2005, F1.

19. Wendy McElroy, ed., *Freedom, Feminism, and the State* (Washington, DC: Cato Institute, 1982), 12–13.

20. O'Neill, *Feminism in America*, xxi.

21. O'Neill, *Feminism in America*, xxii.

22. O'Neill, *Feminism in America*, 61.

23. O'Neill, *Feminism in America*, 25.

24. O'Neill, *Feminism in America*, 26.

25. O'Neill, *Feminism in America*, 70.

26. H.L. Mencken, *In Defense of Women* (New York: Time, 1950/1922), 111.

27. O'Neill, *Feminism in America*, 271.

28. Emma Goldman, "Woman Suffrage," *Red Emma Speaks*, ed. Alix Kates Shulman (New York: Schocken Books, 1983), 191–92.

29. O'Neill, *Feminism in America*, 34.

30. O'Neill, *Feminism in America*, 127–28.

31. O'Neill, *Feminism in America*, 129.

32. *Congressional Record*, May 31, 1924, 9972.

33. O'Neill, *Feminism in America*, 38.

34. O'Neill, *Feminism in America*, 130.

35. Charlotte Perkins Gilman, *The Home* (New York: McClure, Phillips & Co., 1903), ix.
36. Gilman, *The Home*, xi.
37. Gilman, *The Home*, 292.
38. Gilman, *The Home*, 36.
39. Gilman, *The Home*, 39.
40. Gilman, *The Home*, 49.
41. Gilman, *The Home*, 173.
42. Gilman, *The Home*, 237.
43. Gilman, *The Home*, 340.
44. Gilman, *The Home*, 242.
45. Gilman, *The Home*, 131.
46. Gilman, *The Home*, 134.
47. Gilman, *The Home*, 137.
48. Gilman, *The Home*, 303.
49. Gilman, *The Home*, 308.
50. Gilman, *The Home*, 55.
51. Gilman, *The Home*, 60.
52. Gilman, *The Home*, 128.
53. Gilman, *The Home*, 130.
54. Gilman, *The Home*, 170.
55. Gilman, *The Home*, 55.
56. Gilman, *The Home*, 59.
57. Gilman, *The Home*, 217.
58. Gilman, *The Home*, 335.
59. Trish Crawford, "25 Years of Women Making Progress," *Toronto Star*, September 27, 2004, E1.
60. "Swedish Feminists Take Struggle to Halls of Power," *The Star*, <www.thestar.co.za/general> (9 March 9 2005).
61. "Feminists Poised to Create Own Political Party in Sweden," *Agence France Presse*, March 8, 2005.
62. Sue Thomas, *How Women Legislate* (New York: Oxford University Press, 1994), 4.
63. Thomas, *How Women Legislate*, 53.
64. Thomas, *How Women Legislate*, 83.
65. Christine L. Day, Charles D. Hadley, and Megan Duffy Brown, "Gender, Feminism, and Partisanship Among Women's PAC Contributors," *Social Science Quarterly* 82, no. 4 (December 2001): 689.
66. O'Neill, *Feminism in America*, 318. Mary Ann Mason, author of *The Equality Trap* and a family law practitioner with a social feminist bent, argues that the "ERA campaign drained millions of dollars and millions of working hours into the attempt to pass an amendment which would have made little or no change in the fundamental conditions of women's lives." She points out that Californians have lived under a state equal rights amendment since 1964, with no apparent paradise resulting. Mary Ann Mason, *The Equality Trap* (New Brunswick, NJ: Transaction, 2002/1988), 26.

67. Betty Friedan, "Feminism's Next Step," *New York Times Magazine*, July 5, 1981, 14.
68. Susan Page, "The Changing Politics of Abortion," *USA Today*, May 2, 2005, 1A.
69. Laura Barcella, "The A-Word," <Salon.com> (20 September 2004).
70. Friedan, "Feminism's Next Step," *New York Times Magazine*.
71. Janice Kennedy, "The Death of Official Feminism: How a Call to Arms Has Morphed into a Revolution of Stifled Yawns," *Ottawa Citizen*, February 20, 2005, C2.
72. Daly, *Outercourse*, 142.
73. McElroy, *Freedom, Feminism, and the State*, 20.
74. Sommers, *Who Stole Feminism?*, 45.
75. McElroy, *Freedom, Feminism, and the State*, 77.

Chapter Two

Boys Will Be (Damned for Being) Boys

The condition of being a boy has been pathologized. It is, we may say with only mild overstatement, well on the way to being criminalized. In modern America, boys are guilty until proven innocent—and given that the charge on which they are being arraigned is maleness, a guilty verdict is foreordained.

"It's a bad time to be a boy in America,"[1] flatly states philosopher Christina Hoff Sommers in her brave book *The War Against Boys: How Misguided Feminism Is Harming Our Young Men*. Public schools have undertaken an assault on boyness the likes of which have never been seen this side of Andrea Dworkin's reveries. Elementary school students are forced into such productions as *William's Doll*, based on the feminist children's book. William, it seems, is a first-class sissy who wants a dolly to hug and kiss and hold in his arms. Dad, a typical Cro-Magnon American male, tries to interest William in ball games and trains. No go. William wants his doll. So grandmother, who understands the inner William in a way that insensate Pop never can, buys William "a baby doll with curly eyelashes, and a long white dress with a bonnet."[2] The sissy loves it. The end.

De-masculinizing boys, punishing "boyish" behavior and rewarding sissyish acts, is a prime goal of the social engineering feminists of the education bureaucracy. Two of their leading lights, William Pollack, who directs something called the Center for Men at McLean Hospital (the psychiatric teaching facility connected with Harvard Medical School), and Ronald F. Levant, a cofounder of the ominously named Society for the Psychological Study of Men and Masculinity, sigh: "As we raise the next generation, the boys who will become men in the twenty-first century, we look forward to a time when these boys will be able to safely stay in the 'doll corner' as long as they wish, without being taunted...."[3] Oh, brother.

Those who believe that gender is merely a social construct are using the public schools to promote a vision of a world in which boys play with dolls (but not—not on your life!—GI Joe) and girls disdain dolls to play sports—albeit sports in which no score is kept, no winners or losers declared, and the specter of the demoniac Competition never darkens the door.

Christina Hoff Sommers calmly delivers the news to the feminist ideologues: "The natural gender differences between men and women mean we cannot hope to get statistical male-female parity of competence and aptitude in all fields. The same seems true of preferences: there will always be far more women than men who want to stay home with children; there will always be more women than men who want to be kindergarten teachers rather than helicopter mechanics. Boys will always be less interested than girls in dollhouses."[4] Yes, there are Williams, and they should be treated with love and understanding and courtesy, but unless human nature is far more malleable in the future than it has been in the past, they will always be exceptions.

When boys are treated as boys by wise schoolmarms and masters, the pedagogues are accused of enabling "hegemonic masculinist practices."[5] Boys are potential rapists, savages-in-training, while females, in Mary Daly's phrase, are the "touchable" caste, "those condemned by phallocrats to be touched—physically, emotionally, intellectually, spiritually—by those in possession of a penis."[6]

Even dodge ball, that most venerable of gym class games, is said to privilege budding phallocrats. Those with penises seem to do better at dodge ball than do those without, and so since the 1980s numerous school districts across the land of Audie Murphy and Joe Louis and Clint Eastwood have banned dodge ball. It encourages male aggression. Tag and the throwing of snowballs have also been banned in certain exquisitely sensitive school districts.

A substantial number of psychologists believe that discouraging healthy outlets for normal male aggression is unhealthy. Boys need to throw balls, to compete, to test themselves against others in aggressive games. Dodge ball builds men, not criminals.

"According to psychologist and criminologist Edward McGargee," writes Dr. Leonard Sax, "three-quarters of all murders are committed not by overtly aggressive people, but by quiet, seemingly well-behaved men who have never found a safe or appropriate outlet for their aggression."[7] Oh, the lives that a good game of dodge ball might have saved....

For as long as there have been have been frogs with which to make squeamish girls squeal, boys have teased girls on the school playground. And as anyone who has ever actually attended elementary school knows, the teasing goes both ways. In our age, however, that teasing has been upgraded to the slightly more serious category of terrorism.

When the press reported that some boys in Montana elementary schools referred to Friday as "Flip-Up Day," meaning that they flipped up the skirts of their classmates, Nan Stein, located far from the rocky wilds of the Big Sky State at the Wellesley College Center for Research on Women, called the flip-ups "gendered terrorism."[8] That she was not laughed out of Wellesley speaks volumes about that school, though to be fair, Wellesley is not known as a campus of raucous laughter. Those boys in Montana should have been punished for their crude behavior and that ought to have been that. But that is never that in these strange days. A story old as time goes out over the wire services and naughty boys are denounced at "terrorists" by feminist hysterics. Good grief.

When schools aren't cracking down on boys for the crime of boyhood, they are flunking them out of class whilst the special-interest lobbies wail—not about how boys are ill-served by public education, but about how girls are getting the short end of the educational stick!

A primary culprit is the snobbishly named anachronism called the American Association of University Women, or AAUW, and its tendentious research has been refuted with devastating effectiveness by Christine Hoff Sommers. In 1991, the AAUW sponsored an "Initiative for Educational Equity" which included a much-ballyhooed and much-misinterpeted poll of "self-esteem" in children between the ages of nine and fifteen. The sample consisted of 3,000 children, and a central finding was that "The number of boys who aspire to glamorous occupations (rock star, sports star) is greater than that of young women at every stage of adolescence, creating a kind of 'glamour gap.'"[9]

The fatuity of this "finding" boggles the mind. Is the fact that 12-year-old boys are likelier than 12-year-old girls to nurse fantasies of playing in the NFL or playing guitar on MTV really a sign of healthy self-esteem? Or does it suggest that boys are easier prey for delusional pop culture dreams?

An accompanying AAUW documentary featured Dr. David Sadker of American University bleating "If the cure for cancer is in the mind of a girl, there is a chance we will never get it."[10]

Oh, please.

The headlines sparked by this bogus poll suggested that girls were getting the educational shaft while boys soared to Olympian heights. The *New York Times* reported, "Little Girls Lose Their Self-esteem on Way to Adolescence, study finds," while the *Chicago Tribune* headlined its story, "Girls' Confidence Erodes over Years, Study Says."[11]

Congresswoman Pat Schroeder (D-CO), whom no one ever accused of being a rational, logical thinker of the reviled male-model, gave a cursory reading to the AAUW study and proceeded to introduce a $360 million Gender

Equity in Education Act, which would federally subsidize various additional services for girls. Rep. Schroeder declared, "For too long, the needs of girls have been ignored or overlooked in crafting education policy."[12]

These needs were to be met by a cavernous new bureaucracy: the Office of Women's Equity within the Department of Education, which would take on the somewhat shadowy task of ensuring "equity" for girls, who by most accounts exceed boys in school achievements. For instance, as Christina Hoff Sommers notes, the most recently available results from the National Assessment of Education Progress Tests had shown that "males outperformed females by three points in math and eleven points in science. The girls outperformed boys by thirteen points in reading and twenty-four points in writing."[13] Perhaps the plan was that the Office, like not a few bureaucracies, would actually retard the progress of girls, permitting the laggard boys to catch up.

Although the vast majority of studies of self-esteem in young people have found no significant differences between boys and girls, the press reported uncritically on the AAUW study and the concomitant propaganda barrage. Researcher Susan Harter told Christina Hoff Sommers that the AAUW study was "poorly designed and psychometrically unsound." The leading figures in the field agreed. University of Michigan psychologist Joseph Adelson, who edited the *Handbook on Adolescent Psychology*, said, "When I saw the report I thought, 'This is awful. I could prove it is awful, but it's not worth my time.'"[14]

Sommers performed the valiant task of wading through the AAUW study, which the organization did its best to hide from public view by charging $85 per copy and requiring any purchasers to agree to a list of conditions seldom set by legitimate researchers. She found that the AAUW gender gap was traceable to the fact that boys more frequently answered "Always true" to statements such as "I'm good at a lot of things," which may well indicate a lack of self-awareness or maturity on the part of those hyper-confident boys. Girls tended to respond to such questions by answering "Sometimes true," which suggests greater maturity on their part. Expressions of a genuine lack of self-esteem—answering "rarely true" or "never true"—came in about equal numbers from boys and girls.

A follow-up AAUW study, misleadingly titled "How Schools Shortchange Girls," was released in 1992 to such hysterical and mournful headlines as "Powerful Impact of Bias Against Girls (*Los Angeles Times*), "Bias Against Girls is Found Rife in Schools, with Lasting Damage" (*New York Times*), and "Dreadful Waste of Female Talent" (*San Francisco Chronicle*).[15] Like the previous survey, this was unveiled with all the fanfare of a new Tom Cruise movie. The AAUW spent more money promoting it ($150,000) than it did conducting it ($100,000).[16] The money was well-spent, at least from the point of view of an amoral propagandist unconcerned with those bothersome nuisances known as facts. The second AAUW study fed more than 1,400 stories in newspapers around the globe.

The message of this study was summarized by AAUW Educational Foundation president Alice McKee: "The wealth of statistical evidence must convince even the most skeptical that gender bias in our schools is shortchanging girls—and compromising our country."[17]

The evidence does no such thing. Indeed, it convinces only the credulous, the gullible, those who couldn't pass a remedial math or logic class, much less Statistics 101. In almost every index of teenage pathology—rates of suicide, dropping out of school, alcohol and drug use, perpetrating and being a victim of violence—males far outpace females. In 1991, as the AAUW was cranking up its wind machine, the suicide rate for boys exceeded that of girls in every age group (2.1 per 100,000 to 0.8 per 100,000 among ages 10–14; 18.0–4.4 among ages 15–19, and 25.8–4.1 among ages 20–24). This gap has not closed in the years since.

Learning disabilities also afflict boys at much greater rates than girls. Autism, which has increased in incidence more than ten times over during the last two decades and now affects almost one in every 150 children, is overwhelmingly a condition of boys. "It's got to be sex-linked," says Simon Baron-Cohen of Cambridge University, who has studied autism. Baron-Cohen suggests that autism might be understood as an example of an "extreme male brain,"[18] which comprehends math but not the girl next door. The pattern holds for the mild form of autism known as Asperger Syndrome, which affects ten times as many boys as girls.

The grim parade of statistics goes on. Boys are four times as likely as girls to be diagnosed with Huck Finn's Disease (attention deficit/hyperactivity disorder), three times as likely to be assigned to special education classes, four times as likely to not do their homework, and they drop out of school at a rate 25 percent higher than girls. If you believe the U.S. Department of Education, "the average eleventh-grade American boy now writes at the same level as the average eighth-grade girl."[19] Now, one can argue that public schools are designed to suppress genuine spirit and spunk and to produce a compliant cadre of conformists, in which case the inferior performance of boys should be worn as a badge of honor. But this should trouble even the most militant unschooler.

Four times as many boys are dyslexic as girls. Boys are far behind girls in the first of the classic three R's: "[T]he gap in reading proficiency between males and females is roughly equivalent to about one and a half years of schooling,"[20] reports the U.S. Department of Education, and boys—privileged, advantaged, kings-of-the-world boys—are the laggards.

As if its previous studies were not enough balderdash for one organization, in 1995 the AAUW commissioned Valerie E. Lee and a team from the University of Michigan to produce yet another study, this one titled "The Influence of School Climate on Gender Differences in the Achievement and Engagement of Young Adolescents." Lee, a respected researcher and an honest woman, was obviously the wrong choice for the AAUW. She wrote straightforwardly of the superior performance of girls in the classroom, noting carefully those areas in which boys outperform girls, too. She concluded, "The public discourse around issues of gender in school needs some change.... Inequity can (and does) work in both directions."

Wrong answer!

Christina Hoff Sommers notes that not only did the AAUW refrain from shelling out another $150,000 to publicize this study, but that "[a]s far as I have been able to ascertain, Valerie Lee's responsible and objective study was not mentioned in a single newspaper."[21] This news was not fit to print.

Several years after the AAUW's charlatanish studies had set the tone for the male-bashing of the Clinton years, education scholar Diane Ravitch noted sadly, "The AAUW report was just completely wrong. What was so bizarre is that it came out right at the time that girls had just overtaken boys in almost every area.... There were all these special programs put in place for girls, and no one paid any attention to boys."[22] Or if they did, the attention focused on the wickedness of boys, those rapists in training, those fledgling storm troopers of the patriarchy.

David and Myra Sadker, researchers at the American University School of Education, are the very embodiments of the shoddy and even mendacious quality of feminist education research. Consider the case of the evolution of one of the most frequently cited statistics by the "schools shortchange girls" crowd.

In 1981, the Sadkers and coauthor Dawn Thomas wrote in *The Pointer*, a now-defunct journal, that "Boys, particularly low-achieving boys, receive eight to ten times as many reprimands as do their female classmates." A decade later, the Sadkers cited their own work in a paper published by the *Review of Research on Education*: D. Sadker, M. Sadker, and Thomas (1981) reported that "boys were eight times more likely than girls to call out in elementary- and middle-school classrooms. When boys called out, the teacher's most frequent response was to accept the call-out...."[23]

As Christina Hoff Sommers notes, the earlier paper said no such thing. The Sadkers somehow transmogrified the original finding that boys were yelled at eight to ten times more often than girls into a factoid that boys were eight times more likely to "call out" answers or remarks in class, and that teachers accepted these "call outs" with equanimity. This is a Jekyll and Hyde-quality difference!

The math-challenged ladies of the American Association of University Women picked up this error and ran with it. AAUW Executive Director Anne Bryant told the U.S. House of Representatives Subcommittee on Elementary, Secondary, and Vocational Education that "Myra and David Sadker of the American University and other researchers have extensively documented gender bias in teacher-student interactions. . . . Teachers tend to give girls less attention, with some studies showing teachers directing 80 percent of all their questions to boys."[24]

Thus is a myth born. When Sommers called the Sadkers out on their "call-out" nonsense, the happy couple of misstatement responded testily. The Sadkers refused to appear on "Oprah" with Sommers. Oprah's producers caved, Sommers was denied a hearing, and the Sadkers went their merrily unveracious way. This is not atypical behavior by feminist propagandists. Executive Director Bryant of the AAUW, when confronted by Sommers' charge that the AAUW's research was "tendentious and biased," huffed, "Christina, stop it! Do you want to know something? This is the last time you'll criticize the incredibly prestigious and well-run organization—the American Association of University Women."[25] Ms. Bryant, at least, does not suffer from a lack of self-esteem.

The Sadkers, archetypical gender-bias researchers, have a malodorous m.o. A colleague of theirs from American University reported:

> A doctoral student of theirs used one of my classes in her research. At the end of the first visit, she said, "You are screwing up my data." When I showed surprise, she said, "Yes, you're one of the control classes and you're supposed to show bias but you don't." She came to the class two more times, and each time she discovered more bias. In fact, the last time she observed, the numbers looked so lopsided and not at all reflective of the way the class went, I asked my graduate assistant to take a sample poll of students to see how their recollections jibed with the numbers she wrote down. In every case, the male students recalled being called on far fewer times, and the female students several more times than her numbers indicated. I am distrustful of such research.[26]

That's putting it mildly. If American University had a quality control board, the Sadkers could be waiting impatiently in the unemployment line, stewing over the way that the unemployment counselors seem to favor men over women.

Education researcher Dudley Barlow holds a view of American schools that is precisely opposite that of the Sadkers. Barlow writes in *Education Digest*, "Schools favor girls. Teachers think girls are smarter, enjoy being around them more, and hold higher expectations of them."[27]

The numbers, uninfected by Sadkerism, seem to support Barlow. By virtually every index, American schools are failing boys. And this continues right through secondary school.

According to the National Center for Education Statistics, in 2000 the ratio of men to women at U.S. degree-granting institutions of higher learning was 78:100. By 2012, the gap is projected to widen to 74:100. Among historically black colleges, the gap is even more gaping: women compose fourth-fifths of the honor rolls at these schools.

Assessing the changing male-female mix in higher education, Goucher College President Judy Mohraz says that at the current rate, "the last man to be awarded a bachelor's degree would receive it in the spring of 2067."[28]

"My belief is that until women decide that the education of boys is a serious issue, nothing is going to happen,"[29] says Thomas Mortenson, a senior scholar at the Pell Institute for the Study of Opportunity in Higher Education.

Diane Ravitch, a former assistant secretary of education, asks mockingly, "When will it be fair? When women are 60 percent or 75 percent of college enrollments? Perhaps it will be fair when there are no men at all."[30] (That clamorous sound you hear in the background is a thousand radical feminist hearts beating in anticipation of that joyous day.)

Even those federal programs ostensibly designed to assist the poor shower their benefits disproportionately on females. Better than three-fifths (61 percent) of those students who participated in the college-prep Upward Bound and Talent Show programs, which according to Wendy McElroy took in $457.5 million in fiscal year 2005, were girls. Education researcher Jacqueline King has found that the vast majority (68 percent) of college-bound lower income students are female.[31] This gender gap, however, causes no furrowed brows at the AAUW.

Nor does the gap in elementary school provoke anguish or even mild concern in such precincts. The sexual imbalance in the earliest grades is enormous—and the subject of enormous indifference.

Despite the lack of any positive male role model in the lives of so many children, especially the fatherless boys of the inner city, men are discouraged from going into elementary school teaching. Grades K-6 remain a female preserve. For instance, 95 percent of teachers in grades kindergarten through third are women, and while the occasional call is heard for desegregating grade-school teaching, the more common attitude was expressed by counselor Margaret Taylor: "all men who seek careers in nursery education should be regarded with the deepest suspicion." If a young woman wishes to teach four-year-olds, she's a kind-hearted saint; if a young man harbors the same desire, he's a clammy child molester. (As a counterpoint to Taylor's warning, consider this: Fathers are only half as likely as mothers to murder their children; they are nine times less likely than mothers to seriously injure their offspring.)[32]

One consequence of the paucity of male teachers is that "girls' books" about emotions and character are assigned to school children. Boys, who prefer action-oriented adventures, are bored, turned off to reading, and conditioned to think that books are for girls and sissies. Permitting boys to read novels about quarterbacks instead of forcing domestic dramas on them might draw plenty of seemingly obdurate lads into the wonderful world of literacy.

Schools go to ludicrous lengths to favor girls. As one monitor of texts noted, "Modern textbooks and literature often go to extremes to remove male role models as lead characters and examples.[33] Galileo is out. Well, maybe not Galileo, since he can be used as evidence of the Catholic Church's intolerance. But Neils Bohr and Edwin Hubble and William Herschel are out, and Madame Curie and Sally Ride are everywhere. In fictive examples, the brilliant scientist or wise judge is always, inevitably, a woman—extra points if she is "of color," as the phrase goes—while the dolt who can't figure out why the earth goes 'round the sun, or who can't get along with classmates or neighbors, is, inevitably, a boy, and always—always—a white boy. A boy of non-color.

We have rehearsed the grim statistics earlier. But explanations of the apparent inferiority of boys in school take us into some interesting, darkly lit, and very politically incorrect corners.

Historian of feminism William L. O'Neill, in assessing various feminist pedagogues, put the matter with astonishing—one might even say career-ending, but for the fact that he had already established himself as a leading historian—bluntness. O'Neill pointed to

> the tendency of women to favor grade-getting and degree-winning over creative or scholarly work, to focus on the symbols of achievement rather than its substance. . . . Being a "good student" in this sense requires diligence, obedience, and complete faith in the school and its teachings. At some point the student who wishes to do really original work must break with the system and make his own way intellectually. He may often, perhaps usually, be wrong at first, but he cannot grow beyond studenthood until he begins to teach himself. It is easier for boys to do this because their conditioning is not so complete as girls'. Boys are expected to be rebellious and wrong-headed, and sometimes their deviant experiences give them the confidence—arrogance really—to strike out on their own. Girls are given no such latitude. Convention presses heavily on them from the start, they become such "good" students, their intellectual docility is so firmly established, that most can never be anything more than students.[34]

Yes, O'Neill did attribute this "docility" to "conditioning," but still, the American Association of University Women is not amused!

The difference was stated nicely by Sommers: "Daughters want to please their teachers by spending extra time on projects, doing extra credit, making homework as neat as possible. Sons rush through homework assignments and run outside to play, unconcerned about how the teacher will regard the sloppy work."[35]

Yet Christina Hoff Sommers begs us to remember that "the energy, competitiveness, and corporal daring of normal, decent males is responsible for much of what is right in the world."[36]

To educrats, daring and competitiveness are part of what's wrong with the world. If only we played risk-free, cooperative, noncompetitive games in our schools the lion would lie down with the lamb and the world, having been bought a Coke, would sing in perfect harmony.

Alas, that male nature gets in the way of these edenic dreams. Not only do men belch, scratch, and chew with their mouths open, they also play hard, trash talk, and refuse to sit still for hours at a time in brightly lit classrooms. This is hell on young boys, especially. "We sometimes don't make accommodations for boys' development levels," in the opinion of psychologist Michael Thompson, "so we humiliate them and get them mad, or interpret their activity as willful aggression. And so begins the fulfillment of a prophecy where we try to punish and control boys more harshly than girls. They come to resent it and dislike it, and dislike authority and react back against it."

In acting as boys, they violate the rules of the school. It is as if their very nature is being prohibited. Not surprisingly, they rebel.

Matthew Clavel, who taught inner-city students in Harlem and the Bronx, writes that "Modern American teachers are often taught in education school that fairly normal signs of 'male' behavior, like overflowing energy or aggressiveness, must be severely tamped down. . . . Restlessness, high energy, love of games that involve pursuit and moving objects, competitiveness and other traits associated with maleness for eons cannot be squeezed out of boys without quashing their human natures."[37]

Do you think we exaggerate? Surely no one, not even the most grotesque man-hater, wants to use the public schools to squeeze the very nature out of boys. Doesn't the phrase "Boys will be boys" remain an all-purpose response to those who worry that the lads are getting a bit on the wild side?

Well, never underestimate the capacity for tyrannical daydreaming among feminists. Leonard Eron, a University of Michigan psychologist quoted often in the literature of child development in the 1980s, offers these words of curdled wisdom:

> If we want to reduce the level of aggression in our society, we should also discourage boys from aggression early in life and reward them too for other behaviors. . . . Here is where the women's liberation movement has it all wrong. Rather than insisting that little girls should be treated like little boys and be given the same participation in athletic events, Little League, and the like, as

well as all other aspects of life, it should be the other way around. Boys should be socialized the way girls have traditionally been socialized, and they should be encouraged to develop socially positive qualities such as tenderness, sensitivity to feelings, cooperativeness, and aesthetic appreciation. The level of individual aggression in society will be reduced only when male adolescents and young adults, as a result of socialization, subscribe to the same standards of behavior as have been traditionally encouraged for women.[38]

In other words, feminize our boys, drain them of every last drop of masculinity and daring, make them girls in all but anatomy. To William Pollack, assistant professor of psychiatry at Harvard Medical School and the author of *Real Boys*, our sons are deformed by growing up in a "gender straitjacket."[39] Pollack wants boys to share their feelings, get in touch with their feminine sides, and otherwise behave in ways that are approved of within the milieu of Harvard. He wants them to be not real boys, as his title states, but imitation girls.

While an increasing number of education researchers are proposing single-sex education as one possible lifeline to throw to boys—especially African-American boys—the experiments tend to die aborning, strangled in their cribs by interventionist judges. In 1996, the U.S. Supreme Court found that the Virginia Military Institute had violated the Fourteenth Amendment by barring women from its hallowed halls; those women who gained subsequent admission were held to lower physical standards than were the male cadets, but then hey, what are double standards for? As Barnard College president Judith Shapiro argued in an op-ed piece that reeked of hypocrisy even more than most such pieces, "In a society that favors men over women, men's institutions operate to preserve privilege, women's institutions challenge privilege and attempt to expand access to the good things of life."[40] In other words, all-male schools should be abolished by the heavy hand of the centralized state, while all-female schools must be permitted to thrive, to flourish, and of course to enjoy state benefaction. Equality sure has taken on some funny meanings.

For all the dismal news coming out of the classroom, one irrefutable fact continues to drive feminists nuts: Boys do better than girls on standardized tests. They come up big in the clutch. They may screw around all year in class, hand in half-baked (to use a phrase) homework assignments, wise off and act uninterested, but when test day arrives, they outperform girls. Consistently.

Girls tend to score lower on standardized tests such as the SAT than their class rankings would indicate; boys tend to score higher. Boys test well; girls test poorly. That's a gross generalization, but it contains a germ of truth. Boys do better under pressure.

Annually, males outscore females on the Math section of the SAT by a substantial margin (about 35 points) and, surprisingly, by a smaller but not insignificant margin on the Verbal test—a real shocker, since girls are generally agreed to be one to two grades ahead of boys in English language skills. There are mitigating factors, though they are of cold comfort to feminists. For one thing, more females from marginal or at-risk backgrounds take tests such as the SAT, which depresses the average female score.

Amusingly, the Center for Women's Policy, a Washington, DC-based feminist organization, demanded in 1997 "that the College Board, the SAT's sponsor, drop any math questions on which boys get a higher score than girls." Diane Ravitch, incredulous at this demand, asked, "Why stop at dumbing down the SAT? Why not eliminate math altogether? Then, we can be sure of equal results."[41]

Math is, after all, a construct of the patriarchy. . . .

Ah, but we are getting into some awfully contested territory here. Let us enter by confronting the phenomenon stated with admirable indelicacy by social scientist James Q. Wilson: "There are more male geniuses and more male idiots."[42]

Males exhibit far more variability on intelligence tests than do females. We give the world a disproportionate share of whizzes and morons, of Einsteins and O.J. Simpsons. As *Science* magazine reported in 1995, males outnumber females by a factor of seven to one in the top one percent of math ability as measured by standardized tests.[43] University of Chicago researchers Larry Hedges and Amy Nowell, writing in *Science*, noted that boys' advantage over girls in math and science persists in the face of girls' overall superior academic performance. However, "The large sex differences in writing . . . are alarming. The data imply that males are, on average, at a rather profound disadvantage in the performance of this basic skill."[44] And yet even today, the majority of authors on the best-seller list—and certainly the majority of authors whose works appear destined for classic status among generations yet unborn—are male. Geniuses and idiots: we got 'em.

And this is where the hapless Harvardian Larry Summers comes in. Or, rather, where he scurries out. The discreet, the cautious, the prudent, the cowardly will turn tail and run back to the nearest nestling cliché. We press forward.

Larry Summers was an economist who understood well how to play the game of advise, access, and advance. He served as President Clinton's Secretary of the Treasury and from that fetid swamp somehow landed the plum position in the academic orchard: the Presidency of Harvard.

For a time he was making all the right moves—beefing up the African-American Studies department, issuing moderately liberal pronouncements on public matters of the sort that all Right-Thinking People would agree with. But then he committed the cardinal sin of academe: he spoke harsh truths frankly.

He did so in an ostensibly closed session at the Massachusetts Institute of Technology. On January 14, 2005, which shall forevermore be known simply as 1/14, rather as September 11, 2001 has been rendered 9/11, Larry Summers speculated on possible reasons for the shortage of females at the highest levels of math and science.

Summers didn't say that men are better at these subjects. Rather, he offered a trio of possible reasons for the paucity of women scholars in these fields. First was the "high-powered job hypothesis": that is, for reasons of family, women prefer jobs which offer greater flexibility in hours and terms of employment, and which are therefore improbable paths to a Nobel Prize. A second possible reason was discrimination. And third—and fatefully—Summers, evidently believing that as an academic he had some sort of right to engage in the free exchange of ideas, noted the "different availability of aptitude at the high end"[45] of achievement in math and science. Then the floodgates opened. Larry Summers, Harvard President, had observed that men and women are different.

As we have seen, men are disproportionately represented at the highest and lowest levels of mathematical intelligence. We are the geniuses and the morons, to paraphrase James Q. Wilson. Summers acknowledged these incontrovertible facts. But he used a phrase—"intrinsic aptitude"[46]—that set off the alarm bells in the fire stations of political correctness from Boston to Palo Alto. And despite several apologies over a span of weeks, Summers never did succeed in removing his head from the chopping block.

Among those present to hear Summers' *faux pas* was MIT biology professor Nancy Hopkins. Professor Hopkins reacted to Summers' daring exercise of free speech in a manner that will live in infamy (and hilarity). But let us allow her to tell it: "I felt I was going to be sick. My heart was pounding, and my breath was shallow.... I just couldn't breathe because this kind of bias makes me physically ill."

So Professor Hopkins did what all courageous scholars do when confronted with an opposing argument: she left the room. If she hadn't, she said, "I would've either blacked out or thrown up."

Hopkins's overreaction was so egregious that observers on right, left, center, and anywhere common sense is not a liability had a grand laugh over it. But as Pat Buchanan noted, the tribulations of Nancy Hopkins exposed a profoundly depressing fact: "That a Ph.D. at MIT almost collapsed at hearing a central tenet of her liberal orthodoxy questioned, that Summers has been forced to grovel and apologize for an honest opinion, testifies to a neo-Stalinist intolerance of politically incorrect thought at Harvard."[47]

Summers went on, in his memorable Hate Speech of 1/14, to paint an unpretty picture of what happens when affirmative action negates the "intrinsic aptitude" of men: "When major diversity efforts are mounted and special efforts are made, and you look five years later at the quality of the people who have been hired . . . how many of them are what the right-wing critics of all of this suppose represent clear abandonment of quality standards?"

"Diversity," which used to be such a fine and useful word, is used here, as it is throughout the major institutions of the country, as a synonym for "anti-male" and, in particular, "anti-white male." Summers was saying, as Eugene Robinson of the *Washington Post* discovered during his own hissy-fit, that "diversity means lowering standards."[48] Hire on merit and you'll wind up with a math and science faculty that is first-rate but is also virtually all-male.

The redoubtable duo of Christina Hoff Sommers and Sally Satel reported for the *Wall Street Journal* on a post-1/14 conference on "Impediments to Change: Revisiting the Women in Science Question." Sponsored by the Radcliffe Institute for Advanced Study at Harvard University, the conference featured a six-person panel that gave new meaning to the word "imbalanced." The tone of the day was set by panelist Mahzarin Banaji, Harvard professor of psychology, who declared, "In this day and age"—and always be on your guard when a speaker begins with that hackneyed introduction—"to believe that men and women differ in their basic competence for math and science is as insidious as believing that some people are better suited to be slaves and others masters."

It was all downhill from there. Nancy Hopkins, the dyspeptic MIT professor, recounted her tale of nausea and received a standing ovation. Another Harvard professor of psychology, Elizabeth Spelke, said that the case against innate differences between boys and girls "is as conclusive as any case I know in science."[49] This is so flatly untrue that one wonders what other closed cases Ms. Spelke has in mind. The case for alien colonization of Earth, perhaps? The case for the hard-core creationist argument that God created the Earth 6,000 years ago? The case that blondes have more fun?

Professor Hopkins shared in the usual feminist contempt for the non-degreed fellaheen. "It's one thing for an ordinary person to shoot his mouth off like that," she sneered, but quite another for a "top education leader."[50]

Of course few "ordinary" Americans would use so clumsy and half-literate a term as "top education leader," but in any event, few "ordinary" Americans are perhaps affirmative-action hirees at MIT. Ahem.

In one of those exquisitely timed coincidences that suggest that divine providence has one fantastic sense of humor, at the same time that Larry Summers was issuing a thousand abject apologies and Professor Nancy Hopkins was recovering from her sick stomach, a team of Canadian researchers was under blistering attack for a paper in the journal *Intelligence* which suggested that men have faster "nerve conduction velocity," which is a measure of the speed at which nerve impulses are transmitted between brain cells.

"Males had four faster NCVs than females," wrote Zoology Professor Edward Reed of Toronto University and Professors of Psychology Philip Vernon and Andrew Johnson of the University of Western Ontario. "This very significant sex difference in all test conditions in favour of males was most unexpected."

The sample size of this study was 186 men and 201 women; no one has suggested a flaw in the research. No, the problem is that such matters should not even be studied!

Professors Reed, Vernon, and Johnson did not so much as hint that the superior NCV speed in men made males smarter than females. They ascribed the velocity difference to men having a "thicker coating of myeline, a fatty material which protects the nerves and improves conductivity." If men think faster than women they might make better Jeopardy players, à la Ken Jennings, or better chess players, as was implied in a study by Michigan State Psychology Professor Bruce Burns, who found that quicker thinkers were better at chess, but they would not, by nature, be "smarter" than women.

So nerve impulses move faster within male brains. It might mean that men are more rash and prone to stupid impulsive decisions; it might mean that we are better able to make quick decisions in emergencies; or it might mean not much at all. But can't we study the question without having to apply for a special dispensation from the Thought Police?

Reed, Vernon, and Johnson had no apparent political agenda. Indeed, they "appear to have realised only recently that such conclusions could prove political and controversial," noted Roger Dobson and Will Iredale in *The Australian*. Ah, the perils of heterodoxy! Or, rather, and rather more depressingly, the perils of free inquiry! They might have gotten away with this study if it had found that women had faster brains. But a finding favoring men is as verboten as a copy of Hayek's *The Road to Serfdom* in a Moscow library in 1949.

The feminist Bea Campbell sought to put a period on the sentence, if not to put the researchers into the hoosegow, by making an *ex cathedra* pronouncement for which she offered not a scintilla of evidence: "The distribution of intelligence is much the same for all genders and all races," she said, untruthfully. "Our experience and common sense tells us that the quest to prove one or another biological group is brainier than the other is really a vain exercise."[51]

Campbell does not so much refute the Canadian researchers' findings as she does deny that they are possible. It is untrue, she seems to say, because I say it is untrue. That, Ms. Campbell, is vanity—or worse.

Meanwhile, several brave women came to Larry Summers' defense, and to the defense of free inquiry. Doreen Kimura, a neurobiologist at Canada's Simon Fraser University, told Maria Kubacki of the *Ottawa Citizen*, "You'd think that [Summers] was the first person who ever said this. But this has been much discussed in fields where people do research on the topic."[52]

Kimura speculates that the superior spatial ability of men may be a legacy of hunter-gatherer days, when men ventured far from the tribe and needed an internal navigation system to find their way home. Neurologists have learned that in accomplishing spatial tasks, men use a different part of the brain (the hippocampus) than do women (who use the cerebral cortex).

"There is controversy about sex difference," says Michigan State professor of psychology Bruce Burns, "but there seems to be a fair amount of agreement that men do tend to have better visual spatial skills. However, I am not sure we can say that makes them more intelligent."

The social anthropologist Desmond Morris speculates: "Perhaps men's better visual responses came from having to hunt animals while women developed personal skills from child-rearing and co-operating to grow or gather plants."[53]

Larry Summers must be acquainted with this literature—one imagines him reading it by flashlight late at night in a secluded bower, like some Russian dissident devouring samidzat in the wee hours—but one doubts that he will ever say a sensible thing again on the subject after being so badly burned. Which is a real shame.

"He's absolutely right," chimed in Sandra Witelson, professor at the Michael G. DeGroote School of Medicine at McMaster University, when asked about Larry Summers. "How could one ignore that as a possibility?"

Witelson told the intrepid reporter Maria Kubacki of the *Ottawa Citizen* that women may be programmed to prefer nurturing other human beings to exploring the nuances of googolplex. "It may be that the way the female brain is wired—and maybe through the evolutionary development of homo sapiens—that there is a pleasure and a reinforcement that one gets when one is caretaking. This may be something that is more developed on average in women than in men."

It may be. Or it may not be. But surely if academic inquiry means anything it means that scholars must be permitted to study male-female biological and neurological differences without fear of persecution or ostracism. As Dr. Witelson says, "The best message that we could give to the young men and women who are graduating and going out into the real world and trying to make their way is to educate them on the differences that exist, as opposed to trying to give them this politically correct view that we're all the same—except that some people have a uterus and other people don't."

Dr. Steven Pinker, author of *The Blank Slate: The Modern Denial of Human Nature* (2002), has achieved a breakthrough of sorts in discussing male-female differences. Larry Summers achieved a breakdown. His effort to bolster his case by using a homey example drew jeers, even though that example made a cogent point. (He told the increasingly hostile audience that although his twin daughters had received trucks as little girls in an attempt to shatter gender stereotypes, they referred to the vehicles as the "mommy truck" and the "daddy truck."[54] Cute, true to life . . . and not something the Nancy Hopkinses of the world want to hear.)

Summers was not nearly as blunt as Gosta Wrangler, an emeritus professor of electrochemistry at Sweden's Royal Institute of Technology in Stockholm. After surveying the Nobel Prize winners of the second half of the twentieth century and finding, for instance, that 101 of the 102 Physics laureates were male, that all 36 of the laureates in Economics were men, and that 82 of 83 Chemistry laureates were non-females, Wrangler wrote, "With only 8 women (2.3%) out of 343 Nobel laureates in Science and Economics in the last 50 years, we can safely assert: For research in its highest power, testicles are, as a rule, required."[55]

Touché. That is what is known as the freedom of speech of the emeritus professor.

Mary Daly, the influential feminist theologian, God-castrator, and sworn enemy of the phallus whom we shall meet at greater and somewhat jocular length later, writes of the "artificial polarization of human qualities into the traditional sexual stereotypes" and calls for the "becoming of androgynous human persons."[56] This belief that male and female are mere stereotypes and creations of a patriarchal dictatorship runs into an enemy far more formidable than the Religious Right, capitalism, liberal democracy, or even the phallusocracy: that enemy, the real sworn enemy of feminists, is none other than Mother Nature.

Mother Nature, tough old broad that she is, possesses what the feminists call a "false consciousness": she believes that there are two sexes, biologically distinct; that cultural differences result from those distinctions; and that no amount of wishful thinking or crone-chants will make the phallus disappear. The likes of Daly may believe that androgyny, or the merging of the sexes into one amorphous (if penis-less) being, is "psychic wholeness,"[57] but the famously tragic case of David Reimer belies her conceit.

Reimer, born in Winnipeg, Canada, was accidently castrated as an infant during circumcision. To his everlasting infamy, Dr. John Money, a professor at Johns Hopkins University and a believer that sex roles were a product of culture rather than biology, convinced David's parents to raise him as a girl. After all, the penis makes the man, doesn't it? Aren't our sex roles merely social constructs? Cut off the member and a boy becomes a girl in the blink of an eye.

At first, David adapted, in the account of Dr. Money. Renamed "Brenda," he played with dolls and scorned the traditional enthusiasms of young boys. Or so Dr. Money claimed. In fact, Brenda ripped off the dresses "she" was given and stole "her" brother's toy guns. But Dr. Money ignored such behavior. According to Professor Henry Gleitman at the University of Pennsylvania, "Dr. Money's work provides further evidence that most of the differences we observe between girls and boys are socially constructed."[58]

Not so fast, Professor. In May 2004, at the age of 38, David Reimer shot himself. He had discarded the "Brenda" identity years ago and had even had a surgically emplaced artificial penis. He tried to live as a man, even marrying. He felt incredible bitterness toward the persons who had, on the basis of theory alone, forced him to live a lie. (He wasn't told of his birth as a male until he was a teenager.) David Reimer was a suicide, but in a very real sense, he was killed by those who deny the biological basis of gender.

Yet feminists are undeterred by facts, even by messy suicides. Maleness and femaleness are mutable qualities to many feminists; one is not born female, one is made female through "that complex process whereby bi-sexual infants are transformed into male and female gender personalities, the one destined to command, the other to obey."[59]

For instance, we have the bizarre claim, as was made in a profile of a feminist photographer in the estimable *Columbus Dispatch*, that motherhood is bound up in "stereotypes based on sex, class, race, and ethnicity."[60] Well, three of those four may or may not be true, but motherhood is most certainly not based on a "stereotype" of sex. Mothers are all females! Always, inevitably, invariably. No stereotyping about it. And if you don't like that fact, take it up with God or the Intelligent Designer or Charles Darwin or whomever your author of the universe happens to be.

Bizarrely, even tragically, for decades the dominant view of childhood development was closer to that of the bi-sexual fantasists than to common sense. Dr. Leonard Sax, a psychologist and author of the valuable *Why Gender Matters: What Parents and Teachers Need to Know About the Emerging Science of Sex Differences* (2005), recalls the prevailing beliefs during his graduate school work at the University of Pennsylvania in the early 1980s: "'Why do girls and boys behave differently?' my professor, Justin Aronfreed, asked rhetorically. 'Because we expect them to. Imagine a world in which we raised girls to play with tanks and trucks, in which we encouraged boys to play with dolls. Imagine a world in which we played rough-and-tumble games with girls while we cuddled and hugged the boys. In such a world, many of the differences we see in how girls and boys behave—maybe even all the differences—would vanish.'"

Professor Henry Gleitman lectured Sax's class that "most of the differences we observe between girls and boys are socially constructed. We reward children who follow the sex roles we create for them while we penalize or at least fail to reward children who don't conform. Parents create and reinforce the differences we observe between girls and boys."[61]

That such a view—based on non-existent evidence, contrary to everything parents know, but promoted with the zealotry and intolerance of those who wish to remake the world and don't care how many lives they ruin doing it—could ever attain widespread currency in our institutions of higher learning is depressing enough, but the real-life consequences of such fantasies range from the risible to the truly tragic.

In its least harmful manifestation, gender-neutral child-raising is simply ineffectual. As Dr. Sax writes, the claims "that giving dolls to boys will cause boys to become more nurturing, or that giving girls Erector sets will improve girls' spatial relations skills . . . are never questioned. In fact, no scientific evidence exists to support the claim that gender-neutral child-rearing has any measurable benefit."[62] You can lead a boy to Barbie, but you can't make him think pink.

By now, the evidence of biological gender differences extending beyond simple variations in plumbing is so resounding as to have reached the ears of all but the most fortified and isolated denizens of the nation's Women's Studies departments.

I use the imagery of hearing with intention. We have known for decades that women have a more acute sense of hearing than men. Leonard Sax posits this as a possible reason for the virtual epidemic of diagnoses of attention-deficit disorder (ADD) among schoolboys. The lads can't hear the teacher! The solution, in this case, would seem to be simple: put boys, especially those boys whose inattention indicates possible hearing deficiencies, toward the front of the room.

Slowly, here and there, the overwhelmingly female teachers in elementary schools are doing this. But they still opt, all too often, for the ADD door, with its attendant pharmaceutical package. Under a grant from the American Academy of Family Physicians, Dr. Sax discovered that the majority of ADD diagnoses in the Washington area were made not by doctors but by teachers—including those soft-spoken lady teachers whose soothing dulcet voices cannot be heard by the trouble-making boys in the back of the class.

The difference in hearing extends even back unto the crib. A late 1980s study at Florida State University found that girl premature babies who received music therapy left the hospital, on average, nine and a half days sooner than did baby girl preemies who had not had music piped into their cribs. Among boys, however, there was no difference. They seemed not to respond to music therapy.

Subsequent research has confirmed this finding. Girl babies flourish when hearing Brahms' Lullaby, boy babies could care less. This may be indicate poor musical taste by boy babies—perhaps they would respond better to Ozzie Osbourne—or it may mean that girl babies are blessed with better hearing than boy babies.

The latter would seem to be the better bet. Eleven-year-old girls, as Colin Elliot reported in the *British Journal of Psychology* in 1971, are "distracted by noise levels about ten times softer than noise levels that boys find distracting."[63] Again, one implication of this difference is that perhaps boys and girls learn differently; they may require different noise and activity levels within a classroom.

Men and women have different bodies, even different brains. UCLA neuroanatomist Laura Allen reports, "As I began to look at the human brain, I kept finding differences. Seven or eight of the ten structures we measured turned out to be different between men and women."[64]

Men have, on average, slightly larger brains than do women, even if total body size is controlled for. Women, however, have larger cells in certain regions of the brain and seem to have a higher blood flow per gram of tissue. As we noted in the discussion of the Larry Summers contretemps, that doesn't make men smarter, nor does it make women smarter: but it does make them different. One Virginia Tech studied referenced by Dr. Sax noted that "areas of the brain involved in language and fine motor skills mature about six years earlier in girls, while those dedicated to math and spatial skills are about four years ahead in boys."[65]

This may come as unwelcome news to Catherine MacKinnon, who claims, "Male is a social and political concept, not a biological attribute."[66] But it is an irrefutable fact of nature.

Mother Nature is a bitch, ain't she Cath?

From the earliest ages, girls display superior skills at verbal memory and fine motor coordination; boys excel at spatial relationships. Girls, as Dr. Leonard Sax writes, "are better at tasks involving object discrimination—answering the question 'What is it?'—whereas boys are better at tasks involving object location—'Where is it?'"[67]

If men are unwilling by nature to take directions, they are better, on average, at north-south directions than are women, who have been shown in various studies to navigate by landmarks, not by absolute directions. "Neuroscientists have found," according to one account, "that young women use the cerebral cortex"[68] to find their way about, while young men navigate by the hippocampus. And the hippocampus, as we all know, does not permit the rolling down of the driver's window and the asking of a gas station attendant, "How do you get to the stadium?"

"[M]ale brains and female brains are organized differently," notes Dr. Sax, "with functions more compartmentalized in male brains and more globally distributed in female brains."[69] Thus men who suffer strokes affecting the left hemisphere of the brain, which controls their language facilities to a much greater extent than it does for women, suffer a 20 percent drop in verbal IQ, whereas women who suffer strokes affecting the left hemisphere of the brain experience a 10 percent drop in verbal IQ. The situation is reversed when a stroke affects the brain's right hemisphere: women's verbal IQ declines by 10 percent whereas the male verbal IQ is unaffected.

Male-female differences persist from cradle to grave. When 102 boy and girl babies were presented with a mobile and a female human face, boys tended to watch the mobile while girls were transfixed by the lady's face. Given that these were newborns, not yet poisoned by the tyrannical assumptions of patriarchy, their reactions tell us that the sexes diverge almost from the womb.

Boys and girls, and later men and women, also differ in the anatomy of the eye. For instance, a man's retina is thicker than the retina of a woman. Male eyes are more sensitive to movement, while the female eye is more sensitive to color. Not surprisingly, "Girls usually use ten or more colors in their pictures," and these hues tend to be red, green, beige, and brown. Boys, by contrast, seldom use more than six colors when drawing pictures, usually in "cold" colors such as gray, blue, silver, and black. (Wonder why the Oakland Raiders are a perennial boy favorite?) Their artwork depicts "an alien about to eat somebody," cars crashing, linebackers colliding, meteorites destroying Earth, and the like. One child psychologist has said, "girls draw nouns, boys draw verbs."[70]

And yet, as Dr. Leonard Sax and others point out, elementary school teachers—females, as a hard and fast rule—want children to draw pictures of happy people splashed with color. In other words, they wants boys to draw like girls. A boy can suppress his natural style, fitting his round peg into a square hole, or he can receive poor grades, sit in the back with the stupid kids, where his inferior hearing puts him at a disadvantage, and start his doleful journey into dodge-ball-playing gender terrorism. (Two boys in Ocala, Florida, may have gone a little too far in their refusal to conform to feminine rules of classroom drawing. In 2005, the boys, aged nine and ten, sketched a stick-figure classmate being stabbed and hung. They were arrested, though they escaped juvenile detention center by agreeing to anti-aggression counseling. The usual extenuations, among them attention deficit disorder, were offered on behalf of the grisly Picassos.)[71]

We have known now for several years that that part of the brain responsible for fine motor skills develops earlier in girls than in boys. (Thus girls are "smarter" than boys, as any first-grade teacher suspects.) Yet curricula remain unchanged in many ways; kindergartners are encouraged to read, for instance, which is fine and appropriate for many children but spectacularly inappropriate for many boys, who get the message at a precociously young age that they are dumb and that school is for girls.

Dr. Leonard Sax speculates that the explosive growth of anti-depressant medication usage by children—including Zoloft and Prozac—may be because boys are "trapped in a school that just is not geared to their needs. And they have no way out."[72] He adds, in a powerful passage, "Restless boys are drugged with Ritalin and Concerta so that they will sit still and be quiet in classes taught by soft-spoken women who bore them."[73] Whatever the reason, the hypermedication of American children, particularly boys, suggests that it is not only manhood that has been pathologized in recent decades—even boyhood is fast becoming a criminal activity. Huck and Tom would either be on Ritalin or in a juvenile detention center had they the misfortune to be attending school today.

Despite the veritable canyon of evidence to the contrary, the idea that "masculinity and femininity are cultural conceits," as Brown University Professor Anne Fausto-Sterling asserts, is still defended in that last ditch of the ludicrous: the academy. Fausto-Sterling denies that such a thing as a girl or boy even exist: "There is not either/or," she says, but merely "shades of difference."[74]

The fact that boys, no matter how one tries to condition them or extract their maleness from them, will play with trucks and girls will play with dolls is no cultural conceit. Indeed, the same play patterns hold for Larry Summers's kids and male and female monkeys, and surely our simian friends, in any event, are not bent at birth by pink maternity rooms and Allen Iverson posters over their beds.

As Lisa Serbin, a child psychologist at Concordia University, discovered in her study of 77 eighteen-month-old children, boys and girls that young cannot even reliably assign themselves to the correct gender. And yet although a one-and-a-half-year-old boy may not know he belongs to the gender "male," he is far more likely to play with a truck than with a doll. Similar findings have been made time and again with children of every age range: boys are different from girls—even at ages when boys do not know what "boy" means.

In spontaneous play, girls pretend to be mothers. They find babies far more interesting than do boys, who exhibit a kind of benign indifference to infants. And as Dr. Sax notes, "Sons whose parents encourage them to nurture babies are no more nurturing than sons of parents who make no such efforts."[75] (Girls born with an excess of the male hormone known as adrenal androgens, and thereby sufferers of congenital adrenal hyperplasia (CAH), have been found to spend "significantly more time playing with boys' toys"[76] than do girls without CAH.)

Another consistent finding is that boys take risks; they take chances; they act bravely, and they act dumbly. To a far greater extent than girls, boys will jump from a tree, try to perform an Ollie on a skateboard—or fire dad's gun. These behaviors are not learned; the male autonomic nervous system differs from that of the female. Boys get an extra fillip, an extra spark, when danger presents itself. They thrive on risk; they "systematically overestimate their own ability."[77] Scholars from Boston University and the University of Pittsburgh found that men drown at much greater rates than women, whether in swimming pools or in flashfloods. They think they're better swimmers than they really are. Or perhaps they are just imbued with the confidence that makes the seemingly impossible seem possible.

It is that confidence, that willingness to take risks, that essential maleness that is the target of the doctrinaire set, who have affixed bull's-eyes to the backs of those boys whose 12- or 16-year school sentences pass with such agonizing slowness in classrooms in which they are misfits, at best. The very natures of these boys are being pounded, hammered, bent, and twisted by feminist ideologues who seek nothing less than the expurgation of maleness from the public square and the common weal.

Do I exaggerate? Well, consider this. In 1996, the Ms. Foundation, taking heavy fire for its single-sex Take Our Daughters to Work Day, decided to expand the concept to sons. The expansion flopped, for various reasons. In the first place, the concept had lost its appeal, especially once women realized the feminist assumptions behind Take Our Daughters to Work Day, the base assumption being that "work" is something done outside the home, outside the family, for pay. To nurture a child, to prepare a meal, to engage in the countless acts of love and consideration that enrich a family: this is not only not work to the feminists of the Ms. Foundation, it is not even admirable.

In any event, the viragoes of Ms. devised something called Son's Day, which was to be observed on Sunday, October 20, 1996. Note the day of the week selected: boys, unlike the girls who accompany Mom to work, were not to have the day off. October was chosen because, as unreconstructed males may not know, October is Domestic Violence Awareness Month.

What fun activities were planned for Son's Day? In Christina Hoff Summers' account, they read as a parody of feminism—but they are quite real, even as feminism becomes a parody of itself:

- "Take your son—or 'son for a day'—to an event that focuses on . . . ending men's violence against women. Call the Family Violence Prevention Fund at 800-END-ABUSE for information."

- "Plan a game or sport in which the contest specifically does not keep score or declare a winner. Invite the community to watch and celebrate boys playing on teams for the sheer joy of playing."
- "Since Son's Day is on SUNDAY, make sure your son is involved in preparing the family for the work and school week ahead. This means helping lay out clothes for siblings [and] making lunches."
- "Take your son grocery shopping then help him plan and prepare the family's evening meal on Son's Day."

Thank God for small favors: Ms. abandoned its plan for Son's Day, which one wag deemed "a holiday in hell for Junior."[78]

Whether the childless social engineers of Ms. accept it or not, boys are more aggressive than girls. They keep score when they play games, and they play those games hard. To win. They scrap and fight, too, though a few minutes after the fracas, the parties to the fight are once again best friends.

It could be worse, the dispirited American male might mutter. In Australia, that allegedly manly land of Crocodile Dundee and Mad Max, all secondary students receive a government-subsidized booklet titled "If I Was a Lady," whose cover features a "large male foot crushing a woman."[79]

Belated efforts to address boys' lagging test scores in Australia have been dubbed a "What About the Boys?" campaign, but when those boys grow up with images of their bestiality on the covers of the very booklets they read in school, one must conclude that the Australian government is lukewarm at best toward the academic maladies of young males.

Back in the USA, the campaign to de-bestialize boys continues more or less unabated. In the service of gender equity and a risk-free world, the Department of Education has even gotten into the act of writing new stanzas to classic nursery rhymes. In Creating Sex-Fair Family Day Care, underwritten by the DOE's Office of Educational Research and Improvement and just as dreadful as it sounds, daycare providers, after being instructed on the wickedness of Barbies and G.I. Joes and "charming Momma Bears . . . wearing little aprons and holding a broom in one hand," are urged to teach the tykes this sequel to Jack and Jill's unfortunate trip up the hill:

> Jack and Jill went up the track
> To fetch the pail again
> They climbed with care, got safely there
> And finished the job they began.[80]

Truly, any mind capable of producing such drivel, such life-defeating suffocatingly humorless garbage, ought to be kept as far away from impressionable minds as possible.

NOTES

1. Christina Hoff Sommers, *The War Against Boys: How Misguided Feminism Is Harming Our Young Men* (New York: Simon & Schuster, 2000), 13.
2. Sommers, *The War Against Boys*, 79.
3. Sommers, *The War Against Boys*, 86.
4. Sommers, *The War Against Boys*, 88–89.
5. Martin Mills and Bob Lingard, "Masculinity Politics, Myths and Boys' Schooling: A Review Essay," *British Journal of Educational Studies* 45, no. 3 (September 1997): 280.
6. Daly, *Outercourse*, 144.
7. Leonard Sax, *Why Gender Matters: What Parents and Teachers Need to Know About the Emerging Science of Sex Differences* (New York: Doubleday, 2005), 64.
8. Sommers, *Who Stole Feminism?*, 46.
9. Sommers, *Who Stole Feminism?*, 138.
10. Sommers, *Who Stole Feminism?*, 139.
11. Sommers, *Who Stole Feminism?*, 137.
12. Sommers, *Who Stole Feminism?*, 138.
13. Sommers, *Who Stole Feminism?*, 160.
14. Sommers, *Who Stole Feminism?*, 144–45.
15. Sommers, *Who Stole Feminism?*, 158.
16. Sommers, *The War Against Boys*, 21.
17. Sommers, *Who Stole Feminism?*, 158.
18. Maria Kubacki, "Nature or Nurture: How Science Has Helped Us Discover That Boys Will Be Boys and Girls Will Be Girls," *Ottawa Citizen*, March 19, 2005, 13.
19. Sax, *Why Gender Matters*, 8.
20. Sommers, *The War Against Boys*, 164.
21. Sommers, *The War Against Boys*, 34.
22. Sommers, *The War Against Boys*, 22.
23. Sommers, *Who Stole Feminism?*, 165–66.
24. Sommers, *Who Stole Feminism?*, 168.
25. Sommers, *Who Stole Feminism?*, 186.
26. Sommers, *Who Stole Feminism?*, 169–70.
27. Richard T. Hise, *The War Against Men: Why Women Are Winning and What Men Must Do If America Is To Survive* (Oakland, OR: Red Anvil, 2004), 77.
28. Hise, *The War Against Men*, 65.
29. Wendy McElroy, "Missing: Males on College Campuses," <www.lewrockwell.com> (16 June 2005).
30. Sommers, *The War Against Boys*, 14.
31. McElroy, "Missing: Males on College Campuses."
32. Farrell, *Why Men Earn More*, 179–80.
33. McElroy, "Missing: Males on College Campuses."
34. O'Neill, *Feminism in America*, 113.
35. Sommers, *The War Against Boys*, 28.

36. Sommers, *The War Against Boys*, 14.

37. Matthew Clavel, "Save the Males: A Case for Making Schools Friendlier to Boys," *The American Enterprise*, July/August 2005, 31.

38. Quoted in David A. Gershaw, "Children's Aggression," <www.azwestern.edu/psy/dgershaw> (12 April 1998).

39. Emily Gersema, "Expert Says Boys Not Aggressive By Nature," *Omaha World-Herald*, March 8, 2005, 3B.

40. Sommers, *The War Against Boys*, 171–72.

41. Hise, *The War Against Men*, 78–79.

42. Sommers, *The War Against Boys*, 32.

43. Hise, *The War Against Men*, 80.

44. Sommers, *The War Against Boys*, 33.

45. Kubacki, "Nature or Nurture," *Ottawa Citizen*.

46. Patrick J. Buchanan, "Unpardonable Sin of Larry Summers," syndicated column, March 11, 2005.

47. Patrick J. Buchanan, "The Closing of the Harvard Mind," <www.lewrockwell.com> (31 January 2005).

48. Buchanan, "Unpardonable Sin of Larry Summers."

49. Satel and Sommers, "Where Were You on 1/14?" A14.

50. Buchanan, "The Closing of the Harvard Mind."

51. Roger Dobson and Will Iredale, "Males Slow to Realise 'Men Are Quick Thinkers' Claim Could Offend," *The Australian*, February 7, 2005, 6.

52. Kubacki, "Nature or Nurture," *Ottawa Citizen*.

53. Dobson and Iredale, "Males Slow to Realise 'Men Are Quick Thinkers' Claim Could Offend," *The Australian*, 6.

54. Kubacki, "Nature or Nurture," *Ottawa Citizen*.

55. Hise, *The War Against Men*, 80.

56. Daly, *Beyond God the Father*, 15.

57. Daly, *Beyond God the Father*, 26.

58. Sax, *Why Gender Matters*, 3.

59. Sommers, *Who Stole Feminism?*, 22.

60. Julie R. Bailey, "Exhibit Questions Assumptions About Motherhood," *Columbus Dispatch*, January 23, 2005, H1.

61. Sax, *Why Gender Matters*, 3.

62. Sax, *Why Gender Matters*, 6.

63. Sax, *Why Gender Matters*, 18.

64. Sommers, *The War Against Boys*, 89.

65. Kubacki, "Nature or Nurture," *Ottawa Citizen*.

66. McElroy, *Sexual Correctness*, 9.

67. Sax, *Why Gender Matters*, 22.

68. Sax, *Why Gender Matters*, 26.

69. Sax, *Why Gender Matters*, 12.

70. Sax, *Why Gender Matters*, 24.

71. "Ocala Boys Accused of Violent Drawings Accept Counseling Program," Associated Press, February 3, 2005.

72. Sax, *Why Gender Matters*, 98.
73. Sax, *Why Gender Matters*, 239–40.
74. Sax, *Why Gender Matters*, 6.
75. Sax, *Why Gender Matters*, 61.
76. Sommers, *The War Against Boys*, 88.
77. Sax, *Why Gender Matters*, 43.
78. Sommers, *The War Against Boys*, 46.
79. Babette Francis, "Act Has Ruined Our Men," Melbourne, *Australia Herald Sun*, September 29, 2004, 20.
80. Sommers, *The War Against Boys*, 77.

Chapter Three

Bad Characters

The archetypal male, to feminist Mary Daly, is Dracula. Daly imagines an "insatiable lust of males for female blood," which will come as news to any male this side of Vlad the Impaler. But you see, "the Male Machine . . . can continue its obscene life only by genocide. If the Machine dreams, it is of a future filled with megadeaths."[1]

Admittedly, men dream, and some have an insatiable lust, but it is not for genocide, or death, or female blood, or for the naked form of Mary Daly.

The penis is to these women as the Negro is to a Klansman, the internal combustion engine is to Albert Gore, and the Religious Right is to a National Public Radio liberal: the source of all evil. In her seminal (if you will excuse the expression) book, *Against Our Will*, the theorist Susan Brownmiller declared: "Man's discovery that his genitalia could serve as a weapon to generate fear must rank as one of the most important discoveries of prehistoric times, along with the use of fire and the first crude stone axe. From prehistoric times to the present, I believe, rape has played a critical function."[2]

Poor prehistoric man. Rudely parodied as a grunter, a knuckle-dragger, a slope-browed moron, even his two incontestable achievements—figuring out what to do with fire and how to fashion and use tools—are now to be sullied with a third: he scared prehistoric woman with his sex organs.

Which brings us to another axiom: Men are more aggressive than women. Or are they?

Testosterone is the impetus for the male sex drive and also male aggression, "which may help explain why rape is a male crime and why males like casual sex."[3] Aggression is one of those male traits that is both hated and coveted by feminists. They seek to control, dampen, or extract the aggressiveness from boys even as they instill it in girls. But then girls, testosterone-laden as they are not, know a thing or two about aggression, too.

Psychologists verify what even caveparents knew: boys fight. With fists, with rocks, with sticks, with baseball bats. But girls fight, too, though their weapon of choice is words.

Again, our friends the primates offer a mirror. Male chimps, according to primatologist Frans de Waal of the Yerkes Primate Research Center, fight as prelude to friendship. Female chimps, by contrast, are "vindictive and irreconcilable."[4] Once they fight, they are enemies for life.

The same description might be made of human beings. For a growing body of research in the social sciences examines aggression and bullying by girls.

Girl bullies differ from boy bullies in almost every way. Girl bullies are usually popular kids, with many (if not deep) friendships; boy bullies are loners. Girl bullies have mastered the social skills of the pre-teen and adolescent set; boy bullies wouldn't know a social skill if one kicked them in their low-riding pants. Girls bullies congregate and scheme, acting in concert with other bullies or with weak followers to isolate their prey; boy bullies are lone wolves who strike without adjutants. Girl bullies often have good grades; boy bullies are in the dumb classes. Girl bullies often know their targets well, picking on ex-friends or girls of long acquaintance; boy bullies are as apt to pick perfect strangers as their quarry.[5]

It starts early—earlier than you might expect. Craig Hart, professor of marriage, family, and human development at Brigham Young University, found in a study of 328 Utah preschoolers that about one-fifth of the girls—toddlers, really—adopted "aggressive strategies" in preschool. "It could range from leaving someone out to telling friends not to play with someone to saying, 'I'm not going to invite you to my birthday party.' Some kids are really mean and nasty," said Professor Hart.

Hart and his BYU colleagues David Nelson and Craig Robinson published their findings in the journal *Early Education and Development*. They noted that while perhaps 20 percent of the three- and four-year-old girls qualified as "controversial"—that is, mean—the percentage was much lower among boys.

"The typical mantra is that boys are more aggressive than girls," said Hart, "but in the last decade we've learned that girls can be just as aggressive as boys, just in different ways."[6]

When it comes to aggression, researchers Eleanor Maccoby and Carol Jacklin found in their standard *The Psychology of Sex Differences* (1974), "The sex difference is found as early as social play begins—at 2 or 2 1/2."[7]

In a study of 11- and 12-year-olds in the journal *Child Development* (1996), Nicki R. Crick, Maureen A. Bigbee, and Cynthia Howes limn the ways in which aggression by young girls takes a different form from that of young boys. Girls employ "relational aggression" and "verbal insults"[8] whereas boys, who do not by any means neglect verbal insults, prefer physical aggression, which also goes under such names as "punching guys out," "beating the crap out" of a classmate, and "whaling on that sucker."

Now, given the old saw about sticks and stones breaking my bones but names never hurting me, one might think that girls' relational aggression is somehow more benign, or at least less malignant, than boys' physical aggression. Not so. For the girls use relational aggression in manipulative and damaging ways: to blacken a reputation, to exclude other girls, to make classmates cry, to block the formation of friendships.

And these acts can inflict a pain deeper and longer-lasting than that caused by a bop on the nose with a fist. "Little girls know the power of groups, and how to use them," says Alan Leschied of the University of Western Ontario. "They know how to use social networks. We've found in terms of victimization, the wounds experienced from social aggression are much more damaging than wounds from physical aggression. They're long term and they cut deeper."[9]

A trio of Finnish scholars who studied 11- and 12-year-olds in that country found much the same thing. Girls used "indirect" aggression—gossip, exclusion, taking sides, tattling—while boys employed the more direct means of hitting, swearing, and stealing. And though sticks and stones are supposed to be more potent weapons than names, the Finns found that girls stayed angry for a considerably longer period than did boys. Fighting boys will usually make up shortly after the fight; feuding girls may feud for a painfully long time. And when girls are asked to rate their own aggressiveness, they do so much less accurately than do boys: they commit these acts, it seems, without quite knowing the severity of what they are doing.

In sum, conclude the researchers, "the social life of 11- to 12-year-old girls is more ruthless and aggressive than has been suggested by previous research."[10]

In a follow-up study whose authors included two of the same Finnish scholars, girls were found to hone their skills at indirect aggression over the course of several years. Whereas eight-year-olds were relative neophytes in the arts of cruelty, by the time the Finnish lasses turned eleven they were skilled at manipulative acts of indirect aggression. Meanness is in flower.

The authors wonder if boys and men ever do catch up. Or "are backbiting, gossip, and manipulative means still more typically female strategies during adult life?"[11]

To ask the question is to commit career suicide in America, but in Finland, it seems, the wolves of political correctness are not yet baying at the door.

A 2004 survey of Long Island teenagers conducted at SUNY-Stony Brook found a veritable state of war existing between the sexes, with the girls giving as good, or as bad, as they get. A whopping 92 percent of the girls polled admitted that they had insulted or sworn at their boyfriends, while 84 percent of the boys had behaved in a similarly boorish manner.

Spinning the Stony Brook survey as only a feminist can, one Stephanie Nilva of a group called Break the Cycle remarked, "Men have physical intimidation on their side that can speak volumes, so girls are more likely to use words. A boy can intimidate a woman without taking a single step or opening his mouth."[12]

Sure, Stephanie. (Note that use of "boy" as companion to "woman.") We all know what shrinking violets those foul-mouthed Long Island teenaged girls are.

A 2,000-subject Canadian survey, the Teen Relationship Project of York University and Queen's University, produced findings of a like nature. "Considerably more boys than girls say their dates yell at them, demean them, pinch them, slap them and out-and-out attack them," as the Canadian press reported.

Lead researcher Debra Pepler, a York psychology professor, said that "we have done a disservice by only looking at one side of the issue. . . . By suggesting that it's only the boys and men who are aggressive, we've actually overlooked girls."[13]

The girls of the Teen Relationship Project were more aggressive in every measurable category: major abuse, minor abuse, and verbal abuse. They kick, they needle, they sneer and they snarl.

Those who believe that impressionable youngsters ape what they see on the big and small screens will note the profusion of ultra-aggressive females in pop culture, from the scheming sluts of *Desperate Housewives* to the Amazonian Angelina Jolie to the glaring Career Monsters of *The Apprentice* to the sullen whining of a hundred disposable pop singers who dress provocatively enough so that the boys in the audience aren't bothered by their bratty anti-male rants.

The British publication *Sugar*, one of those annoyingly titled magazines for teenagers, polled 2,000 girls between the ages of 13 and 19 and found that fully 43 percent believed that it was acceptable under some circumstances for a boyfriend to hit a girl. Wes Cuel, a director of the British charity that subsidized the survey, said that it "reveals a generation of girls, many of whom are growing up believing that aggression is an acceptable part of life."[14]

He means violence, not aggression—at least one hopes that he does—but one wonders what will become of this generation of free-swinging—fistically—young British women.

Britain's Crown Prosecution Service has encouraged authorities to press domestic violence cases even when the victim wishes the case dropped. As

Philip Jenkins of Penn State University has provocatively argued, domestic violence law is the one area in which a key tenet of Judeo-Christian ethics—forgiveness—is thrown out the window. Depending on the jurisdiction, wives and girlfriends are either discouraged or actually barred from dropping charges against the creeps who hit them.

But the complications of what has come to be known, somewhat misleadingly, as "domestic violence," will be taken up a bit later. For now, let us consider what study after study has shown: the real target of aggressive girls is not boys but other girls.

The "mean girls" media phenomenon of the early twenty-first century shone long-overdue light on the ways in which relational aggression by girls and young women leaves lasting scars. Petty acts of cruelty, exclusive cliques, and backbiting as a daily exercise are part of a girls' life in public school. "Name-calling can be just as damaging as a punch,"[15] says New Zealand anthropologist Donna Swift, who has studied female aggression, and while the coldcocked boy clutching his broken jaw might disagree, the good doctor has a point.

As Elaine Cassel writes, "When boys get too rough or aggressive, when their physical aggression tips over into violence, parents, teachers, and even law enforcement step in and draw the line. At least boys learn when they are going too far. But girls' aggression . . . is insidious. Rarely do outsiders step in."[16]

Picking up on Rachel Simmons' popular work, *Odd Girl Out: The Hidden Culture of Aggression in Girls* (2002), Emily Warne of the *Buffalo News* interviewed teenaged girls in one affluent Buffalo high school. Representative comments paint a picture of a perpetual catfight:

- "Girls will talk about each other behind their backs until one of them breaks. They'll make up rumors if they feel threatened. And no matter how ridiculous it is, [somebody] will believe it."
- "Girls can always deny something. Punching someone is a visual—you know they did it. You can't know exactly what someone is whispering."
- "A lot of time if you're trying to get into the 'popular' group sometimes you need to bully and sometimes put down your own friends in order to get into the 'popular' group."
- "Between guys and girls—there's a really big difference. [Guys] will get mad and two seconds later they're patting each other on the back and it's completely forgotten. Girls hold grudges."[17]

Yet most schools lack any programs to curb aggressive behavior among girls. Interventions start as early as kindergarten or first grade for boys, whose more unruly specimens play the Good Behavior Game, in which the urchins receive points and praise for walking single file to the lunchroom, saying please and thank you, and not punching their classmates. Perhaps a Good Behavior Game might be designed for girls in which the bonny lasses win credits when they refrain from gossip, tattling, lying, and not inviting Marissa to the birthday party.

In some girls, relational aggression crosses the line into physical violence. Yes, girls remain somewhat less likely than boys to throw a roundhouse right. As Dr. Erika Karres of Chapel Hill, North Carolina, remarks, "You don't see too many second-grade girls punching each other out." But you see a lot more 16-year-old girls dropping the gloves. For instance, the number of U.S. girls arrested for assault skyrocketed by 40.9 percent from 1992 to 2003, while the rate for boys increased by only 4.3 percent.

"Girls look on physical violence as much more acceptable now," in the opinion of Penn State College of Medicine Professor Cheryl Dellasega, author of *Girl Wars*. She credits this, in part, to pop culture, where "women are not only gorgeous but they beat another woman up without thinking twice about it."[18]

Or maybe they do think twice about it. In *Child Development* (1979), David M. Brodzinsky, Stanley B. Messer, and John D. Tew of the psychology department at Rutgers surveyed the aggression fantasies of 127 fifth graders. Asked to make up stories to describe a series of pen-and-ink drawings, boys were more likely than girls to fill their tales with punching, hitting, guys taking awesome spills, etc. But girls embroidered their stories with much more indirect aggression: stealing, tattling, lying, etc. The researchers concluded that "girls are not consistently less aggressive than boys."[19] It is the form the aggression takes that separates the sexes.

Subsequent studies have confirmed this research; they have in fact ratified it into stone cold fact. And at the same time, crime rates among girls have risen, suggesting that girls are transferring that indirect aggression into direct form. Or in the odd locution of the Canadian Public Health Agency, girls are choosing "violent strategies."[20] ("Bonnie, what say we adopt a violent strategy the next time we visit a bank?" "Capital idea, Clyde!")

When *Boston Magazine* investigated the juvenile justice system of Massachusetts, it found that the number of female juvenile delinquents in state custody tripled between 1995 and 2005. But talk about a curious twist: the authors of the piece, Lindsay Taub and Alexandra Hall, complained that the Massachusetts Department of Youth Services and the Bay State bureaucracy were "hamstrung" in dealing with girl criminals "by a system that has historically catered to boys."[21]

Catered to boys? Incarceration is catering?! Them boys get all the breaks!

None of this is to deny that many males do commit acts of violence. Cruelty to animals is more common among boys than girls. "Hypermasculinity," the macho posing found among fatherless male adolescents, is a real problem; with their bravado backed by cowardly acts of violence, these boys are petty thugs.

In one troubling study published in *Developmental Psychology*, "Heterogeneity of Popular Boys: Antisocial and Prosocial Configurations" (2000), authors Philip C. Rodkin of Duke, Thomas W. Farmer of the University of North Carolina, and Ruth Pearl and Richard Van Acker of the University of Illinois at Chicago found that, contrary to prevailing beliefs, highly antisocial boys were popular—at least among African-American peers.

"Tough boys" in the fourth through sixth grades—that is, those who are "cool, athletic, and antisocial"[22]—were the most popular, socially connected, and admired boys in African-American elementary classrooms. These boys are bullies with low academic achievements, but their athletic ability, defiance of authority, fashionable clothing and personal styles, and refusal to learn algebra give them a disturbing popularity among their peers, especially their male peers. Much as we may admire the rebel spirit that perhaps animates certain of these boys, their antisocial behavior and contempt for learning bode disastrous for their futures, and those of persons unfortunate enough to live within mugging distance of them.

Alternative explanations of male aggressiveness abound. James Spilsbury of Case Western Reserve University found that African-American boys aged eight to eleven were four times as likely as other children of the same age to have a bedtime after 11:00 p.m.[23] These children also exhibit more aggressive behavior, leading the good don to the conclusion that lack of sleep makes boys aggressive. Yawn.

Some researchers point to the influence of nitwitted video games or television shows. "There is clear evidence that playing violent video games is related to aggressive behavior, hostility toward others," says Rachel Linebarger, a professor of communications at the University of Pennsylvania. "It leads to more physical fights among boys, it leads to more relational aggression in girls."[24]

Video games are today's culprit, but yesterday it was TV: too much *Starsky and Hutch* was thought to lead straight to the hoosegow. Now, this is not to deny that some connection may exist between viewing violent TV shows and behaving aggressively. Children are imitative creatures, and if they watch six hours of violence on television every day they may well insert violence into their own daily scripts. But the relationship between TV viewing (or video-game playing) and violence may be spurious. Other, more potent factors—social class, socioeconomic status, intelligence, a single-parent upbringing—may in fact be controlling variables. But TV is easier to blame. Thus when four social scientists from the University of Michigan presented their findings that "childhood exposure to media violence predicts young adult aggressive behavior for both males and females,"[25] they did not advise parents to just turn the damned idiot box off. Indeed, they seemed not to hold parents responsible at all, saying that "it is unrealistic to expect parents to control completely what children watch in a society with multiple TVs in each household, VCRs everywhere, and both parents working."

Oh really? What statute requires parents to have TVs in every room? Where is it written that parents have no control over what DVDs their children rent at the video store? The authors also disparage the "people watch it so we give it to them" defense made by the producers of these entertainments, saying that this First Amendment, freedom-based defense is "not valid in a modern, socially conscious society."

The Michiganders conclude that further research ought to be aimed at "elaborating and testing the kinds of interventions"[26] that government and the government's schools (and, yes, parents, too, in a no doubt subordinate role) might undertake to correct aggressive behavior in children. Freedom of speech and parental choice, we can be sure, will be off the table in those discussions.

Video games are also a popular explanation for aggression in teenaged boys. Hands were wrung and teeth were gnashed when in 2004 the best-selling video game, with over five million sold in the U.S. alone, was "Grand Theft: Auto," which offered players the chance to participate vicariously in such edifying acts as assaulting prostitutes in dark alleys. Links between game-playing and actual violence are tenuous at best. One 15-year-old exasperatedly told the *Columbia Missourian* that even though he enjoys "Grand Theft: Auto," he is aware that it's just a game: "It's not like we're going to shoot hookers in real life."

An 11-year-old named Cody told the paper, "One day I got mad and broke the game disk for 'Grand Theft: Auto.'" Conclusive proof that video games cause violence! Don't forget that Columbine, Colorado teen rampagers Eric Harris and Dylan Klebold liked to play the video game "Doom." And that's about as deep as the evidence goes. Messed-up kids are attracted to dumb games.

Nevertheless, child psychologist Douglas Gentile, director of research at the National Institute for Media and the Family, frets, "Kids who play violent video games, regardless of the time spent playing them, seem to be more aggressive and less pro-social." Perhaps if our education mandarins would start designing elementary, middle, and high schools that engage boys instead of denying them, fewer would waste their time pushing buttons and clutching joysticks as they sit dazedly in front of their Play Stations.

An auxiliary issue — or maybe it's the real issue — is that, as the *Missourian* puts it, "Stereotypical gender roles are often portrayed, with few strong female characters and an overabundance of hyper-masculine male characters." Psychology professor Bruce Bartholow of the University of Missouri adds, "Within games, very traditional gender stereotypes are perpetuated . . . players are often saving the damsel in distress or brutalizing the women."[27]

Well, there's a rather large difference between saving a damsel in distress and brutalizing a woman. But to feminists, they're all the same. In each case a man lays a hand on a woman, and a helping hand is just as bad as a harassing hand. Might boys respond to damsel-in-distress games because there is something deep inside them, intrinsic to their natures, that wishes to protect women? And since chivalrous behavior has been pretty much wiped out of popular culture by the feminist onslaught, who can blame them if they find a fantasy refuge in video games?

Others claim that the hormone cortisol is at fault. According to a study in the *Archives of General Psychiatry* (2000), boys with low levels of cortisol were more likely to be voted "meanest kid in the class"[28] than were boys with high levels of cortisol. The meanness persisted, as did the low cortisol levels, over the four-year course of the study.

Finally, the mere fact of, and pressure attendant on, being male is cited as a reason for extreme acts of violence. In perhaps the most ludicrous headline of its short and banal life, *USA Today* told us, after yet another teenaged boy shot up a classroom, that "Teen Killers Feel Trapped by Masculine Stereotypes."

The writer, one Jessie Klein of the City University of New York-Lehman's Department of Sociology and Social Work, fretted that "injured manhood" motivated many of the rogue's gallery of schoolyard killers, from Klebold and Harris of the 1999 Columbine shooting to Kip Kinkel's 1998 rampage in Oregon.

Certainly Professor Klein is correct that many of the teenaged shooters were teased by the jocks and preppies of the school. They nursed the usual revenge fantasies; alas, they had wide enough sociopathic streaks that they actually acted on these fantasies. One might well feel pity for these boys, thrown into the snakepit of the modern public school and forced to sink or swim in an environment that gave them no ballast.

However, Professor Klein goes the proverbial one step beyond. She blames as inspiration for the schoolyard snipers . . . GI Joe![29]

Yes, that's right, good old GI Joe, camouflage-clad friend of many an American boy for four decades. You see, GI Joe's biceps have doubled in size since the 1960s. This, we are to assume, shames boys into feeling like major-league wusses, unable to measure up to the doll's musculature, and so those lads who have the misfortune of playing with GI Joe follow one of two paths: they become hyper-masculine bullies, or they become sullen, withdrawn, scrawny loners who shoot the hyper-masculine bullies.

Oh, to be a boy: you can't win for losing!

In fact, something called GenderPAC, or the Gender Public Advocacy Coalition, has exploited the school shootings and the work of Michael Kimmel, who says, like Professor Klein, that the vast majority of shooters were teased for being sissies, to urge the federal government to do something about the "harsh codes of masculinity and the aggression it [*sic*] breeds"[30] in America. This has not heretofore been regarded as a legitimate activity of the federal leviathan, but then feminists do have a thing for Big Brother. Expect a federal initiative on de-masculinization during the administration of President Hillary Clinton.

Boys grow into men, and then their wicked acts against women really start.

"Why are certain feminists so eager to put men in a bad light?" asks Christina Hoff Sommers.[31] As much as our texts prettify the early feminists, many of them, too, were misanthropists. Even the more moderate tended to "think of themselves as a kind of super race condemned by historical accident and otiose convention to serve their natural inferiors,"[32] wrote William L. O'Neill in his history of feminism. Their descendants have even devised elaborate mathematical formulae intended to demonstrate the inferiority—and iniquity—of the male.

There is no infamy, it seems, of which the vile penis-clad monsters are not capable. In 1992, Gloria Steinem made the preposterous claim that "in this country alone . . . about 150,000 females die of anorexia each year."[33] This was the fault of men, of course, who in feminist myth refuse to so much as look at a woman who weighs over, say, 80 pounds. Karen Carpenter *in extremis* represents our ideal woman. Steinem's assertion is found in her book titled *Revolution from Within: A Book of Self-Esteem*. The subtitle is revealing. To Steinem, self-esteem amounts to building a straw man—the Male, not as he is but as feminists imagine him to be—and then knocking him over with any weapon one might find, including ludicrous statistics.

Naomi Wolf, the fetching author of *The Beauty Myth* (1992), made the same wild claim in her best-selling account of how women distort, poison, and ultimately kill themselves for the approval of uncaring men. Wolf compares the death toll of anorexia to the Holocaust, thus placing each American male in the role of Hitler.

Fortunately, the idiocies of Steinem and Wolf were exposed by the courageous Christina Hoff Sommers in her powerful work *Who Stole Feminism? How Women Have Betrayed Women* (1994). Sommers performed an act of detection so clever that it barred her forever from the sorority of the professional women's movement: she tracked down the source of the anorexia=Holocaust statistic.

Naomi Wolf, it seems, plucked it from a book (*Fasting Girls: The Emergence of Anorexia Nervosa as a Modern Disease*) by a former director of

Women's Studies at Cornell named Joan Jacobs Brumberg. *Fasting Girls* was published by Harvard University Press, which, perhaps due to Harvard's notoriously meager endowment, cannot afford fact-checkers. Brumberg, too, claims that 150,000 American women perish each year from anorexia, a calamity she attributes to "a misogynistic society that demeans women . . . by objectifying their bodies."

Brumberg cited the American Anorexia and Bulimia Association, so Sommers rang up its president, Dr. Diane Mickey, who said flatly, "We were misquoted."[34] The Association had pegged at 150,000 to 200,000 the number of women who suffer from anorexia, not the number who die from it. The actual number of deaths seems to range from 50 to 100 per year. Which is about 50–100 more deaths per year than occur from bulimia, another disease forced on helpless women by the patriarchy.

The ever-gullible Ann Landers repeated the lie-stat about anorexia, and since the number of her readers dwarfs that of the readers of Christina Hoff Sommers, another urban legend has been loosed on us.

Yet the incredible shrinking anorexia death toll is but one of the feminist hoaxes revealed by Sommers. For instance, a feminist academic named Deborah Louis, president of the National Women's Studies Association, sent out a circular e-mail on November 4, 1992, reading, "According to [the] last March of Dimes report, domestic violence (vs. pregnant women) is now responsible for more birth defects than all other causes combined. Personally [this] strikes me as the most disgusting piece of data I've seen in a long while." The fact-averse NOW president Patricia Ireland passed along this choice morsel to Charlie Rose on PBS: "Battery of pregnant women is the number one cause of birth defects in this country."

Again, Sommers to the rescue. She tracked the source of this startling claim to one Sarah Buel, a product of Harvard Law School active in the domestic violence industry. Buel, it seems, had misunderstood a North Carolina nurse named Caroline Whitehead when Ms. Whitehead had said, "We screen for battery far less than we screen for birth defects." Just how Sarah Buel could possibly misinterpret Whitehead's remark as saying that wife-beating causes birth defects is almost beyond imagining. Indeed, Caroline Whitehead, when reached by Sommers, said of Buel's interpretation, "It blows my mind. It is not true."

Unfortunately, this egregiously untrue contention also received wide circulation. *Time* magazine, that citadel of responsible journalism, declared, "Especially grotesque is the brutality reserved for pregnant women: the March of Dimes has concluded that the battering of women during pregnancy causes more birth defects than all the diseases put together for which children are usually immunized."[35]

Time retracted the story and apologized to the March of Dimes, which concluded no such thing. But the damage had been done. Millions read the story in *Time* and the numerous newspapers that ran with this falsehood. No untruth, it seems, is too outrageous when it serves the greater purpose of showing up men as brutish, nasty, and short-tempered. We rape to impregnate women, then batter the fetus into deformity or death. Why not just castrate us?

It's hard to know just how to ascribe responsibility for the feminist myths. To call them "lies" seems harsh, but the alternative—that these women do not understand how to use numbers—leads us into Larry Summers territory, from which few men ever escape.

Perhaps the biggest lie, or at least the myth with the most colorful public life, was the claim made in January 1993 that on Super Bowl Sunday domestic violence runs 40 percent higher than on other days of the year.

This falsehood, which confirmed pretty much everything that upper-middle-class white feminists believe about working-class men, spread like chickenpox in a day-care center. As Sommers notes, it seems to have originated—with malice aforethought—with one Sheila Kuehl of the California Women's Law Center. On January 27, 1993, or the Thursday before the big game, Ms. Kuehl participated in a joint press conference of California feminists who wished to denounce football and its associated brutalities. Statistically challenged, Kuehl claimed that a study by scholars at Old Dominion University had found that men beat women on Super Bowl Sunday—renamed the "Abuse Bowl"[36] by the laughably p.c. sports columnist Robert Lipsyte of the *New York Times*—at a rate 40 percent higher than on the typical day.

The news conference also featured a woman from the ironically named FAIR (Fairness and Accuracy in Reporting), an organization whose contribution to this unfair and inaccurate story consisted of sending out a mass mailing warning women, "Don't remain at home with him during the game."[37] Another FAIR operative appeared on the ABC-TV pabulum "Good Morning, America," the next day, after which all hell broke loose.

Nancy Isaac, a research associate at the Harvard School of Public Health (and do you notice how often Harvard turns up on the wrong side of the truth?), lectured the *Boston Globe*, "It's a day for men to revel in their maleness and unfortunately, for a lot of men that includes being violent toward women if they want to be."[38] Isaac, spewing the sort of venom that only the most virulent men-haters can spew, assumed the voice of the Man of the House: "I'm supposed to be king of my castle, it's supposed to be my day, and if you don't have dinner ready on time, you're going to get it."

The media, ever credulous, found the story too meretriciously tempting to pass up. The *Globe* reporter, Lynda Gorov, buttressed her retelling of the 40 percent canard with a vague reference to a "study of women's shelters out West"[39]—a cryptic claim that the *Globe*'s editors apparently found convincing.

NBC, which carried the 1993 Super Bowl, "made special pleas to men to stay calm."[40] (Given the dullness of most Super Bowls, the request may have been superfluous.) CBS, perhaps miffed that it wasn't carrying the game, sniffed that Super Sunday was "a day of dread." It was—but mostly for fans of the Buffalo Bills, who lost yet another Super Bowl.

The hero of this story was Ken Ringle of the *Washington Post*, who, unlike Lynda Gorov and other reporters, bothered to verify the facts. And he found them utterly unverifiable. One of the authors of the Old Dominion study which was the slender reed on which the 40 percent claim rested told Ringle, "That's not what we found at all." Indeed, she and her colleagues discovered that the level of emergency-room admissions "was not associated with the occurrence of football games in general."[41]

The prevaricators were not amused at being caught in their falsehoods. Instead of dropping to her knees and begging apologies, the ineffable Lenore Walker, author of *The Battered Woman* and retailer of the 40 percent myth, said of *Post* reporter Ken Ringle that he "decided to use his pen as a sword as a batterer does with his fist when he does not get what he thinks he is entitled to."[42]

Ringle exposed this Super Lie. Yet to this day, one hears credulous nitwits repeating the Abuse Bowl story every Super Bowl season.

To the knuckle-dragging oaf who is the American Male, every day is Super Bowl Sunday. Mainstream media outlets have claimed that six million wives are "abused by their husbands in any one year" (*Time*), that "an American woman is abused by her partner" four to five million times a year (*Christian Science Monitor*), and that "[t]here are 3 million to 4 million women beaten by husbands or lovers every year" (*Chicago Tribune*).[43] That's a lot of beating.

The problem, again, is that the feminist propagandists who distribute such "factoids," to use Norman Mailer's lingo, are either liars or math-challenged. In the case of wife and girlfriend-beating statistics, as Sommers points out, the feminists ignore the most reliable figures—for instance, those compiled by veteran scholars Richard J. Gelles and Murray A. Straus, who estimate that well under one percent of women (perhaps 100,000 total) require medical treatment for abuse in any year. I will offer the obligatory "even one battered woman is too many," because the cliché is true: domestic abuse is assault and ought to punished as such by the criminal justice system. (Although there are problems with the loaded term "domestic abuse," for a vastly disproportionate number of these assaults are committed not by husbands but by boyfriends who are not, in any real sense, part of a "domestic" arrangement with the victim.)

Indeed, as chief probation officer Andrew Klein of Quincy, Massachusetts discovered in a study for the Ford Foundation, 80 percent of the "domestic abusers" in the Bay State had previous arrests for assault. They "were generally violent, assaulting other males as well as female intimates."[44] In other words, these are not football-watching slobs who hit the old lady because she's late putting the Hamburger Helper on the table, as the Super Bowl hysterics imagine; no, these are serial criminals, creeps who get their jollies or their pelf by beating people up. Their prey are not exclusively women; they attack bipeds of either sex.

Domestic abuse statistics are often puffed by including as "abuse" behavior that clearly is not. For instance, a 1993 Louis Harris and Associates survey found that 34 percent of women in a sample of 2,500 had had a spouse or partner "insul[t] you or [swear] at you" within the last year; 34 percent had also had a spouse or partner who "stomped out of the room or house or yard."[45] By classifying such normal, if sometimes impolite or inconsiderate, acts as "abuse," feminists are able to paint a statistical fairy world in which a man's day is not complete if he's not abusing the little lady.

When studies find, as did a 1992 Family Violence Prevention Fund survey of 397 California emergency rooms, that far fewer women are diagnosed with domestic-abuse injuries than feminist rhetoric would have us believe, then the fault is laid at the door of those lunkheads who answer the survey. In the case of the Family Violence Prevention Fund, the surveyors explained away their findings in this way: "The low identity rates reported in this survey might be explained by the marked lack of domestic violence-specific training."[46] In other words, the nurses and physicians in emergency rooms are too obtuse, dim-witted, and beguiled by the patriarchy to recognize a battered woman when they see one.

Nor is the typical nurse, let alone the average American dunce, capable of recognizing a woman who has been raped—or at least that is the conceit of the Ms. Foundation.

The Foundation has played a key role in inflating rape statistics—a disreputable act that diminishes the very real and horrific crime of rape by defining it so broadly that women who were willingly sweet-talked into a night in the sack by some collegiate Casanova are afforded the same rape-victim status as are women who have been violently attacked by psychopaths.

The Ms.-ascription of rape was the product of Kent State University professor Mary Koss, a feminist whose viewpoint is that "rape represents an extreme behavior but one that is on a continuum with normal male behavior within the culture." In other words, a rapist is just a typical guy, albeit one with a bit more gumption than the rest of us. (Catherine MacKinnon, feminist legal theorist, concurs. She has claimed that rape, "by conservative definition happens to almost half of all women at least once in their lives.")

Mary Koss and her researchers asked more than 3,000 college women about the degree to which their sexual experiences had been voluntary. Had the women ever "had sexual intercourse when you didn't want to because a man gave you alcohol or drugs?" Had a woman ever been violated by either a penis or other object because a man held you down or twisted your arm?

More than one-quarter of respondents (27.5 percent) answered yes to such questions. Yet only one-quarter of those women who responded in the affirmative believed themselves to be victims of rape or attempted rape. About half—49 percent—chalked it up to "miscommunication."

Such nuances and complications do not register with orthodox feminists. The Ms. Foundation reported the Koss project as follows: "The Ms. project—the largest scientific investigation ever undertaken on the subject—revealed some disquieting statistics, including this astonishing fact: one in four female respondents had an experience that met the legal definition of rape or attempted rape."[47]

No, Ms., what is disquieting and even astonishing is the flat falsity of that statement. Three in four of those women deny that they were raped or the victims of an attempted rape, and the Koss definition is not the legal definition of rape, but no matter: Another urban myth was born. It has since been used to justify a vast expansion of the "rape industry," especially on college campuses, where anti-male busybodies find employment delivering stern lectures about another myth, "date rape." (The ever-credulous Naomi Wolf repeated Koss's canard in *The Beauty Myth*, writing that "One in four women respondents had an experience that met the American legal definition of rape or attempted rape."[48])

More reliable estimates give the incidence of rape in America at about one in every fifty women—a number that is in itself disturbingly high. These victims are overwhelmingly lower income and nonwhite; they live on the mean streets of the cities, not in college dorms. But then as the heroic Christina Hoff Sommers notes in her critique of Koss's work and its consequences, "privileged young women in our nation's colleges gain moral parity with the real victims in the community at large . . . . [Expansive definitions of rape] justif[y] the salaries being paid to all the new personnel in the burgeoning college date-rape industry. After all, it is much more pleasant to deal with rape from an office in Princeton than on the streets of downtown Trenton."[49]

Well and sharply said.

But then American feminism has always been an upper-middle-class concern. Poor women may be useful tokens when one must burble on about "diversity," but the number of inner-city women who subscribe to Ms. is about as minuscule as the number who subscribe to *Foreign Affairs*.

Reputable social scientists were aghast at the Koss survey. Retired Purdue University Professor of Sociology Eugene Kanin called it "highly convoluted activism rather than social science research."[50] To give a graphic idea of just how sensitive these activists really are to rape victims, Sheila Kuehl—you remember her; she is the California Women's Law Center director who started the ball of lies rolling about Super Bowl Sunday—said of Neil Gilbert, a professor at the University of California's School of Social Welfare who had easily debunked the Koss report, "I found myself wishing that Gilbert, himself, might be raped and . . . be told, to his face, it had never happened."[51]

The obscenity of this remark hardly needs comment.

But then to many feminists, sex (between men and women, that is) equals rape. As Catherine MacKinnon says, "Politically, I call it rape whenever a woman has sex and feels violated."[52]

Taking MacKinnon one step further, if such a thing is possible, Wendy McElroy reports that the *New York Radical Feminists Manifesto* speaks of men as though they are repulsive aliens come to earth to wage wrack and ruin for no real reason other than that they feel like it: "He has found ways to enslave her . . . as a final proof of his power and her debasement as a possession, a thing, a chunk of meat, he has raped her. The act of rape is the logical expression of the essential relationship now existing between men and women."[53]

Think of men as the malevolent and hideous aliens in Steven Spielberg's film version of *War of the Worlds* (2005) and you get an idea of how these women regard men.

After the debunking of a date-rape hoax at Vassar in which several male students were falsely accused of this crime, Assistant Dean Catherine Comins—who might have been expected to give support to the wronged students—smugly said of the unfortunate lads, "They have a lot of pain, but it is not a pain that I would necessarily have spared them. I think it ideally initiates a process of self-exploration. 'How do I see women?' 'If I did not violate her, could I have?' 'Do I have the potential to do to her what they say I did?' These are good questions."[54]

Dean Comins obviously sees every male student as a potential rapist. And, as Wendy McElroy observes, when it comes to the influential feminist law professor Catherine MacKinnon, we may as well remove the qualifier "potential." For MacKinnon has written that "the social relation between the sexes is organized so that men may dominate and women must submit and this relation is sexual—in fact, is sex."[55]

That's right. Sex between a man and a woman is always, in every case, an act of domination by the male and an act of submission by the female. [One might ask: Where is a dominatrix when you really need her?] Elsewhere, MacKinnon has argued—or rather she has stated with authority, in the way that a sane person might announce that the sun is shining today—that rape and marriage and prostitution are basically the same thing.

Andrea Dworkin, MacKinnon's late sister in arms, raged, "We must destroy the very structure of culture as we know it, its art, its churches, its laws; we must eradicate from consciousness and memory all of the images, institutions, and structural mental sets that turn men into rapists by definition and women into victims by definition."[56]

So there you have it. Men are, by very definition, rapists. Even the art they create is thinly disguised violence—music to commit rape by.

The beleaguered male cannot even take refuge in the world of classical music. Beethoven's Ninth Symphony, we are told by Professor Susan McClary of the University of Minnesota, contains "one of the most horrifying moments in music, as the carefully prepared cadence is frustrated, damming up energy which finally explodes in the throttling, murderous rage of a rapist incapable of attaining release."[57] So there you are: listen to Beethoven and not only are you a vicarious rapist, but an impotent one at that!

Contrary to the sclerotic conventional belief, husbands and wives, in those fortunately rare instances in which one kills the other, commit homicide in roughly equal numbers. Indeed, among those statistics that invariably causes a raised eyebrow in she-who-hears-it-first is the fact that men and women commit acts of violence in the home at roughly the same rate.

The early and seminal study of husband-wife homicide was performed by criminologist Marvin E. Wolfgang and published in 1966. Using data from Philadelphia in the years 1948–1952, Wolfgang found that 53 percent of spousal homicides were committed by husbands, 47 percent by wives. They differed, however, in the weapon of choice: wives opted for knives more than twice as often as they did for guns, while husbands were more versatile in their choice of murder weapons, using guns, knives, and fists in roughly equal measure.

As Margaret Howard wrote in "Husband-Wife Homicide: An Essay from a Family Law Perspective," in *Law and Contemporary Problems* (1986), Wolfgang also found that "the bedroom is a more lethal place for wives"—an observation that it is best to let pass without comment— "with 45% of wives, but only 23% of husbands, killed in that room. On the other hand, kitchens are more lethal for husbands"—as Rodney Dangerfield told us all along— for 40 percent of men and 19 percent of women met their demise therein.

The wifely weapon of choice—the knife—can be explained by "the tendency of wives to kill their husbands in the kitchen, where knives are readily available."[58] Colonel Mustard, Miss Scarlett, and Clue players of the world, take note.

The next major survey of the subject used 1967 data from 17 big cities. The Task Force on Individual Acts of Violence of the National Commission on the Causes and Prevention of Violence found that wives killed husbands in a bare majority (51 percent) of 1967 spousal murder cases. Unlike in Wolfgang's study of Philadelphia, the men in this survey used firearms with the same frequency as did the women. Death by beating was down, death by gunshot was up.

Subsequent studies have confirmed the findings of Wolfgang and the National Commission on the Causes and Prevention of Violence. As Margaret Howard summed it up: "the risk posed to husbands and wives by spousal homicide is roughly equal."[59] This information seems not to have penetrated the crania of feminist scholars just yet.

Parenthetically, studies of spousal murders from Wolfgang's to those of the present day give no comfort to would-be banners of guns. Wolfgang opined that "a gun is used because it is in the offender's possession at the time of incitement, but that if it were not present, he would use a knife to stab, or fists to beat his victim to death."[60] Margaret Howard, after surveying the literature on the subject, also concludes that banning guns would not save lives but rather cause them to be taken by other means. Moreover, she writes that the "most noticeable effect a handgun ban" would have would be "to remove a battered woman's best defense weapon."[61]

In a study published in *Criminology and Public Policy* (2001), Terrie Moffitt, Richard Robins, and Avshalom Caspi charged that the "male-dominance model guiding feminist-oriented intervention programs"[62] is based on a misreading of domestic violence and ought to be scrapped. Violence within the home is no likelier to be a male than a female occupation.

Yet the domestic violence shelters that have sprouted like mushrooms after a rainstorm across the United States offer services to women and angry glares at men. Within the home, women are just as violent toward men as men are toward women, but this simple statement of fact, backed by volumes of empirical research, has yet to break into the feminist integument of the domestic violence industry. There's too much satisfaction to be gained, and grants to be won, by depicting men as the enemy, women as the helpless victims.

Again, the wackiest purveyors of cockeyed (if you will excuse the word) statistics are not necessarily embedded in the armpit-hair wing of Women's Studies departments. Take Katherine Hanson, who as director of the Women's Educational Equity Act Publishing Center was at the head of what was termed the "primary vehicle" through which Rep. Pat Schroeder's noxious Gender Equity in Education Act, that misbegotten bastard of the AAUW pseudo-studies, would blanket the nation's schools like the Red Death come a-calling.

Hanson, as the invaluable Christina Hoff Sommers discovered, has written that "Every year nearly four million women are beaten to death."[63] This is, Sommers notes with incredulity, the single most astonishing misstatement she has ever come across. Four million American women are beaten to death every year: that number is four times the amount of American women who die each year from all causes, natural and unnatural, combined! Surely Hanson is onto the most invisible epidemic in the history of humynkind!

Hanson claims to have based her work—which is transmitted to schools and education researchers across the country by virtue of the U.S. Department of Education—on figures from the Department of Justice. Alas—or happily, relatively speaking—Justice annually pegs the number of women who die due to homicide at fewer than 4,000. Hanson, perhaps confused by such male inventions as decimal points and commas, stuck to the four million number when quizzed by Sommers. Your tax dollars at work again.

The ubiquitous Nan Stein and her Wellesley College Center for Research on Women have produced—with the subsidy of your money via the U.S. Department of Education—a curriculum guide titled "Gender Violence/Gender Justice." Under this charming program, seventh-graders are told to "close their eyes" and "imagine that the woman you care about the most (your mother, sister, daughter, girlfriend) is being raped, battered or sexually abused. . . . Give them at least 30 seconds to think about the scenario before asking them to open their eyes."[64] The 12-year-old boys undergoing this classroom torture are experiencing a form of child abuse, though instead of being punished Nan Stein just receives bigger grants. (Among the other pearls of wisdom produced by the Women's Educational Equity Act Publishing Center and spread around the country with the financial backing of the U.S. Department of Education is a publication titled *Gender Equity for Educators, Parents, and Community*. This fount of feminist wisdom informs us: "We know that biological, psychological, and intellectual differences between males and females are minimal during early childhood. Nevertheless, in our society we tend to socialize children in ways that serve to emphasize gender-based differences."[65] More utter tripe paid for by your tax dollars, Chapter 12,257.)

Christina Hoff Sommers, who describes herself as "a feminist who does not like what feminism has become,"[66] believes these misstatements to be part and parcel of the feminist campaign to convince American women that a gender war rages in which not only the basic rights but the very lives of women are at stake. The patriarchy that tyrannizes women, that teaches them their worthlessness (even as they outscore boys on standardized tests and outnumber boys in colleges and universities), that imposes male hegemony over that eternal victim, Woman, must be smashed, and if it requires lies to smash it, well, you can't make an omelette without breaking a few eggs, as the Stalinists used to say. And these women have all the respect for truth and liberty once exhibited by Uncle Joe Stalin.

The rampant misuse of statistics fed the Clinton administration's Violence Against Women Act, which defined something called a "gender-motivated crime" as a violation of a woman's civil rights, "thus converting domestic violence into a hate crime."

As Wendy McElroy observed, VAWA "recognizes men and women as antagonistic classes to be governed by different standards of law."[67] Which, of course, is exactly how Nan Stein, Catherine MacKinnon, and the feminist law professoriat see men and women: as antagonistic classes who are infinitely better off finding sexual pleasure and lifelong companionship with members of the same sex. If you have to be in the same room as a member of the opposite sex, Stein and MacKinnon seem to advise, be sure to have a lawyer present.

If anyone is to be protected, perhaps it ought to be men. A 1989 study in the *Canadian Journal of Sociology* found that of the married couples surveyed in Calgary, Alberta, "the rate of severe husband-to-wife violence was 4.8 percent, while severe wife-to-husband violence was 10 percent." Another Canadian study, this one conducted in 1990 and 1992 by the Manitoba Centre for Health Policy and Evaluation, revealed that the women surveyed committed acts of "minor" ("throw object at partner," "pushed, or grabbed") and "severe" ("slapped, punched, or kicked," "used weapon") violence against men more often than the men committed these same acts against women.[68]

A 1994 study of 1,800 married or cohabiting heterosexual men and women by Dr. Malcolm George of the neuroscience department at London University found that more than twice as many men (11 percent) as women (five percent) had been subjected to an act of domestic violence (defined as anything from pushing to stabbing) by their partner. Dr. George's report was given the silent treatment, for as Melanie Phillips wrote in the *London Sunday Times*, "academics who publish" findings such as this "are victimised [*sic*] and vilified, and other commentators omit such data from reports." Cowardice, in this case, gets much the better of valor. Careerism trumps truth.

Phillips discerned "gender fascism" at work in British sexual politics. She noted that the government has encouraged children to rat on their parents, or rather on their fathers, if they detect "emotional abuse" within the family. To help the tykes understand the somewhat diffuse nature of this abuse, the women's unit of the British Home Office came up with a television advertisement depicting a man who arrives home from work and is informed by his devoted wife that dinner is late. He hollers. And then . . . nothing. Except that a telephone number appears on the screen and children in the audience are instructed to call that number if they see such a horrifying scene enacted in their own households. If dad yells at mom, call the cops. Somewhere Mr. Orwell is grimacing.[69]

The American Father has, since the 1950s, been maligned as an indifferent, almost bestial figure who is so focused on bringing home the bacon that he neglects the little piggies back home. One infamously specious statistic claimed that the average father spent only five minutes a day with his kids—a factoid that might conceivably be true of incarcerated parents or presidential fathers, but not the average male in real-life America.

The child poverty numbers in this country point to one undeniable truth: the best way to avoid poverty is to have a father who lives within the household. Children born out of wedlock are seven times likelier to be poor than are children born to married parents who live together. Overwhelmingly, male prison inmates report being raised by single mothers. In one study in Wisconsin, fully 87 percent of the inmates had been brought up in single-parent families.[70]

The phrase "single-parent" household really means single-mother household, at least in 90 percent of the cases. The vast majority of custodial arrangements, as men's rights author Richard T. Hise of Texas A&M University notes, favor women. Barely one in ten (11.4 percent) such cases involve children living with a father.[71] Yet feminists "have shown little interest in custody issues,"[72] writes family lawyer Mary Ann Mason. After all, children are a burden, a drag, an albatross. The goal of the divorced spouse should be to transfer as much as possible of the responsibility for child-raising onto his or her ex-partner. Or at least that's the feminist viewpoint. Real-life men and women behave quite differently, fighting for custody with a sometimes feral tenacity.

In purely financial terms, women suffer much more from divorce than do men. In California, one study found that "a woman can expect a 73 percent drop in disposable income one year after divorce, while her ex-husband experiences a 42 percent increase."[73]

Meanwhile, a report by the Department of Health and Human Services notes that "women (the majority of whom are natural mothers) murder children 31.6 times more often than do natural fathers."[74]

Are mothers natural born killers? No, of course not. Infanticide and pediacide are, thankfully, extremely rare crimes. But, keeping in mind their infrequency, they are still committed far, far more often by women than by men. Yet women receive custody of children in divorce cases far, far more often than do men. Is there an injustice here or am I just another paranoiac patriarchalist?

But if he once was necessary to the procreation of the species, the male is now hopelessly obsolete. Suzi Leather, the provocatively named British feminist, spits that "the view that a child needs a father is a social anachronism."[75] The vast majority of ordinary persons, male and female, in Britain and elsewhere, would say that Ms. Leather is daft. But her view has much greater currency in academia and even in the halls of political power. Just south of Britain an organization called Non-Disposable Daddies of Ireland (NODDI) fights for the rights of fathers, and who would ever have thought that such a group would be needed in the land of St. Patrick?

Gloria Steinem, some years before she married, famously quipped that a woman without a man is like a fish without a bicycle. Female separatists take Steinem's point even further, claiming not that men and women are incompatible but that they are enemies. Defending female-only communities, Marilyn Frye states that "it is nothing extraordinary for a master to bar his slaves from the manor, but it is a revolutionary act for slaves to bar their master from their hut."[76] In fact, any persons who could do such a thing would not be slaves at all, but Ms. Frye evidently needs her persecution fantasies. In any event, there are single-sex gathering places for men, too: they are called bars.

Feminist separatists wish to establish all-womyn colonies, which thanks to the wonder of science may now perpetuate themselves by in vitro fertilization, though the question lurks—what to do about the male babies? Well, that's why God created abortion, as the feminists say.

Men are "separate knowers," in feminist argot, who wage "the game of impersonal reason" with a vengeance. Separate knowers, who dominate math and the sciences, are ornery bastards, according to the quartet of authors of *Women's Ways of Knowing*: "Presented with a proposition, separate knowers immediately look for something wrong a loophole, a factual error, a logical contradiction, the omission of contrary evidence."[77] Logic and reasoning are like knives and guns in the hands of men, with their scientific minds and grim commitment to accuracy.

It is nigh impossible for men to defend themselves against charges like this. Maybe all we can say is, "Well, um, yes. . . ." Just why a scientist or mathematician should be ashamed of searching for factual errors, logical contradictions, or the omission of contrary evidence is never quite made clear.

Women are widely believed to have superior intuition, or a cognition not based on rational processes. They just know. Intuition is considered yet another woman's way of knowing—unlike, say, math. Women are empaths; men write books debunking pseudo-science.

According to Dr. David G. Meyers, author of *Intuition: Its Powers and Perils*, while a majority (six in ten) of men are categorized as "thinkers" (that is, users of logic) on personality tests, the preponderance of women grade out as "feelers" (which are—sorry to disappoint the sophomoric—subjective decision makers). Psychologists have noted that women tend to be better at recognizing emotional messages within behavior; for instance, in one test women were better than men at guessing whether or not a male-female couple was romantically involved or merely a setup.

Before getting carried away by women's superior ways of knowing, Dr. Meyers cautions us to remember that "intuition often errs." No less a personage than Diana Spencer, Princess of Wales, remarked in the last interview she gave before her death: "I work through instinct, and instinct is my best counselor."[78]

Perhaps that trusted instinct could have told her not to get into a speeding car packed with decadent drunks and druggies?

The late Princess Di notwithstanding, intuition counselors and self-labeled "intuitives" are peddling their logic-free methods of superior knowledge—for a price. Rather than rely on such patriarchal vestiges as ratiocination and reasoning, they teach women to base decisions on feelings—nothing more than feelings. That their classes are virtually men-free should be worn as a badge of honor by patriarchs.

Men die earlier than women, but don't think for a moment, fella, that you're off the hook when feminists turn their attention to medicine. As the founders of the Foundation for Women's Health put it in 1996, "Women are invisible in the health care system beyond their reproductive systems. The medical model using male science, male body, male culture is still the norm. Women die unnecessarily due to this male perspective."[79]

Where to start? Women make up 31 percent of all physicians and surgeons in the United States, and that number rises every year, since more than half of all medical school graduates in 2004 were female. Half of all medical administrators are women, too, as are the vast majority (95 percent) of nurses. Sixty-eight percent of bachelor's degrees in health and related sciences and 69 percent in biological and life sciences are earned by women. And as for patients, 60 percent of those in the age group receiving the most medical care, persons 65 years of age and older, are female. If this is "invisible," the directors of the Foundation had best get their eyes examined.

One wonders if the "male body, male culture" is the "norm" in one of the largest fields of medicine, obstretrics and gynecology. (Let us hope not.) It is true that as recently as 1970 this field was dominated by men (when 90 percent of obstetricians and gynecologists were male), but today one-third of practicing ob-gyns and two-thirds of ob-gyn residents are women.

Women visit the doctor more than men. Even women past fertility visit the doctor more than men. Women take more drugs than men. Women whine about their aches and pains more than men. And of course women live longer than men. Usually unmentioned in the stories of women as victims of a patriarchal medical establishment is the uncomfortable fact that the average lifespan of an American woman now exceeds that of men by almost six years (79.4 to 73.9).

Alas, the feminist take on medicine and medical research is not limited to some lunatic fringe of lesbian therapists. During his campaign for the presidency in 2000, Vice President Albert Gore said, "Throughout my career, I have fought for more research funds for those diseases so recently considered less important because they benefit only women, such as breast cancer."

Psychiatrist Sally Satel, a lecturer at Yale University School of Medicine and author of *P.C., M.D.: How Political Correctness is Corrupting Medicine*, threw up her hands at this complaint:

> It is hard to imagine what more Gore could do. Women represented 62 percent of the more than six million participants in NIH-funded research in 1997, according to the NIH's Office of Research on Women's Health. Breast cancer research has received more money than any other type of cancer research each year since 1985, when the National Cancer Institute began keeping track of disease-specific funding. It has always received many times the funding of prostate cancer—about five times the amount in 1997 and triple the expenditure in 1999. These imbalances have prompted the Men's Health Network, a Washington-based group, to lobby Congress for redress.[80]

Lotsa luck, guys. The clichèd view, expressed by that mistress of clichè, former Rep. Pat Schroeder (D-CO), that "male researchers were more worried about prostate cancer than breast cancer,"[81] retains common currency.

Satel notes that invasive prostate cancer is somewhat more common than invasive breast cancer (147 diagnoses per 100,000 men annually versus 115 diagnoses per 100,000 women annually) and mortality rates are similar, though prostate cancer kills twice as many men over 65 as breast cancer kills women, while breast cancer kills five times more young women than prostate cancer kills young men.

Lung cancer kills almost twice as many women each year than does breast cancer, and heart disease kills more than both lung cancer and breast cancer—indeed, it kills more women than all cancers put together—but lung cancer and heart disease, as illnesses that are not sex-specific, have of late been surpassed as fashionable charities. Prostate cancer, too, has not caught the imagination of donors. (Writing in the *New England Journal of Medicine*, Cary P. Gross found that breast cancer ranked with AIDS, dementia, diabetes, and yes, heart disease, as the diseases funded most "generously."[82])

Utterly without foundation, Hillary Clinton has referred with scorn to the "appalling degree to which women were routinely excluded from major clinical trials of most illnesses."[83] Senator Olympia Snowe (R-ME) went so far as to claim that women were excluded even from breast cancer research! (This did not cause Snowe to go back to first principles and ask whether or not the federal government really ought to be in the business of funding medical research.)

Clinton and Snowe were parroting a favorite canard of Dr. Susan J. Blumenthal, an appointee of Mrs. Clinton's husband who headed the Office of

Women's Health within the Department of Health and Human Services. The claims of special pleaders like Blumenthal were effectively demolished by Dr. Andrew G. Kadar of the UCLA School of Medicine in the August 1994 *Atlantic Monthly*. Dr. Kadar found that in fact, women were more likely than men to be the subject of single-sex research.

From 1977–1993, pregnant women were excluded from toxicity tests of new drugs, but the reason for this exclusion was to protect the women and their babies. Women were also excluded from some AIDS clinical trials when that condition was thought to be exclusive to male homosexuals. Men, the elderly, and those with specific health conditions are frequently excluded from trials when they are determined to be irrelevant (men in pregnancy trials) or at risk (weak older people are not subjected to tests requiring vigorous exercise). But a systematic exclusion of half the population from clinical trials as a patriarchal conspiracy? Not quite.

Yet the myth is too valuable a propaganda tool to let go. Dr. Satel writes of being pestered by promotional materials from the Harvard Women's Health Watch newsletter claiming that "nearly all drug testing has been done on men." Phyllis Greenberger, speaking for the Society for Women's Health Research, sighs, "It's going to take some time before it's generally accepted that women and men have to be in clinical trials."[84] And that weathervane of conventional opinion, the *USA Today* editorial page, platitudinized, "The habit of overlooking women in medical research is deeply ingrained and hard to shake. For decades, women have been alternatively ignored or overprotected. And the research hierarchy is still largely dominated by the interests and concerns of white males."[85] One gathers that as white males, it is now our bounden obligation to apologize for producing so many doctors and scientists. It is as if each white male surgeon represents the denial of opportunity for an African-American woman.

Sally Satel points out that in 1979, the first year for which such data were available—and presumably a year smack in the middle of those dark ages during which medical researchers studying, say, menstrual cycles, ovulation, and menopause used only male subjects—268 out of the 293 clinical trials funded by the National Institutes of Health included women. Of the single-sex studies, 13 studied only women and 12 studied only men.[86]

Complicating matters—or uncomplicating them, as it were—is the fact that the vast majority of drugs have identical effects on men and women. In 1987, the Food and Drug Administration reported: "The number of documented gender-related pharmacological differences of clinical consequence is at this time small and conducting formal effectiveness studies to detect them may be difficult. . . . Such studies are not therefore routinely necessary."[87]

In 1999, the Clinton-era U.S. Commission on Civil Rights, ever on the lookout for examples of gender bias against which to set its lance, denounced medical schools for "steering... female students toward the more 'accepted' specialities such as pediatrics and general practice,"[88] while the boys, who always get all the breaks, waltz into such cushy niches as brain and heart surgery.

The problem, of course, is that female medical students choose freely those specialities that are most accommodating to those women who may want to bear and raise children.

Dare to point this out and you are accused of being kin to U.S. Supreme Court Justice Joseph Bradley, whose words in the 1872 case *Bradwell v. The State of Illinois* are a staple of feminist history. The Court upheld the right of Illinois to refuse to issue licenses to women to practice law. Bradley wrote: "Man is, or should be, woman's protector and defender. The natural and proper timidity and delicacy which belongs to the female sex evidently unfits it for many of the occupations of civil life. The constitution of the family organization, which is founded in the divine ordinance, as well as in the nature of things, indicates the domestic sphere as that which properly belongs to the domain and functions of womanhood.... The paramount destiny and mission of woman are to fulfill the noble and benign offices of wife and mother. This is the law of the Creator."[89]

Ouch!

That *Bradwell* is now an anachronism on the order of periwigs and birch beer seems not to calm the roiled waters of feminist agit-prop. Much less often quoted is the 1971 California State Supreme Court decision that stated the doctrine of equalitarian economic liberty: "Laws which disable women from full participation in the political, business and economic arenas are often characterized as 'protective' and beneficial. Those same laws applied to racial or ethnic minorities would readily be recognized as invidious and impermissible. The pedestal upon which women have been placed has all too often, on closer inspection, been revealed as a cage."[90]

Nevertheless, the special privileges demanded by feminists would seem to mark them as closer to *Bradwell*, in spirit, than to the California court decision. Demands for equal treatment grow dimmer when, in the light of day, women are found to be incapable of matching men in certain fields.

In Camille Paglia's admiring formulation, "Masculinity is aggressive, unstable, combustible. It is also the most creative cultural force in history."[91] Paglia has been kicked ass over syllabus for making such remarks, but by their behavior, feminists seem to ratify her insights.

In Britain, for instance, the Orange Prize for fiction is awarded to a female novelist each year—as though in the land of Jane Austen women writers need an affirmative action boost. Work by female artists makes up just seven percent of the collection of London's Tate Gallery, leading one female gallery owner to complain that "the art world remains dominated by a male perspective and male power."[92] And male talent? (That that perspective and power is to a considerable extent homosexual is of no comfort, one gathers, though heterosexual male artists have been complaining about this bias ever since the days of Thomas Hart Benton.)

Men create. Men also fight. And the degradation of standards in the U.S. military is a story so widely known, yet underreported, as to be scandalous. Women are simply unable to meet the physical requirements that men meet and have met for years. So the standards are lessened, or de-emphasized, or quietly dropped.

In one of the most notorious cases in the modern military, that of the carrier Theodore Roosevelt, about 15 percent (45 of 300) of female sailors in one 1999 deployment "either could not begin the cruise or complete it due to impending childbirth."[93] This may be good for the morale of male sailors, or at least it is nine months before childbirth, but the consequences for military readiness are catastrophic. This story was largely swept under the rug by a compliant media, but it has achieved a legendary status in naval circles.

The queen may be the most powerful piece on the chess board, but in real-life combat our martial queens are rather less nimble.

In 1975, the U.S. Congress ordered West Point, the Naval Academy, and the Air Force Academy to admit women the following school year. They did so, despite grumbling of the sort done by former West Point Superintendent William Westmoreland: "Maybe you could find one woman in ten thousand who could lead in combat, but she would be a freak, and we're not running the Military Academy for freaks."

Thirty years later, substantial numbers of men at the academies still believe that to be so, but they have learned that among the prices one pays for military service is keeping your mouth shut. West Point Dean Gerald Galloway is said to have once informed a faculty meeting, "If you don't think women should be at West Point, please leave by the door behind you."[94]

Dean Galloway's frank denial of dissent is by now a commonplace in our culture. Erin Solaro, author of *Beyond GI Jane: American Women, the War on Terror, and the New Civic Feminism*, has urged President George W. Bush to tell cadets, "There is no place here for men who do not believe women should be here."[95] It matters not, apparently, how fine a soldier a man is. What matters is his political viewpoint, his willingness to conform to feminist teachings, to deny the evidence of his own senses and internalize political correctness.

So active duty military men, learning that silence is the better part of valor, speak not a discouraging word about the sexual integration of the academies. No doubt the service academies have been enriched in various ways by female students, but their putative primary function—training the next generation of officers—has been compromised. As West Point grad Karl Day, a policy analyst with the Family Research Council, says, "Feminization has degraded the Academy and required a broadening of academics to accommodate women who are not particularly engineering-focused."[96]

Oh, Mr. Day: how many points of feminist etiquette can you violate in one sentence?!

A report in early 2005 alleged that one in seven women at the service academies had been the victim of a sexual assault, and while that number seems high, it also indicates that the training grounds for warriors, for men who are learning to fight and kill and not feel all guilty about it, are—just maybe—not the best place for 19-year-old women to live and study.

The classic exposition of the case for single-sex service academies remains James Webb's essay "Women Can't Fight." Webb—Naval Academy graduate, Vietnam veteran, best-selling novelist, Reagan's Secretary of the Navy and now the Democratic U.S. Senator from Virginia—wrote, "There is a place for women in our military, but not in combat. And their presence at institutions dedicated to the preparation of men for combat command is poisoning that preparation."[97]

Webb wrote that essay more than 25 years ago. While women are still technically prohibited from engaging in combat, they serve in support roles that invariably bring them into combat, and harm's way. Women have returned in body bags from the Iraq War. If this is the sort of equality feminists seek—an equal right to die on the other side of the world wearing a government uniform—then it is no wonder that so many women refuse to bear the feminist label.

NOTES

1. Daly, *Beyond God the Father*, 173.
2. McElroy, *Sexual Correctness*, 25.
3. Kubacki, "Nature or Nurture," *Ottawa Citizen*.
4. Sax, *Why Gender Matters*, 58.
5. Sax, *Why Gender Matters*, 75.
6. "Study: Meanness in Girls Can Start at 3," <www.kotv.com/home/stories> (9 May 2005).
7. Sommers, *The War Against Boys*, 63.
8. Nicki R. Crick, Maureen A. Bigbee, and Cynthia Howes, "Gender Differences in Children's Normative Beliefs about Aggression: How Do I Hurt Thee? Let Me Count the Ways," *Child Development* 67, no. 3 (June 1996): 1003.
9. Sandy Naiman, "'Little Girls Know the Power of Groups,'" *Toronto Sun*, August 1, 2004, 14.
10. Kirsti M.J. Lagerspetz, Kaj Bjorkqvist, and Tarja Peltonen, "Is Indirect Aggression Typical of Females?" *Aggressive Behavior* 14 (1989): 412.

11. Kaj Bjorkqvist, Kirsti M.J. Lagerspetz, and Ari Kaukiainen, "Do Girls Manipulate and Boys Fight?" *Aggressive Behavior* 18 (1992): 126.

12. Bridget Harrison, "Girls' Date Hate—Meaner Than Boys: Study," *New York Post*, November 18, 2004, 29.

13. Jenny Jackson, "Girls More Aggressive When Dating: Study," *Saskatoon Star Phoenix*, December 6, 2004, A1.

14. John Carvel and Steven Morris, "Alarm at Acceptance of Abuse by Teenage Girls," (London) *Guardian*, March 21, 2005, 3.

15. Sally Kidson, "Violent Girls Target of Pilot Programme," *The Nelson* (New Zealand) *Mail*, April 2, 2005, 1.

16. Elaine Cassel, "Girls and Relational Aggression: A Review of Odd Girl Out," <http://college.hmco.com/psychology/resources/ students/shelves> (4 February 2007).

17. Emily Warne, "Mean Girls? Teens Discuss 'Odd Girl Out' and the Culture of Bullying," *Buffalo News*, March 30, 2005, N2.

18. Susan Llewelyn Leach, "Behind the Surge in Girl Crime," *Christian Science Monitor*, September 15, 2004, 16.

19. David M. Brodzinsky, Stanley B. Messer, and John D. Tew, "Sex Differences in Children's Expression and Control of Fantasy and Overt Aggression," *Child Development* 50, no. 2 (June 1979): 377.

20. "Aggressive Girls—Overview Paper," Public Health Agency of Canada, <www.phac-aspc.gc.ca/ncfv-cnivf/familyviolence> (11 Jan. 2005).

21. Lindsay Taub and Alexandra Hall, "Female Juvenile Delinquents in Massachusetts, Overburdened System," *Boston Magazine*, April 2005, 118.

22. Philip C. Rodkin, Thomas W. Farmer, Ruth Pearl, and Richard Van Acker, "Heterogeneity of Popular Boys: Antisocial and Prosocial Configurations," *Developmental Psychology* 36, no. 1 (2000): 14.

23. "Sleep Problems for Black Boys," *Pittsburgh Post-Gazette*, October 12, 2004, D1.

24. "Do You Know What Video Games Your Child Is Playing?" <www.nbc10.com> (12 May 2005).

25. L. Rowell Huesmann, Jessica Moise-Titus, Cheryl-Lynn Podolski, and Leonard D. Eron, "Longitudinal Relations Between Children's Exposure to TV Violence and Their Aggressive and Violent Behavior in Young Adulthood: 1977–1992," *Developmental Psychology* 39, no. 2 (2003): 201.

26. Huesmann, Moise-Titus, Podolski, and Eron, "Longitudinal Relations Between Children's Exposure to TV Violence," 219.

27. M. Zapp, "Do You Know What Games Your Kids are Playing?" *Columbia Missourian*, May 8, 2005, 10A–13A.

28. "Hormone Linked to Severe Aggression in Boys," <www.mercola.com> (13 Jan. 2000).

29. Jessie Klein, "Teen Killers Feel Trapped by Masculine Stereotypes," *USA Today*, November 12, 2003, 13A.

30. "Gender Public Advocacy Coalition Applauds Bush Focus on Boys and Young Men," *U.S. Newswire*, February 3, 2005.

31. Sommers, *Who Stole Feminism?*, 15.

32. O'Neill, *Feminism in America*, 37.

33. Sommers, *Who Stole Feminism?*, 11.
34. Sommers, *Who Stole Feminism?*, 12.
35. Sommers, *Who Stole Feminism?*, 13–14.
36. Sommers, *Who Stole Feminism?*, 193.
37. Sommers, *Who Stole Feminism?*, 189.
38. Sommers, *Who Stole Feminism?*, 15.
39. Sommers, *Who Stole Feminism?*, 189–90.
40. Sommers, *Who Stole Feminism?*, 15.
41. Sommers, *Who Stole Feminism?*, 190.
42. Sommers, *Who Stole Feminism?*, 192.
43. Sommers, *Who Stole Feminism?*, 193–94.
44. Sommers, *Who Stole Feminism?*, 199.
45. Sommers, *Who Stole Feminism?*, 196.
46. Sommers, *Who Stole Feminism?*, 204.
47. Sommers, *Who Stole Feminism?*, 210–11.
48. Naomi Wolf, *The Beauty Myth: How Images of Beauty Are Used Against Women* (New York: Doubleday, 1992), 165.
49. Sommers, *Who Stole Feminism?*, 220.
50. Sommers, *Who Stole Feminism?*, 217.
51. Sommers, *Who Stole Feminism?*, 222.
52. McElroy, *Sexual Correctness*, 22.
53. McElroy, *Sexual Correctness*, 23.
54. Sommers, *Who Stole Feminism?*, 44.
55. McElroy, *Sexual Correctness*, epigraph.
56. McElroy, *Sexual Correctness*, 8.
57. Sommers, *Who Stole Feminism?*, 28.
58. Margaret Howard, "Husband-Wife Homicide: An Essay from a Family Law Perspective," *Law and Contemporary Problems* 49, no. 1 (Winter 1986): 68.
59. Howard, "Husband-Wife Homicide," 67.
60. Howard, "Husband-Wife Homicide," 81.
61. Howard, "Husband-Wife Homicide," 88.
62. Christine Stolba, *Lying in a Room of One's Own: How Women's Studies Textbooks Miseducate Students* (Arlington, VA: Independent Women's Forum, 2002), 13.
63. Sommers, *The War Against Boys*, 47–48.
64. Sommers, *The War Against Boys*, 57.
65. Sommers, *The War Against Boys*, 75.
66. Sommers, *The War Against Boys*, 18.
67. McElroy, *Sexual Correctness*, 112.
68. Men Against Libelous Editors, "Oh Judgment, Thou Art Fled to Brutish Beasts: Feminism's . . . err . . . Mistakes!" <file:///c:/DOCUME-1/GTAS/LOCALS> (Nov. 1996).
69. Melanie Phillips, "Who Will Speak for the Battered Men?" (London) *Sunday Times*, November 15, 1998, 17.
70. Gene Edward Veith, "Father's Day," *World Magazine*, February 5, 2005, 28.
71. Hise, *The War Against Men*, 100.

72. Mason, *The Equality Trap*, 80.

73. Mason, *The Equality Trap*, 22.

74. Stephen Baskerville, "Violence Against Families," *The American Conservative*, August 29, 2005, 25.

75. Babette Francis, "Act Has Ruined Our Men," (Melbourne) *Herald Sun*.

76. Fionola Meredith, "Wanted: Single-Sex Zones for Our Sanity," *The Irish Times*, March 4, 2005, 15.

77. Sommers, *Who Stole Feminism?*, 67.

78. David G. Myers, "The Powers and Perils of Intuition," *Psychology Today* 35, no. 6 (November/December 2002): 45.

79. Sally Satel, *PC, M.D.: How Political Correctness Is Corrupting Medicine* (New York: Basic Books, 2000), 107.

80. Satel, *PC, M.D.*, 109.

81. Hise, *The War Against Men*, 21.

82. Satel, *PC, M.D.*, 110.

83. Satel, *PC, M.D.*, 109.

84. Satel, *PC, M.D.*, 116–17.

85. Satel, *PC, M.D.*, 126.

86. Satel, *PC, M.D.*, 117.

87. Satel, *PC, M.D.*, 127.

88. Satel, *PC, M.D.*, 112.

89. Quoted in Haig Bosmajian, "Sexism in the Language of Legislatures and Courts," in Alleen Pace Nilsen, Haig Bosmajian, H. Lee Gershuny, and Julia P. Stanley, *Sexism and Language* (Urbana, IL: National Council of Teachers of English, 1977), 82–83.

90. Quoted in Bosmajian, "Sexism in the Language," 99.

91. Camille Paglia, *Sex, Art, and American Culture* (New York: Vintage, 1992), 53.

92. Beverley Knowles, "A Woman's Place Is on the Wall," (London) *Guardian*, April 6, 2005, 10.

93. Hise, *The War Against Men*, 173.

94. Bill Kauffman, "West Point Story," *The American Enterprise*, July/August 1999, 37.

95. Erin Solaro, "Time to Halt Sexual Assaults at Military Academies," *Baltimore Sun*, March 31, 2005, 17A.

96. Kauffman, "West Point Story," *The American Enterprise*, 37.

97. Kauffman, "West Point Story," 38.

Chapter Four

Rewriting His-Story, from God to Hillary Rodham Clinton

At the height of the mania of political correctness, a former "Tonight Show" writer named Edward P. Moser came up with *The Politically Correct Guide to American History*, a funny retelling of the American story using the stilted, clumsy, and ridiculous diction of the p.c. academic. A decade later, it no longer seems quite so funny, perhaps because our world, or at least that part of it that exists on a college campus, keeps moving in Moser's direction—alas, very unfunnily.

For instance, Moser recasts Paul Bunyan, lumberjack, as "the vertically endowed lumberjane Paula Bunyan," who practiced "such unfortunate local customs as the asphyxiation of maritime companions (fishing), the slaughter of forest animal companions (hunting), and, above all, the mass murder of botanical companions (lumbering)."[1] This will not seem so farfetched to parents of young schoolchildren, who learn about the Revolutionary War (when they do learn about the Revolutionary War) through novels and ostensibly factual stories of cross-dressing girls who fight and spy and pretty much win independence for the colonies on their own, with minimal help from the slave-owning likes of George Washington, whose birthday has been squeezed into the puzzlingly meaningless President's Day.

In Moser's burlesque, the "Founding Parents"[2] were "lifestyle bigots who frowned on out-of-wedlock births"[3] and insisted that married women drop their "pre-domestic incarceration name,"[4] formerly known as the maiden name.

But it has gotten harder to tell the parodies from the real world. Some feminist academics no longer conduct seminars: rather, they conduct "ovulars." Who could make this up?

As in such dystopian novels as Aldous Huxley's *Brave New World* (1932) and Ray Bradbury's *Fahrenheit 451* (1953), feminist activists seek to remold the minds of the next generations through schooling and the recasting of history. Little nuisances—facts, the families of their subjects, human nature—are to be disposed of with all the casual unconcern of a wanton girl pulling the wings off a fly.

The remolding begins early. As it does, coincidentally, in *Fahrenheit 451*, in which the kindergarten age is lowered to infancy so that the state can snatch children from their parents before they can walk or talk or absorb any illicit social or political ideas from mother or father.

Since the 1960s and 1970s, school textbooks have been rewritten with an eye—no, with two eyes, a brain, and indeed the entire body with the obvious exception of the heart—towards ramming feminist assumptions down the throats of children. John Wiley & Sons, among the most prominent textbook publishers, began its 1977 *Wiley Guidelines on Sexism in Language* with a Soviet-style picture of an androgynous-looking woman sawing while a young girl looked on. The caption read:

Sara got the boards.
Then her mother showed her how to use the hammer and the saw.[5]

This was no simple token, a gesture to women who were pursuing unconventional lives. No, almost en masse, textbooks for young children started featuring hammering ladies, baby-carriage-pushing men, and a decided paucity of images of men and women doing things that men and women usually do. For women, mothers were out, and lady cops were in. Male doctors virtually disappeared (unless they were nonwhite), but male nurses multiplied.

Old textbooks were thrown out in what might have made one massive book-burning bonfire. You see, in the early 1960s the federal government, just getting its tentacles into the formerly local field of education, subsidized the mass purchase of science textbooks. The Sputnik launch had convinced U.S. policymakers that the Soviet Union had become our equal, if not our superior, in several scientific disciplines, and what better way to catch up than to throw taxpayers' money at the problem? However—and this became a huge however— "[m]any of the books were historical accounts of scientific discoveries, and, because men have made most of the discoveries, these were books about men."[6]

Heaven forfend! In the newly enlightened late 1960s and 1970s, these male-dominated science texts had to be scrapped and replaced by texts that (1) removed the names of scientists from their discoveries; and (2) installed Madame Curie as the greatest scientist in the history of the world.

Wiley did not urge text writers to be conscious of sexual stereotypes in writing; it mandated conformity. "Books that treat both sexes equally are better books, and they sell better than those that do not," the publisher declared in its corporate voice. Those that do not bow to the new orthodoxy, it need not be added, were not published.

Wiley cracked the whip on adherents of traditional language and English grammar. Its grim guideline writers warned textbook authors against such crimes as use of the generic "man." For instance, the phrase "man became civilized" is altered to "human beings became civilized." Thus felicity is sacrificed to make a point that any cretin understands anyway: that "man" in this case refers to all persons of both sexes. The use of the generic "he" is treated as an offense deserving of the Chinese water torture. Though of course "Chinese water torture" is no doubt verboten as an ethnic slur. The Wileyites counsel the use of "they" and "their" as a substitute for he—as in "Everyone will get their comeuppance." This is flatly wrong and ungrammatical—but bad grammar is to be preferred to anything hinting of sexism.

The poverty of imagination exhibited by the feminist language police is on sorry display in Wiley's list of words and phrases to avoid—that is, in its (not "their") list of forbidden words. "Saleslady" must be replaced by the lumpish and less informative "salesperson." In fact, "lady" is gone, "woman" is in. "Manpower" becomes "personnel," though once the lady sleuths catch on that "personnel" contains the word "son" that will be tossed into the rubbish heap of forbidden words, too. "Middleman," a fine word with an alliterative poetry to it, is out, replaced by the boring "intermediary." "Foreman," which conveys an image of blue-collar authority, is erased from the Wiley dictionary in favor of the antiseptic white-collar "supervisor." Several fine words that tell us about the person described—"bachelor," "spinster," "divorcee"—are junked for the vague "single person."

The purpose of Wiley's speech code—and it is mirrored at other textbook publishing companies—seems to be to rob the English language of beauty, subtlety, and history. Some phrases, such as "henpecked husband," are so far beyond the pale that they don't even make the Wiley list of banned words. They are considered "trite," though in fact "henpecked husband" is an evocative phrase that conjures up a host of images.[7]

Wiley is far from the only censorious publisher of texts. By the mid-1970s, virtually every publisher of schoolbooks was squeezing writers in the vice of political correctness. Scott, Foresman had proscribed such useful words and even resonant phrases as the common man, businessman, early man, the fair sex, housewife, mailman, repairman, sculptress, and the attachment of the pronoun "she" when referring to an elementary school teacher.[8] The only surprise is that Scott, Foresman had not instructed writers to use "he or she" when referring to, say, an NFL quarterback or a heavyweight boxing champ.

Writing in the *English Journal*, one particularly maniacal Remolder of Youth actually proposed that textbook publishers devise sexism scores as a means of judging a book's worthiness. Under this plan, the publisher would award "bonus points to the author who depicts women as truck drivers and heavy equipment operators while giving negative points to the author who pictures women as mothers, housewives, or teachers." That these three last named vocations are motivated by love, by affection, and by kindness would seem to elevate them in any recognizable moral system—except feminism. (Fittingly, the communist regimes of the Eastern Bloc made heavy and heavy-handed use of propaganda images of women driving trucks and engaging in manual labor. The purpose was not liberation but industrialization: in post-World War II Czechoslovakia, for instance, women had to be coerced into hopping into the tractors and dumping their children in government-controlled daycare centers, where the children could read abecedenaries showing Mom aboard a tractor laboring to create a New Socialist Man.)

"Guidelines," as Albert J. Kingston and Terry L. Lovelace of the University of Georgia argued in the *Journal of Reading Behavior* in 1977, "is usually a euphemism for the words 'regulations' or 'musts.'"[9] Textbook authors who violate the guidelines have their work rejected or expurgated; the offending phrases are removed with the indelicacy of a drunken surgeon, or if an author commits too many offenses her work may never see the light of publication day. Kingston and Lovelace wrote with an admirable directness, saying that "these guidelines constitute a form of censorship!"[10]

Of course they did, and do. But the same sanctimonious goobers who walk around wearing t-shirts that say "I Read Banned Books" and who get their panties tied in knots whenever a school board in the deepest darkest mining town in West Virginia expresses doubt that *Catcher in the Rye* should be read by their seventh-graders submit meekly, even gratefully, to the censorious commands of the feminist bowdlerizers. There is phony courage, and then there is real courage.

Those who seek to control the language we use also want to control the images that enter our heads. Ban words, ban images. And what starts in elementary school continues right on through college.

Christine Stolba, an Emory University Ph.D. and senior fellow [*sic*! according to the language police] at the Independent Women's Forum, exposed and then demolished the propaganda barrage in *Lying in a Room of One's Own: How Women's Studies Textbooks Miseducate Students* (2002).

Stolba's cool, reasoned, amused detonation of feminist textbooks is a classic piece debunking the frauds and charlatans of the Women's Studies division of the academy. She did not, as so many are tempted to do, discredit these departments by quoting their most *outré* or lunatic members. Rather, she examined the mainstream, or at least what passes for the mainstream in those parts. She examined the syllabi of the leading and not-so-leading

Women's Studies departments from 30 colleges and universities ranging from Vassar to Lexington Community College. The most commonly used textbooks were:

- *Thinking About Women: Sociological Perspectives on Sex and Gender* by Margaret L. Andersen;
- *Women's Realities, Women's Choices: An Introduction to Women's Studies* by the Hunter College Women's Studies Collective;
- *Issues in Feminism: An Introduction to Women's Studies* by Sheila Ruth;
- *Women in American Society: An Introduction to Women's Studies* by Virginia Sapiro; and
- *Gender and Culture in America* by Linda Stone and Nancy P. McKee.

The authors, Stolba found, seldom bothered to hide behind even the pretense of objectivity or scholarship. Their purpose was, frankly, ideological and didactic. As Stone and McKee wrote in *Gender and Culture in America*, their goal and that of Women's Studies in general is to "challenge students to consider that addressing gender inequality in America involves not just activism or new laws and policies, but new modes of thought, a rethinking of our deepest, most accepted premises about the world."[11]

The object is nothing less than the transformation of the student: a pliable ball of putty in the hands of instructors who are as convinced of their rightness and as uninterested in opposing points of view as is the most jihad-crazed extremist imam. And don't think for a moment that such trifles as scholarly standards or the scientific method will be allowed to stand in the way of the construction of new persons. After all, as Sheila Ruth writes in *Issues in Feminism*, "Feminist theoreticians in every field . . . are convinced that no purely factual studies exist." What the rest of us believe are facts have "all developed within a framework of male bias."[12] That the earth orbits the sun, that the square root of 25 is five, that George Washington was the first president of the United States: all developed within a framework of male bias. They are not "purely factual" but rather the constructions of biased males.

The collective authors of the ironically named *Women's Realities, Women's Choices* actually put quote marks around the word "knowledge,"[13] for in achieving the "intellectual revolution" they advocate we must dispense with such archaic concepts as knowledge as well as logic, reason, a competent use of statistics, and even basic math skills. For these are tools of the patriarchy, weapons of phallocentrism that are more dangerous, more lethal, more anti-woman, and even more repulsive than the penis.

Stolba is as kind as she can possibly be when she writes, "Women's Studies textbooks support a large number of factual inaccuracies" and "deliberately misleading sisterly sophistries."[14] Moreover, they are "themselves purveyors of bias—skewing information, telling only part of the story, and failing to include facts that might inconvenience their arguments."[15] A less charitable observer might call them mendacious mishmashes of agit-prop and outright untruths.

The range of misinformation in the most popular Women's Studies textbooks is truly staggering. Without exception, they trumpet the so-called "wage gap": that hoary myth that women who work full time make only 70 cents (or 59 cents, or 65 cents—the myth is protean) of what their male counterparts make. I shall deal more fully with this fairy tale in Chapter Six, but for now let us note Stolba's remark that this quintet of "mainstream" Women's Studies texts consistently offer a "deliberately misleading presentation of the wage gap," attributing it to sexist discrimination, pure and simple.

"In 1890, a woman earned 46 cents for every dollar a man earned," mewls *Women's Realities, Women's Choices*. "A century later, we still earn only 69 cents."[16] As economist June O'Neill has discovered, the real wage gap amounts at most to a few pennies; others have found that single women with college degrees make more money than their male opposite numbers.

What is perhaps most nauseating about these Women's Studies texts is the contempt they display for women who make choices of which the authors and editors disapprove. Stolba finds auctorial disdain for "the fact that women physicians are more likely to work in pediatrics or family medicine."[17] In other words, they are people-oriented, more eager to work with children and families than are, say, brain surgeons or podiatrists. Just why this should be a source of dismay is something of a mystery. Healthy women might regard it as a source of pride.

In *Issues in Feminism*, Sheila Ruth disparages women who wish to devote something less than their hearts and souls to work and Mammon. "To meet home demands," sneers the ruthless Ruth, women "may settle for part-time shifts (such as 'Mommy Tracks'), poor hours, or local jobs, all of which can be terribly exploitative." The idea that "local jobs" are somehow inferior to jobs with global corporations comes as something of a surprise; but then Ruth seems not to have the faintest clue as to what women really want. As Stolba writes, "women do not find flexible work arrangements exploitative; on the contrary, many women (and an increasing number of men) rate job flexibility high on their list of priorities for achieving work/family balance."

The notion of work/family balance is an obscenity to many feminists, unless that family consists of two lesbians and a menagerie of cats.

Women who hold traditional "pink-collar" jobs come in for scorn. Their work is "often highly impersonal and routine, as in a typing pool," hiss the authors of *Women's Realities, Women's Choices*. They may scorn secretaries, but in the real world, pink-collar workers appreciate that "skill sets for these jobs deteriorate slowly, allowing women to move in and out of the workforce in those jobs without their skills becoming obsolete."

Barely able to contain their anger at their women students, "nearly all" of whom "plan to curtail or cease their paid employment after the children are born," *Gender and Culture*'s Stone and McKee chalk it up to dunces who "are apparently unaware that in these decisions they are following traditional gender stereotypes,"[18] i.e., behaving as generations of women have behaved. Stone and McKee, a higher form of the species, know better.

Perhaps the most distasteful aspect of that traditional gender stereotype is the love of men, or at least the assumption that "women need men for sexual arousal and satisfaction," as Andersen puts it in *Thinking About Women*. (The problem is that these authors think about *nothing but* women.) This is part and parcel of the cruelty of what the lesbian poet and polemicist Adrienne Rich calls "compulsory heterosexuality."[19] (If you have ever seen a photo of Ms. Rich, you'll realize that her abstention from heterosexuality has an element of compulsion about it as well.)

Glimpsing the male member is horrid enough, but to actually marry the owner of such an organ? Perish the thought! The collective authors of *Women's Realities, Women's Choices*, proudly admit to taking a "uniformly critical stance" on marriage, which they "regard as an instrument of social oppression."[20]

Indeed, these texts call to mind the immortal chant of the demure ladies of WITCH (Women's International Terrorist Conspiracy from Hell), who in 1969 protested a bridal fashion show with this little ditty: "Here come the slaves/Off to their graves."[21]

Bad poetry, bad manners, an appalling contempt for other women—all the hallmarks of feminism in a mere two lines.

"[T]he role of 'wife,'" write the authors, who for some odd reason consistently place "wife" in quotation marks, as though they can't quite bring themselves to believe that such a thing exists, is "intimately connected with the subordination of women in society in general."[22] By marrying "wives," those monsters known as "husbands" thereby "gain domestic servants, sexual companions, and producers of children but also political assets and instruments for acquiring allies." Sound like your home life? A married man, it appears, lives a sybaritic life of ease and power; his "wife" is maid, sexpot, cranker out of babies, campaign manager, and the means by which France, Spain, and Madagascar will seek alliance with him. What a bargain!

And the riches and glory just keep on coming. As Sheila Ruth complains in *Issues in Feminism*, "Because women do the 'shitwork' of society . . . men are free to spend their time on socially valued activities for which they receive all kinds of material and psychological rewards."[23] Sure, that janitor swabbing the toilet in the McDonald's bathroom is a man, as are most janitors, but just think how much tougher and less rewarding his work would be if hadn't the exquisite advantage of a penis. Who knows what valuable allies he is acquiring with mop and bucket!

For an ideology that in theory promotes the empowerment of women, feminism seems to take an awfully jaundiced view of the female of the species. Sheila Ruth, in *Issues in Feminism*, snipes, "As individuals within an oppressed group, we tend to accept the stereotypes of ourselves formulated by the dominant group in society, setting up a pattern of low self-esteem and isolation."[24] This low self-esteem is manifested by such self-deprecating acts as marrying men, bearing children, and, perhaps worst of all, caring for the children rather than turning them over to impersonal bureaucratic nurseries run by the state.

Keeping a house, which many women (and men) find a challenge and a reward, is "boring, ugly, tiresome, repetitive, unsatisfying, and lonely work."[25] So how do you like it now, Ms. Housewife?

Ruth reveals a repulsive mixture of scorn and pity for those who have gone before—those "mothers who themselves were bent to the yoke as we are meant to be." This is a fool's pity, the poisonously unctuous compassion that immature minds feel for the billions of human beings who have lived since the dawn of time without benefit of modern enlightenment and feminist consciousness-raising.

Their powers of perception limited by "mind control as an instrument of patriarchy," women are as "slaves . . . unaware of their condition, unaware that they were controlled, believing instead that they had freely chosen their life and situation."[26]

If ever a male chauvinist pig has expressed more contempt for women than has Ruth, I have yet to see it.

"Women's Studies textbooks err on the side of portraying motherhood as a burden for women, something to be overcome,"[27] writes Christine Stolba. The texts uniformly advocate government-subsidized daycare, despite mounting evidence that placing one's child in an impersonal bureaucratic setting to be cared for by strangers is inferior to virtually every other form of child nurturing this side of turning the pesky kid over to wolves.

If you must have a child, these books seem to suggest, at least do it without benefit of a live-in father. As Stolba notes incredulously, *Women's Realities, Women's Choices* devotes two pages to "the supposed ubiquitousness of incest and child abuse perpetrated by fathers"—a canard of feminists. "Our relationships with our fathers can be fraught with tension and instability. Daughters often find ourselves in league with our mothers against the foreign male element represented by the father." But there is hope on the far horizon, promise the authors, for "domineering fathers may provoke reactions in their daughters that release our feminist impulses and creative potential."[28]

There is no aspect of American womanhood which these authors are unwilling to turn into a burden, an onus, a badge of oppression. American women are living, on the average, five-plus years longer than men. Is this a source of pride or at least satisfaction to the authors of Women's Studies textbooks? Well, of course not. Margaret L. Andersen, author of *Thinking About Women*, chalks it up to male recklessness, in an example of what might be called "blaming the victim" were not the victims so un-p.c.

"Mortality differences between men and women are determined by men's greater risk of death by accident," Andersen writes, adding that this is "itself a function of men's engagement in risky behavior, violent activity, and alcohol consumption."[29] We get drunk, drive fast, and shoot off guns. That's how we all die.

As Christine Stolba notes, men are more likely to be uncovered by health insurance than are women, but that is of no significance to the author of these texts. For "what Women's Studies textbooks view as the real sickness," in Stolba's view, is "masculinity"[30]—and the only cure for that is death. The only good male, to paraphrase that notoriously masculine DWM Andrew Jackson, is a dead male.

In any event, the parade of errors and slanders against the male of the species continues throughout the medical sphere. "Women's Studies textbooks are riddled with errors about women's access to health care and about the causes and consequences of many women's health issues," writes Stolba. The books consistently make the flatly wrong claim that women are typically excluded from major tests and studies "of heart disease, lung cancer, and kidney disease."

The sources for such misstatements of fact are those legendarily mendacious ghosts known as "many experts." For instance, in Virginia Sapiro's *Women in American Society*, "many experts point to the shocking lack of research on women's bodies and health as one of the most serious health care problems for women."

"Many experts" are apparently not so expert enough as to know that "since 1985, when the NIH's National Cancer Center began keeping track of specific cancer funding, it has annually spent more money on breast cancer than any other type of cancer research."[31] A substantial majority—over 60 percent—of people in tests funded by the National Institutes of Health are women. As we detailed in the previous chapter, claims that American medicine shortchanges (longer-living) women are so absurd that it takes an Albert Gore to believe them.

Bring up the matter of prostate cancer to Women's Studies crowd and one is met with silence, if not outright cheering. Does the NIH annually spend three to five times less on prostate cancer than on breast cancer despite similar mortality rates for the diseases? Ah, so much the better. Let the bastards die. For you see, men are never being truer to their fundamental natures than when they are beating the crap out of women. They do it on Super Bowl Sunday, they do it on the final day of the Masters, they do it on Flag Day, they do it on Arbor Day, they do it on Gloria Steinem's Birthday.

We have already examined the inflated statistics for this despicable crime. One of the textbooks asserts that "a fairly large proportion of women who show up in emergency rooms of hospitals for treatment of injuries are victims of a phenomenon known as wife battering" (and note the use of "wife" when in fact a live-in girlfriend is likelier than a wife to be the object of an assault; mustn't waste any opportunity to show marriage in a bad light). Yet studies by the National Center for Health Statistics and the U.S. Bureau of Justice estimate that, at most, one percent of women treated in emergency rooms are being treated for assault by a husband or boyfriend.

Sapiro, in *Women in American Society*, makes the patently false assertion that "most research agrees that even when both partners engage in violence, men tend to be the primary perpetrators." Not true. Nor is the even stronger claim, in Andersen's *Thinking About Women*, that "studies indicate that the overwhelming amount of domestic violence is directed against women."[32]

Although doctrinaire feminists seldom listen to what men say, they are convinced that our language is one long tapestry of profanity punctuated by images and threats of violence. One of the texts in Stolba's sample provided this helpful example of how men and women speak:

"Women's Language: Oh dear, you've put the peanut butter in the refrigerator again, haven't you? Men's Language: Shit, you've put the damn peanut butter in the refrigerator again."[33] We may only hope that this exchange of sweet nothings did not occur on Super Bowl Sunday.

We'll put the peanut butter in the fridge and you'll like it, bitch! Or at least that's what we're supposed to say. For there is no wickedness in the world for which we men are not responsible. The always reliable Sheila Ruth asks, in *Issues in Feminism*, "Who creates weapons and marches off to war? Who hunts and kills living creatures for fun? Who fights for kicks? Who pillages the earth for profit? Who colonizes and exploits?"[34]

Who does? We do! One might add, "Who invented the refrigerator?" but some things are better left unsaid.

The fantasies of the American Association of University Women regarding bias against girls in education—so memorably debunked by Christina Hoff Sommers in one of the classic exposures of charlatanry—are repeated as gospel truth in Women's Studies textbooks. College frosh are exposed to such manifestly fraudulent claims as that in *Women's Realities, Women's Choices* that irrefutable evidence proves the "unequal treatment girls receive in a wide range of areas, including curricula, materials used in classrooms, testing, and teacher attention."[35] The authors go on to pass off as truth the infamously false claim of the Sadkers' that "as compared to boys, girls receive less attention and praise from teachers; request less help; and are less dominant in class.... Even at the college level, teachers pay more attention to male students than to female students.[36]

As for the political bias embedded in these books: well, let's just say that Margaret Thatcher is as invisible as Hillary Rodham Clinton is lauded. And the Republicans? On those infrequent occasions when they might merit mention, they are barely conceded the status of human beings. Sheila Ruth writes in *Issues in Feminism*: "Anti-feminist, antiwoman forces on the right have whittled away at our demands for human parity, for reproductive autonomy, and for economic justice, and today they promise continued assault. The 1990s have given us the Contract on America [it was called the Contract with America, but when in full hysterical mode Ms. Ruth cannot be bothered to identify her opponents accurately], the virulent racism and misogyny of the religious and political right, attacks against the poorest and most vulnerable among us." The villains go beyond mere Republicans and kindred subhumans to include "antiwoman pseudo-feminists, to patriarchy-worshipping 'Promise Keepers,' to social 'scientists' [there's that dismissive and juvenile use of quotation marks again] suddenly discovering and suddenly becoming concerned about absent fathers and negative (or nonexistent) male role models."

Wow. That's an even-handed presentation of the political scene for you. Just for laughs—actually, she is in deadly earnest, but anyone with a sense of the absurd will take it as just for laughs—Ruth tells readers a couple of pages later that "most of us [in Women's Studies] try to encourage and be open to ideas even when they are very different from our own."[37]

Outstanding work, Sheila! If ever a writer has utterly undercut her own work, has thoroughly discredited everything she might say, it is Sheila Ruth and her grim totalitarian sisters of the Women's Studies textbook racket. They "present only one side of a question, omitting arguments or facts that are relevant but that prove an uncomfortable fit with their feminist agenda,"[38] concludes Christine Stolba. "[T]hese texts also teach Women's Studies students that dismissive—even contemptuous—and shoddy summaries of their opponents' work is an appropriate intellectual response to ideas that challenge one's own."[39]

Amen, Dr. Stolba.

Dr. Margaret L. Andersen, whose textbook, *Thinking About Women: Sociological Perspectives on Sex and Gender*, has gone through five editions since first appearing in 1983, is considered one of the more moderate of feminist textbook writers. Dr. Andersen goes so far as to thank Richard Rosenfeld for his "love" as well as his "management of our household,"[40] which both fits the model of the femininist activist (having a househusband) but also breaks it by, well, loving a man.

Yet Andersen's book is the same dreary compilation of half-truths whose transmission depends on auditors who are easily manipulated ("women college graduates who worked full time earned, on average, 70 percent of what men college graduates earned working full time")[41] and laughable contortions of fact whose purpose is to always depict women as victims. ("Although women live longer than men, they report more ill health than men do"[42]—well, yes: 75-year-old women suffer from osteoporosis—and 75-year-old men are dead.)

Women are victims, women are oppressed, women are everywhere in chains. "[W]omen have been wiped out of history," pules Mary Daly.[43] Margaret Andersen means to wipe them back in by wiping out the men. (Except, one supposes, useful househusbands.)

"It may occur to you one night as you are walking through city streets that the bright lights shining in the night skyline represent the thousands of women—many of them African American, Latina, or Asian American—who clean the corporate suites and offices for organizations that are dominated by White men,"[44] writes Andersen. It might not occur to the indoctrinated 18-year-old student that those buildings didn't build themselves but rather were built by the sweat and blood and ingenuity of those White men whose sole aim in life, in the view of Andersen and her ilk, is to keep Latina room cleaners down. It might also not occur to that 18-year-old text reader that male janitors are in those skyscrapers, too, and that they are typically assigned those tasks that require strong stomachs (cleaning toilets) and strong bodies (moving heavy objects).

The alleged invisibility of women is a favorite trope of feminist literature. "As the river of a girl's life flows into the sea of Western culture, she is in danger of drowning or disappearing," gushed Carol Gilligan.[45]

Opting for rather more gruesome imagery, Mary Pipher, author of the best-selling *Reviving Ophelia: Saving the Selves of Adolescent Girls* (1994), panicked: "Something dramatic happens to girls in early adolescence. Just as planes and ships disappear mysteriously into the Bermuda Triangle, so do the selves of girls go down in droves. They crash and burn."[46]

My oh my. Are these the same girls who dominate American colleges and high school national honor societies? If they are crashing and burning into the Bermuda Triangle, what, pray tell, is happening to the boys?

Given this luridness, it is no wonder that certain fantastic tales find their way into textbooks, where they are enshrined as incontrovertible facts. Among the hoariest if most ridiculous myths of male oppression of women is that expressed in 1982 in the government publication *Under the Rule of Thumb: Battered Women and the Administration of Justice—A Report of the United States Commission on Civil Rights*. As Sommers found, the commission report erroneously claimed, "American law is built on the British common law that condoned wife beating and even prescribed the weapon to be used. This 'rule of thumb' stipulated that a man could only beat his wife with a 'rod not thicker than his thumb.'"[47]

An irresistible anecdote, repeated often in Women's Studies texts—and utterly untrue. Despite its widespread, almost ubiquitous presence in American folklore, and its frequent repetition in mainstream journals and on television talk shows, the "rule of thumb" story has no basis in fact or history. "The real explanation of 'rule of thumb' is that it derives from woodworkers," as Christina Hoff Sommers quotes a Canadian folklorist, "who knew their trade so well they rarely or never fell back on the use of such things as rulers. Instead, they would measure things by, for example, the length of their thumbs."[48]

So there you have it: a phrase whose provenance reflects well on the skill of male woodworkers is transmogrified into a feminist fantasy whereby men—those same woodworkers, presumably—may beat their wives with impunity so long as the weapon of torture is not fatter than their thumbs. Another patch in the feminist quilt of lies.

Women's Studies may be a joke, but it is no longer a sideshow. One study of syllabi in 55 leading American universities found that 54 of them (Princeton was the holdout) offered more undergraduate courses in Women's Studies than in Economics. Yet ten times more students major in Econ than in Women's Studies. Do you sense an agenda?[49]

The only hope for a white male to get a fair shake in these texts is if his sexual appetite runs to other men. Leave women for the women! For instance, Abraham Lincoln may well undergo a new vogue with the publication of C.A. Tripp's dubious work, *The Intimate World of Abraham Lincoln* (2005), in which Tripp declares that the Great Emancipator was into men. The book was widely trashed by mainstream historians—Rutgers professor David Greenberg called it "tendentious, sloppy, and wholly unpersuasive,"[50] and Tripp's one-time coauthor Philip Nobile devastated the book and the plagiarism-prone late author in the *Weekly Standard*—but no matter: the cat is out of the bag, the genie has escaped the bottle, and the highly questionable "fact" of Abraham Lincoln's homosexuality is about to become an embedded myth of higher education.

Tripp's work is laughably bad, his evidence scandalously thin: that Lincoln signs letters to one man "Yours forever" is adduced as proof of his lusting heart, even though he often signed his epistles "Yours forever" when writing to persons that no one in his wildest imagination could peg as Lincoln love partners.

"Male history," as a distressingly typical pair of "male" historians (Martin Mills and Bob Lingard) assert, "has been a history shaped by xenophobia, homophobia, and misogyny."[51] It is distinguished by "privileges accruing to heterosexual men simply on the basis of their manhood"[52]—including, presumably, dying in wars, slaving away on the pyramids, working 60 hours a week in coal mines to support their families. You know, the whole range of male privilege that makes life such a tea party for those of us cursed with penises.

The State Department of Education in California requires of public schools: "Whenever an instructional material presents developments in history or current events, or achievements in art, science, or any other field, the contributions of women and men should be represented in approximately equal number."[53] This leads to distortions of our cultural and scientific histories that become parodistic. Since almost every significant scientific discovery in recorded history has been made by a person possessing male organs, those who write texts and pamphlets for California science classes have the aforementioned choice that has bedeviled text writers for 30 years now: lie or devote inordinate space to Madame Curie.

Female scientists like the nineteenth-century astronomer Maria Mitchell, a fine if hardly Galileo-quality figure, are inflated into veritable Newtons of the age. (Racial correctness leads to the same distortions: African-American almanac writer Benjamin Banneker has become perhaps the best-known scientist in American history.)

In areas such as physics, where the distaff presence has been an absence, confounded text writers can solve their problem by simply dropping males from the account. But perhaps that is better than the feminist take on physics. In *The Science Question in Feminism*, academic Sandra Harding refers to Newton's Principles of Mechanics as "Newton's Rape Manual."[54]

In Christine Stolba's study of Women's Studies textbooks, she found such claims as that "these people—scientists—are like all human beings, products of their culture . . . their investigations and conclusions about female and male characteristics necessarily reflect the perspectives and expectations of the dominant male culture." Margaret L. Andersen, in *Thinking About Women*, puts it in wackier terms, informing the unsuspecting college freshpersyns who are forced to buy her book that "despite the strong claims of neutrality and objectivity by scientists, the fact is that science is closely tied to the centers of power in this society and interwoven with capitalist and patriarchal institutions."[55]

Naturally, most female scientists utterly reject the absurd effusions of the feminists. Mathematician Margarita Levin asks, "One still wants to know whether feminist airplanes would stay airborne for feminist engineers."[56] The laws of physics have a funny way of not bending for gender.

Writers with the great misfortune of possessing male genitals—say, Shakespeare—are *persona non grata* in departments run by feminists. Richard T. Hise notes that in one celebrated case, Arizona State University theater professor Jared Sakren was fired when he insisted on teaching Shakespeare instead of a sublime work called "Betty the Yeti," the heartwarming tale of "a female Sasquatch" who "seduces a conservative, gun-toting logger and turns him into a sensitive, enlightened environmentalist."

Explaining Sakren's crime against Betty the Yeti, an Arizona State teaching assistant remarked, "The feminists are offended by the selection of works from a sexist European canon that is approached traditionally."[57]

The anecdotes about anti-sexism run riot over common sense and freedom of speech and are as numerous as grains of sand on the beach, or the hairs under a Women's Studies instructor's armpits. Their number is legion, countable perhaps only by God—but then God, as we shall see, is an implacable foe in the view of feminist intellectuals.

"The church is the enemy,"[58] stated Betty Friedan, godmother of the 1960s feminism.

That parodist of political correctness, Edward P. Moser, dubs God "the Patriarchal Oppressor,"[59] which is actually rather mild given the fervency of most feminist denunciations of the Old Testament God. Moser also refers to Delilah's consort as "Samdaughter—or Samanthadaughter, or Samanthason, or Samson"[60]—which is absurd, you say, until you read feminist theologians and see that this is how they really write!

The queen bee of such theologians, even though she disdains the T-word almost as much as she loathes the G-word, is Mary Daly, whose *Beyond God the Father: Toward a Philosophy of Women's Liberation* (1973) is the touchstone volume—the bible, you might say—of the movement. It is the key to understanding just where these women are coming from—and just where they would like to send organized religion.

Which is to a God that is not only not a father, but a God to whom no masculine pronoun can be attached. It hasn't happened yet, of course. Despite a push by feminists who claim that the Bible is a sexism-ridden book that perpetuates the patriarchy, the editors of the New Revised Standard Version have resisted—so far—efforts to refer to God as "She" and "Her." The scholars were reluctant to alter the pronouns as they had appeared in the original Hebrew and Greek, they have explained sheepishly after each revision. The feminist fallback position—removing all pronouns—has also failed because it would render the language of the Bible repetitive, what with God this and God that and nary a Him or He. Not that an argument from felicity appeases feminist critics: they don't care in the least about the beauty of the language.

But then many "religious" feminists are scornful of Christianity itself and dismissive of the Bible. Just why editors of biblical revisions should pay attention to women who despise them, their work, and their book is a matter that no one has ever bothered to explain. But then to do so would be to understand Mary Daly, and that is a challenge that even God might shy from.

Mary Daly wrote *Beyond God the Father*, as she recalls in a spectacularly incoherent "original reintroduction" for the 1985 paperback edition, in the midst of "Be-Friending, which means 'the creation of a context/atmosphere in which leaps of Metamorphosis can take place.' Be-Friending is Realizing the Lust to share happiness, and it is possible when women begin to re-member our Elemental potency and therefore experience Be-Longing, the Lust for happiness."[61]

Got that?

Daly uses hyphens the way truck drivers in Manhattan's garment district use the f-word. You must remember, or re-member, to borrow Daly's orthography, that *Beyond God the Father* was not just some kooky New Age effusion but a seminal—if you will excuse the masculine implications of that word—book on which the feminist revision of Christianity, a process that has crippled and may well eventually kill off the mainline Protestant denominations, was based.

Daly is given to erratic capitalization, but then so are many poets. Alas, her prose is about as far from poetical as can be. Make sense of this, if you will: "Weaving our own Time/Space on the boundaries of clockocracy, Websters Doom these doomers."[62]

You betcha, Mary!

But Daly has a valid excuse for her abuse of the language: she denies its validity. "We denounce both good usage and bad usage, proclaiming the termination of usage," she says of those patriarchal artifacts known as "words." She continues, "Journeying Websters are enabled to declare words free from usage insofar as we Speak our lives in an Other context."[63]

She chucks women into categories—Crones, Norns, Nags, Sirens—as carelessly as the most arrant sexist. Time she dismisses as a male construct: after all, we call him Father Time, don't we?

As for men . . . well, they are pigs, that's for sure, in Mary Daly's world. Or as she puts it in a typically felicitous passage: "Re-membering/Musing women know that man continues to manufacture memories for himself and that to this end he is escalating the use of torture, blood, sacrifice—physical and psychic. The man-made memories embedded in women—particularly through the masterminded media—torture, batter, and bury Deep Memory, afflicting women with amnesia."[64]

The years of Ronald Reagan's presidency drove her into a deep dolor: "The horrors of the 1980s—experienced concretely in the day-to-day struggle to survive with our bodies/minds intact—have been Lived through." But just as Helen Reddy roared with the realization of her own indomitable womanhood, so does Daly find those "horrors" to have been "surmounted to the degree that we have been able to Realize our own potency." I am Woman/Hear Me Bore!

Still, as long as one penis is still attached to one functioning hetero-male, the Crones are not safe. For "the dis-ease of phallocracy is extending its organs everywhere."[65] The ultimate goal of the phallocrats—that's you, Mister!—is gynocide, or the murder of women. Just what the phallocrats will do with their phalluses when all the women are dead is a matter not mused on by Ms. Daly. Expect a burgeoning trade in blow-up dolls.

Pretty much all evils flow from the phallus: "the nuclear arms buildup, racism, man-made poverty, chemical contamination." For "rapism" is the "paradigm of all oppression."[66] Men, by definition, are rapists. Even the loneliest hermit, or the kindliest saint, is a rapist if he is a he. And there ain't nothin' he can do about it. God is on his side. Which is where Mary Daly's problems with God start.

Daly casts a cold eye on those namby-pamby feminists who wish merely to change God to Goddess. This is a mere "transsexual operation on the patriarchal god," she complains. Risking offense to transgendered persons, she observes that "a 'transsexed' male is still male"—a she male, in crude parlance. And a she-male goddess will not do! For she/he still "serves the cockocratic establishment,"[67] remarks this long-time professor at the putatively Catholic Boston College. (To "cockocrat" and "phallocrat" Daly adds the flaccid "bore-ocrat" in her never-ending lexicon of abuse.)

Women who fail to follow Daly away from the "godfather, son and holy ghost theology" are deluded by "the propaganda of patriarchy." If only they would follow the author, they would learn about "shifting the shapes of space and time, rearranging energy patterns, breaking through and relocating boundaries,"[68] and perhaps they would meet a few congenial lesbian witches to boot.

It is not enough to reform the phallocracy—to make it, well, less phallic. It must be smashed. (Or severed, if that term doesn't cause too much Lorena Bobbitt-esque wincing.) "Witches/Hags," Daly's ideal women, understand that "assimilation is deadly."[69] The enemy—whose name is embedded backwards in the three middle letters of "enemy"—must not be propitiated, humored, or made dinner. He must be destroyed. The models here are the "Moon-Goddesses—Gorgons," who "look toward men and turn them to stone." This may sound physically impossible, but if you've ever seen a photograph of Mary Daly you will Re-alize that it just might work.

To sum up, "Surviving women Realize Presence. Conjuring the Courage to See, Viragos/Gorgons expel the phallic presence of absence—that glut of non-sense which expands meaninglessly, suffocating meaning. As Sibyls, we are becoming prescient, presentiment. As Soothsayers, Survivors are learning to presentiate Other reality, causing this to be Realized as present."[70]

Thus speaketh the most influential female "intellectual" in American theology today.

Beyond God the Father, while using a more conventional lexicon than her bizarre reintroduction, is no less loopy than the later Daly. She is out to expose "antifeminism in the Judeo-Christian heritage," which ever since the scapegoating of Eve has been a cesspool of misogyny, exploitation, and the subjugation of women by the malign patriarchy. She adduces such examples as Pope Pius XII's remark that "the mother who complains because a new child presses against her bosom seeking nourishment at her breast is foolish, ignorant of herself, and unhappy."[71] Most mothers might agree with the Pope, or at least chalk the miserable new mom's blues up to postpartum depression, but they would be the victims of false consciousness in the world of Mary Daly. So beguiled and brainwashed are they by the hetero-patriarchal dictatorship that they actually accept, even, horrors, enjoy, the role of "mother." That Mary never experienced motherhood should perhaps go unremarked.

Daly eschews both theology and philosophy as "male-created" disciplines; her goal is "to transform human consciousness" and thereby encounter "what some would call God."[72] (Imagine if at the end of her transformation she came on God and the old trickster was the stern white-bearded man of Sunday School! Oh, the furies!) She looks forward to the arrival of the Antichrist, which is synonymous with "the Second Coming of women."[73]

Say this for Mary Daly: she doesn't mince words. She wants the Antichrist to come, and by God she is doing all she can to hasten his/her arrival. It is time, she declares, to "castrate . . . that great 'God-Father' of us all which indulges senselessly and universally in the politics of rape."[74] Daly pronounces herself a "deicide,"[75] a God-killer, who places her faith in the Fall and the "Antichurch." All of which she has a perfect right to do. But how, one wonders, did this man-hater, this God-hater, this sworn foe of "Christolatry,"[76] which would seem to be synonymous with Christianity, come to have a deep and lasting influence on Christian feminists?

In her occasional explicable passage, Daly explains that her God is a verb, not a noun; it is in fact found in women's liberation, to use her now archaic term. "The unfolding of the woman-consciousness is an intimation of the endless unfolding of God." By rejecting patriarchy and the phallus, women become. Become Gods? Not quite. But they are able to become something transcendent (a favorite fuzzy word of Daly's, though we must remember that words were created by oppressive cockocrats and are thus inadequate to express the magnificent thoughts she is cerebrating). Women create new space, new time, they . . . well, they transcend.

"[I]n some sense we must share [Marxism's] insistence upon atheism,"[77] writes Daly. An atheist theologian would seem to be an exercise in self-negation, but Daly is willing to use "God" in a noninvidious way: her "God is form-destroying, form-creating, transforming power that makes all things new."[78]

God, in other words, equals Mary Daly's philosophy.

Daly's employer, Boston College, which at last report was a Roman Catholic institution, upholds a curious idea of academic freedom when it comes to its Transcendent Castrating Gorgon. Daly, who like a peevish child disparages her employer by refusing to capitalize the "C" in Catholic or the "J" in Jesuit, insisted upon teaching an all-female class in feminist ethics. That she is permitted to do so by the Jesuits suggests that Catholic discipline has gone awfully lax in these later days. Not that Mary Daly concurs: she sees her oppression by BC as emblematic of "the universal condition of women in all universities and in all institutions of patriarchy."[79] Which is true if that universal condition consists of being coddled and cosseted and having special rules set up for her and only her.

When a luckless or intrepid young man named Duane Naquin tried to penetrate, if you will excuse the verb, Daly's class, she refused to hear anything of it. She would furnish the class readings to males, but they could not sit in the class with the female students. When the Center for Individual Rights, a public-interest law firm, filed suit for Mr. Naquin, Professor Daly responded that the Center consisted of "dickheads,"[80] which as we know is a term of very great disapprobation in Mary Daly's world. (Indeed, given her aversion to the male member, it is remarkable that Daly solicited a blurb for one book from Harvard Professor Harvey Cox. As far as we know she never did receive the endorsement of Herman Balz.)

Daly may exclude men from her classrooms, but she has been unable to devise a way to keep men from reading her books. Well, her prose is actually a fairly effective deterrent to readers, male and female, but those with a cast-iron stomach and a taste for what can only be called insane narrative may plunge into her autobiography, the accurately titled *Outercourse* (1992), which she immodestly subtitles *The Be-Dazzling Voyage*.

Give Daly this: she does not lack confidence. Pronouncing herself not a rigorously unattractive professor but rather a "Pirate, Righteously Plundering and Smuggling back to women gems which have been stolen from us by the patriarchal thieves," she decides that in order to "Throw off mindbindings/ spiritbindings," an act which is central to the achievement of Feminist Creativity, she must "break rules which restrict creative expression."[81] These rules presumably include the most basic rules of punctuation.

Mary Daly is big on some rules—for instance, those restricting the freedom of expression for men—but not so big on others. After all, she is after

"Outercourse," which is defined, if this is a definition, as "moving beyond the imprisoning mental, physical, emotional, spiritual walls of patriarchy,"[82] not to mention grammar.

Ms. Daly, in her own account, was nothing if not precocious. She remembers even her "preconception," those days in the womb in which she was more "reflective and critical" than other fetuses. It was within this matrix that she made the crucial decision to be born female. After considering "the extremely poor showing, that is, the wretched record of the majority of males wielding patriarchal power on this planet,"[83] she willed herself a vagina and out she popped, into a world too damned obtuse to appreciate her manifold, or womynifold, charms.

Although to an outside observer Daly might appear to have led a life favored by the powers that be, as she professes her faith for a substantial salary at a respected college and travels the world delivering incoherent lectures to bedazzled lesbians, she sees nothing but dolor and prison walls as far as the eye can see. She apparently accepted her appointment at Boston College under false pretenses. She neglected to tell the priests who hired her that "for years I had found the christian fixation on the 'divinity of Christ' and on the figure of Jesus disturbing and profoundly repulsive." Christ "profoundly repulsive"? Yes, one imagines that the priests at Boston College might have hesitated to hire a professor with such beliefs. She likely kept them to herself—until her job was secure.

The purpose of Christianity, or christianity in her orthography, is merely "to legitimate patriarchy."[84] This is the purpose of everything in Mary Daly's world, from toasters to Tang to tiddlywinks. Patriarchy is being legitimated as we speak, as we write, as we sleep. It never stops.

Mary Daly has left christianity behind. She sees it as hideous superstition. As a rational being too sophisticated to fall for that bunkum, she instead holds to a more solidly grounded faith. As she sums up in words of utter clarity, "I See that it is in The Fourth Spiral Galaxy that the Craft of the Crafty Voyager can truly begin to Move as the Craft of the Fourth Dimension."[85]

At last, a religion based on self-evident truths! No more superstitious hokum!

The more one reads about the voyages of Mary Daly, the crazy aunt of feminist theology, the more one realizes that she has dissembled and dissimulated when it suits her purposes. In October 1971, Professor Daly was invited to be the first woman ever to preach of a Sunday at Harvard Memorial Church. She might have said "no" on principle, but that would have required her to have principles. Instead, she accepted the invitation and plotted an exodus, a walkout, and what she calls, in a typical delusion of grandeur, "an historic Moment of Breakthrough and Re-Calling."[86] (What, you've never heard of this historic moment? The patriarchy has kept you stupid!)

Mary "mounted" what she calls "the gigantic, phallus-like pulpit" on November 14, 1971, declared, "We cannot really belong to institutional religion as it exists,"[87] and walked out together with dozens of other women in a carefully planned and choreographed march. Daly assumed that this petulant act by a few privileged upper-middle-class feminists at Harvard would bring down the whole of religion crashing around her. It did not. Indeed, no one outside Mary's narrow circle of friends even knows about it, because "the patriarchs . . . have in large measure managed to erase it from history."[88]

The megalomania here is overwhelming. His-story books exclude her not because she is a marginal kook with bad manners but because men, those penised monsters, conspire to minimize her role in the his-story of humankind. It's enough to drive a gal over the edge.

The dogged reader is struck by the banality of this "radical's" concerns: she spends much of her autobiography whining about tenure, sniping at campus critics, even committing that gaucherie of all auctorial gaucheries: replaying favorable reviews of her books. It's all just so . . . middle class.

Sure, one minute she's writing "In The Third Spiral Galaxy I continued my work as a Pirate sailing through the Mist of the Subliminal Sea, taking on the massive symbol system of patriarchal religion,"[89] but a few paragraphs later this Pirate is applying for and receiving "a very substantial grant"[90] from the Rockefeller Foundation. Some Pirate!

Daly is not exactly an outcast living on crumbs in her garret. Whilst "vowing that I would dare to Spin Wildly, always,"[91] she is seeking tenure. She befriends a cow, a gentle bovine soul she names Catherine, urging her "Be Free, Catherine!"[92] but she is always careful to put first things first: no sooner does she bid farewell to the cow than she's bitching about money, about the "zero salary increment"[93] she received from Boston College one year.

This career-mongering becomes downright embarrassing. When a BC committee tells Daly that her work is "unscholarly," she goes into a rant so puerile, so boastful, so full of cockalorum—a word she would run from screaming—that the sensitive reader must avert her eyes. "I richly deserved the rank of full professor," sneers Daly, speaker to cows, spiraling pirate, and "Boston College's long denial of that rank did not dishonor me, but rather that institution itself."[94]

Oh, Mary. Please, stop. Go back to the lesbian cows.

When female students accuse the BC administration of committing "gynocide"[95] by not paying Mary what a world-class scholar of her rank deserves—"Mary Daly is being starved out," they chanted, though one look at Mary's photo suggests otherwise—the genius takes a break from grubbing money and coveting status to be "Touched" by the "New Surge of Hope"[96] that she, Mary Daly, had inspired among the women of Boston College.

A prophet's work is never done. Though with her obsessive raise-craving we might take a page from Daly's creative spelling book and call her a Profitess.

Finally, as enjoyable as wacky Mary the Spinning Pirate can be, the hatred of men is just too much to bear. It's as if some bizarrely goofy Stalinist or Nazi is holding court about his time travels: one might listen for more minutes than one is comfortable admitting, but sooner or later—sooner, one hopes—the nausea wins out. Daly detests men, whom she calls "bores, botchers, butchers, jocks, plug-ugles, rippers, and other snools"—that's you, fellas—and views them as "driven by phallic lust, which is violent and self-indulgent, leveling all life, dis-membering spirit/matter, attempting annihilation."[97] She leaves no doubt about just what she'd like to do to each and every member on earth: cut the damned thing off.

And snools, every time you pick up a missal in your church pew and find the fatherhood of God diminished or the androgynous qualities of God emphasized, remember that the goal of the revisionists is to go beyond God the Father into not God the Father and Mother but . . . God the Nothing.

NOTES

1. Edward Moser, *The Politically Correct Guide to American History* (New York: Three River Press, 1996), 88.
2. Moser, *The Politically Correct Guide*, 11.
3. Moser, *The Politically Correct Guide*, 12.
4. Moser, *The Politically Correct Guide*, 20.
5. *Wiley Guidelines on Sexism in Language* (New York: John Wiley & Sons, 1977), second frontispiece.
6. Alleen Pace Nilsen, "Sexism in Children's Books and Elementary Teaching Materials," *Sexism and Language*, 169.
7. *Wiley Guidelines on Sexism in Language*, unpaginated.
8. Albert J. Kingston and Terry L. Lovelace, "Guidelines for Authors: A New Form of Censorship?" *Journal of Reading Behavior* 9, no. 1 (1977): 91.
9. Kingston and Lovelace, "Guidelines for Authors," 90.
10. Kingston and Lovelace, "Guidelines for Authors," 92.
11. Stolba, *Lying in a Room of One's Own*, 6.
12. Stolba, *Lying in a Room of One's Own*, 8.
13. Stolba, *Lying in a Room of One's Own*, 7.
14. Stolba, *Lying in a Room of One's Own*, 8.
15. Stolba, *Lying in a Room of One's Own*, 16.
16. Stolba, *Lying in a Room of One's Own*, 8.
17. Stolba, *Lying in a Room of One's Own*, 9.
18. Stolba, *Lying in a Room of One's Own*, 10.
19. Stolba, *Lying in a Room of One's Own*, 19.

20. Stolba, *Lying in a Room of One's Own*, 20.
21. McElroy, *Sexual Correctness*, 107.
22. Stolba, *Lying in a Room of One's Own*, 20.
23. Stolba, *Lying in a Room of One's Own*, 21.
24. Stolba, *Lying in a Room of One's Own*, 18.
25. Stolba, *Lying in a Room of One's Own*, 21.
26. Stolba, *Lying in a Room of One's Own*, 18.
27. Stolba, *Lying in a Room of One's Own*, 22.
28. Stolba, *Lying in a Room of One's Own*, 23.
29. Stolba, *Lying in a Room of One's Own*, 11–12.
30. Stolba, *Lying in a Room of One's Own*, 10.
31. Stolba, *Lying in a Room of One's Own*, 11.
32. Stolba, *Lying in a Room of One's Own*, 13.
33. Stolba, *Lying in a Room of One's Own*, 24.
34. Stolba, *Lying in a Room of One's Own*, 27.
35. Stolba, *Lying in a Room of One's Own*, 14.
36. Stolba, *Lying in a Room of One's Own*, 15.
37. Stolba, *Lying in a Room of One's Own*, 25.
38. Stolba, *Lying in a Room of One's Own*, 28.
39. Stolba, *Lying in a Room of One's Own*, 31.
40. Andersen, *Thinking About Women*, xiii.
41. Andersen, *Thinking About Women*, 1.
42. Andersen, *Thinking About Women*, 3.
43. Daly, *Beyond God the Father*, 134.
44. Andersen, *Thinking About Women*, 4.
45. Sommers, *The War Against Boys*, 17.
46. Sommers, *The War Against Boys*, 18.
47. Sommers, *Who Stole Feminism?*, 207.
48. Sommers, *Who Stole Feminism?*, 204.
49. Farrell, *Why Men Earn More*, 184.
50. Quoted in Cathy Young, "Co-Opting Lincoln's Sexuality," *Boston Globe*, January 31, 2005, A15.
51. Mills and Lingard, "Masculinity Politics, Myths," 282.
52. Mills and Lingard, "Masculinity, Politics, Myths," 284.
53. Sommers, *Who Stole Feminism?*, 62.
54. Sommers, *Who Stole Feminism?*, 66.
55. Stolba, *Lying in a Room of One's Own*, 12.
56. Sommers, *Who Stole Feminism?*, 73.
57. Hise, *The War Against Men*, 87.
58. Quoted in Daly, *Beyond God the Father*, 155.
59. Edward Moser, *The Politically Correct Guide to the Bible* (New York: Three Rivers Press, 1997), 24.
60. Moser, *The Politically Correct Guide*, 77.
61. Daly, *Beyond God the Father*, xi.
62. Daly, *Beyond God the Father*, xii.

63. Daly, *Beyond God the Father*, xxvi.
64. Daly, *Beyond God the Father*, xv.
65. Daly, *Beyond God the Father*, xi.
66. Daly, *Beyond God the Father*, xvi.
67. Daly, *Beyond God the Father*, xviii.
68. Daly, *Beyond God the Father*, xx.
69. Daly, *Beyond God the Father*, xxi.
70. Daly, *Beyond God the Father*, xxiii.
71. Daly, *Beyond God the Father*, 3.
72. Daly, *Beyond God the Father*, 6.
73. Daly, *Beyond God the Father*, 96.
74. Daly, *Beyond God the Father*, 10.
75. Daly, *Beyond God the Father*, 12.
76. Daly, *Beyond God the Father*, 69.
77. Daly, *Beyond God the Father*, 36.
78. Daly, *Beyond God the Father*, 43.
79. Daly, *Outercourse*, 7.
80. Hise, *The War Against Men*, 83.
81. Daly, *Outercourse*, xii.
82. Daly, *Outercourse*, 1.
83. Daly, *Outercourse*, 19.
84. Daly, *Outercourse*, 85.
85. Daly, *Outercourse*, 109–110.
86. Daly, *Outercourse*, 137.
87. Daly, *Outercourse*, 138.
88. Daly, *Outercourse*, 140.
89. Daly, *Outercourse*, 195.
90. Daly, *Outercourse*, 212.
91. Daly, *Outercourse*, 240.
92. Daly, *Outercourse*, 246.
93. Daly, *Outercourse*, 278.
94. Daly, *Outercourse*, 386.
95. Daly, *Outercourse*, 392.
96. Daly, *Outercourse*, 393.
97. Daly, *Outercourse*, 240.

Chapter Five

Pulling Out Our Tongues: The Assault on Language

"The liberation of language is rooted in the liberation of ourselves," wrote radical feminist theologian Mary Daly.[1]

But I must beg a thousand pardons for using that word: theologian. Daly does not wish to be called a theologian or a philosopher, for as she says, these are "male-created" disciplines, not unlike quantum physics, football, and cartography. It is an unhappy fact for Daly that "the symbolic and linguistic instruments for communication"—in other words, words—"have been formulated by males under the condition of patriarchy."[2] Thus words, languages, even gestures, must be purged in an act of cultural revolution that would make the Khmer Rouge under Pol Pot and the Maoist Chinese Cultural Revolution look like a nursery-school game of Duck Duck Goose. Mary Daly, and indeed her branch of feminism, would cut out our tongues.

Actually, there are other organs Mary Daly and Crew would like to cut out even more than our tongues. Daly, in using the term "sisterhood of man," seeks thereby to "emasculat[e] the pseudo-generic 'man.'" That she would like to emasculate real men as well is implied in her writings. With glee she writes of the "castrating of language," for this sinister creation—language and culture—has "amounted to a kind of gang rape of minds as well as of bodies."[3]

Language even causes rape, or so it seems that certain feminist linguists claim. Jackson Katz, who goes through life bearing the cringe-inducing label of "anti-sexism activist," which we are sure is nice work if you can get it, told a December 2004 conference on violence at the University of Wisconsin-Parkside that men are encouraged to bad behavior when they hear women referred to in the passive voice.

"Women were raped. Women were abused. Women got pregnant," said Katz. "No one says how men raped women, how men impregnated women."

Notice how Katz lists rape, abuse, and pregnancy as a trio of hostile acts that men commit against women. There is no such thing as consensual sex, apparently; women do not conceive children of their own volition but rather have the little brutelings forced on them by primitive men whose animal instincts take over when they hear people speaking in the passive voice. Sex equals rape. Abuse equals pregnancy.

"Why do we have so many abusive men?" asks the sensitive Mr. Katz. "What's the process from becoming a little boy to a rapist or an abuser?"[4] To feminist analysts, it's a natural progression. How does a calf become a cow? How does a seed become a flower? How does a boy become a rapist? Just let nature take its course.

But there is one way that potential rapists and abusers can be cut off at the pass, and that is by reducing the American-English vocabulary, by bowdlerizing the dictionary, by eliminating those combinations of letters and sounds that keep women in thralldom and men holding the whips and chains.

For thirty years now, a concerted attack has been waged on the English language—and, by extension, on the men whose existence is acknowledged in the daily usage of this tongue.

The language feminists seek to purge useful, venerable words and replace them with often bloodless terms. The words under attack are not odd words, $64,000 curiosities known only to sesquipedalians and crossword puzzle fanatics. No, the words go to the very core of our existence. For instance, Casey Miller and Kate Swift proposed in the *New York Times Magazine* in April 16, 1972 that the generic "man" be replaced by their own artificial coinage: "gen."[5]

Well, you can't keep a good man down, but men and women have had no trouble in the ensuing three-plus decades in keeping "gen" out of their mouths and off their pages. It never caught on, and never will unless the jackbooted feminists someday act out their deepest totalitarian fantasies.

Longshoreman, however, which suggests virile stevedores working on the waterfront, is a candidate for elimination by feminist language police. It is to be replaced by the non-word longshoreworker. The honorable word sportsmanship, which calls to mind a host of desirable qualities and evokes memories of good sports throughout the decades, is also recommended for the scrapheap, to be succeeded, or so suggest the editors of *The Handbook of Nonsexist Writing*, by the prolix "the highest ideals of fair play."[6] Never use one good word when six okay ones will do.

Amusingly, the crusaders for narrowing the language have sometimes been men from, ah, unexpected quarters. In 1970, Benjamin Bradlee, executive editor of the *Washington Post*, purged divorcee, grandmother, blonde, vivacious, pert, dimpled, and cute from his newspaper. Bradlee, you may remember, was a courtier journalist in the circle of President John F. Kennedy, the ultimate objectifier of women. It's okay, apparently, for the President of the United States to leer at, fondle, and commit adultery with blonde, pert, vivacious, cute girls (if not grandmothers) with dimples, as long as he doesn't actually use those words to describe them in writing.

Among the words and phrases that some feminists seek to scratch from the language are "input," "plugs into," "thrust," and "penetrate,"[7] because they might remind the dirty-minded of . . . well, you know.

Manhole cover, which is not a word that particularly privileges the men of the species, must be scrapped and replaced not by personhole cover, which at least has the virtue of being so ridiculous that it is amusing, but by the bland access cover or utility-hole cover.[8] Ho-hum.

Bachelor and spinster are also said to carry "underlying negative attitudes toward women,"[9] but don't you dare think of equalizing them by using bachelorette, which includes one of the verboten "ette" or "ess" suffixes. Similarly, poetess and actress, prettily sibilant words that conjure up Emily Dickinson and Katherine Hepburn, are on the way out the stage door.

So are tomboy and sissy, which one publication of the language police orders should be replaced by "adventurous/daring girl" and "sensitive/caring boy," respectively. Thus excellent words that may sting but that also carry a fund of meaning are to be banned in favor of mushy euphemisms.

Ships and automobiles—"objects that are containers," in the strange and dark formulation of one virago—are no longer to be referred to as "she." So the lovely sentence "The ship set forth with her sail billowing in the wind"[10] is provided as an example of forbidden speech. Ships may pass in the night, but only as Its. And as for hurricanes and tropical storms, don't even think about using a gender-specific pronoun. Unless, one supposes, Florida is threatened by a his-icane. Since 1979, hurricanes have become androgynous, equally male and female, though only the most insensate lout of a weatherperson would deny that Hurricane Camille or Hurricane Katrina somehow sound more elegantly devastating than, say, Hurricane Fred.

Still, even the most determined of language police let a male syllable slip through, so to speak, now and then. When in January 1971 the Women's Strike for Equality held a prayer service, its adherents ended prayers not with "amen" but rather "ah-women"[11]—which, alas, ends with those three nasty letters M-E-N. You can't get away from it!

Mary Daly, at least, appreciates one aspect of the English language: the prefix mal, meaning bad. She adds an e and voilà, words like male-functioning take on new and more sinister meaning. Daly's loathing of the language is such that she refers with obvious disgust to the "dick-tionary."[12]

Yet the preposterous assertions and demands of radical feminists have a way of entering the mainstream, transmuted, perhaps, or modified, but still intact at the core. They define the terms of debate and, in so doing, push the boundaries so far into crazed misandry that all sorts of insidious proposals seem moderate by comparison. Organizations that represent real people living real lives find themselves infected by the anti-male virus.

In 1977, the National Council of Teachers of English published *Sexism and Language* by the fearsome foursome of Alleen Pace Nilsen, Haig Bosmajian, H. Lee Gershuny, and Julia P. Stanley. The book carried the imprimatur of the NCTE's Committee on Doublespeak—an ironic appellation, to be sure, for the council was counseling the English teachers of America to twist and contort the language almost beyond recognition—certainly beyond felicity—in the service of gender neutralism.

Coauthor Nilsen went so far as to bemoan the existence of the word "masterpiece,"[13] which is somehow supposed to be a bar to the creation of art by women. Presumably "manager" is also on her list of words to be execrated, if not erased from the very language.

The battle against "waitress" and "waiter," which feminists insist be replaced by "server," also points up the beauty gap within the feminist language police. We are to employ a lifeless term—server—instead of the evocative waitress and waiter, which breathe the smoky air of experience, of literature, of all those four a.m. coffee-drinking jags that supply so many fond memories.

The blandly titled Committee on Equality of Opportunity at the University College Cork in Ireland provides other examples of words and phrases to be discarded in the dustbin of lexical history. For instance, "To each his own" ought to be replaced by "To each one's own." "One man's meat is another man's poison" is to be supplanted by "What is food to one is poison to another." And "Time waits for no man" is to give way to "Time waits for no one."[14]

Besides adding nothing to the clarity of these adages, the proposed changes serve to suck all the life and pith and heart out of the expressions. So do demands that such fine words as workmanship and craftsman be eliminated. At bottom, those who insist on such censorship are the enemies not only of men, history, and custom but of beauty and even of language itself.

Beauty once may have been a concern of philosophers, but the American Philosophical Association put its imprimatur on the most un-beautiful and anti-felicitous "Guidelines for Non-Sexist Use of Language" by the estimable Virginia L. Warren of Chapman College. This plier of Plato's trade, in the foreword to her little hectoring handbook, writes of the APA's "conviction that philosophers should take special care to avoid giving needless and unintended offense."[15]

Forget the pursuit of truth, the asking of hard questions—inoffensiveness is paramount to American philosophers! Professor Warren has the nerve to piously intone that "as scholars and teachers we pursue truth wherever it leads"—unless, it appears, that the truth or the pursuit thereof might offend an ultrasensitive reader, in which case it's time to call off the pursuit and let truth gallop into the next county.

Warren instructs her fellow (or sister) philosophers that "every occurrence" of such generic terms as "man" and "he" is "problematic." However, "'Person' and 'human' are genuinely gender-neutral."[16] Excuse me, Professor: Man is offensive, but human is okay? He repels, but person is dandy?

The philosopher is only getting started. She lectures her colleagues that they must not label "some roles as predominantly male or female." For instance, "homemaking and child rearing" are not predominantly female tasks but rather, in the world of her pipe dreams, are gender-neutral. Any suggestion that women are either better suited or more likely to engage in homemaking or child rearing will be frowned on most severely. Presumably only an editor with a modicum of sense prevented Warren from adding "childbearing" to her list of gender-neutral jobs.

She supplies the philosophical community with a long—a painfully long—list of words that are henceforth forbidden in philosophical discourse. He and man lead the list, and though we shall revisit this controversy a bit later in the chapter, it is worth noting that Warren recommends "deleting 'he,' 'his,' and 'him' altogether."[17] Deleting men altogether is the next step, one suspects.

Women must always be addressed as Ms., no matter what their preferences may be. No one shall be permitted to be referred to as "Miss" or "Mrs."[18] Period. What individual women happen to want is not important. "Coeds," an evocative word, is too evocative: we are instead to call them females.

Whenever possible, philosophers are urged to choose the wordy over the concise and the confusing over the precise.

And always, but always, any hint that men exist or are represented in the English language must be repressed. "He knows" must be changed to the ungainly "This person knows."[19] A resonant phrase like "the common man" is exsanguinated into "ordinary individuals."[20] No wonder no one reads feminist poets or philosophers except under academic compulsion!

"Males and females" must be altered to "females and males" if one absolutely, positively has to acknowledge the existence of men. However, "fraternity" and "brotherhood," perfectly fine words, are out of bounds for philosophers who wish to be published in the major journals. Einstein may not be called the "Father of relativity theory" but rather its "founder." And yet, Ms. Warren, Albert Einstein was a man—deal with it!

Congressman and congresswoman are out; the awkward "member of Congress" is in. "Founding Fathers," a term that calls to mind a cluster of patriotic and historical images and memories, must become "founding leaders."[21]

In this way, one assumes, we will forget the Founding Fathers and all they thought or stood for.

As for Mother Earth . . . she escapes the Banned Words list.

The ungrammatical they is acceptable. (As in "As someone grows older, they grow more reflective.")[22] Grammar is a male concept, after all, and its rules are automatically suspect.

Thankfully, the Professor Warrens of the world are not philosopher-kings. The feminist assault on language has met with resistance from the start. In 1975, Boyd Wright, an associate editor at *Women's Wear Daily*, defended none other than that locus of all lexical evil: man. "Man, as all dictionaries agree, can be as much a generic, sexless word as horse or dog," argued Wright. "We have not yet resorted to racemare or seeing-eye bitch. Why, then, chairwoman or the even clumsier chairperson?"

He continued, "The irony is that violating the language in this fashion undermines the cause of women's liberation, in whose name this battle is being waged. The result is not a more adequate recognition of women's equality, but a verbal ugliness that makes a valid cause seem unnecessarily dubious."[23]

In 1972, L.E. Sissman compared the feminist language police to communist bullies. They "distort and corrupt further the language already savaged by the Establishment politicians when they conspire to eliminate the innocuous, and correct, locution, 'Everyone knows he has to decide for himself,' and to substitute the odious Newspeakism 'chairperson.'"[24]

But the chairs have been known to revolt. Rosa Monckton wrote in the *London Sunday Telegraph* in May 2004 that "The English language, on which the whole culture and civilisation of our country is based, is being distorted beyond recognition. Creeping political correctness, which has seeped into our society over the past decade, is now in full flood, and it will take more than a finger in the dyke (a word probably not allowed anymore) to stop it."

Monckton told readers of her chairmanship of KIDS, a children's charity for the handicapped. She accepted the position because her daughter, Domenica, has Down's Syndrome, though she was quickly instructed not to use the word "handicapped" and to instead use such wretched euphemisms as "special needs" and "learning disabilities."

Monckton fought back against the Orwellians. She refused to be called "chair," since it "would give the impression that I could be easily sat upon." She also rejected "chairperson," insisting on the standard title "chairman."[25]

The word chairperson is a "ridiculous and cacophonous usage," wrote the much-honored late novelist Anthony Burgess, whose novel, *A Clockwork Orange*, remains a classic dystopian tale of what happens when an all-powerful state tries to remold human beings. "You can't outlaw attitudes by outlawing words," pled Burgess, though no one listened to him.

Burgess defended the use of "man" as a gender-neutral pronoun, suggested "Mistress" as a venerable substitute for the horrid "Ms.," exalted "'man,' being short and Anglo-Saxon," over "person," and asked us "to love language rather than fear it and to refuse to attach partisan meanings to words."[26] Perhaps he was asking too much. After all, he assumed that the feminists to whom he was addressing his arguments shared his love of Western civilization and the English language. They were, as it turns out, every bit as hostile to it as were Alex and the Droogs who rampaged through *A Clockwork Orange*.

As philosopher Kelly L. Ross has noted, "the ideology that there is 'sexist language' in ordinary words and in the ordinary use of English . . . rarely comes under sustained criticism." Yet grammar, as Ross explicates, "is used to express meaning—it does not determine meaning."[27] Still, the furrowed-brow feminists fret over the endurance of "chairman" and the failure of the bulky "chairperson" or the ridiculous "chair" to take its place. And they are not content to rely on mere suasion. They positively exult in compulsion.

Take the Australian professor who found that in 2000, only 5.4 percent of classified ads in newspapers she had studied contained gender-specific language. This, comrades, is success; it is nirvana: Banning the word mailman from the English language! The professor, after surveying classified ads in other nations, opined that the success in purging such odious terms as "cleaning lady" from the want ads was "due to the more regulated nature of the former genre: i.e., in principle, advertisers can be fined for using gender-based language in job classifieds."[28] Thus coercion is seen as the key to the enforcement of feminist ideology.

Compel. Force. Dictate. These are the action verbs on which the campaign against men relies. Free men and women, acting by their own lights, are problematic. Too often they choose to do the wrong thing. They fall in love. They marry. They have children. The woman may love and care for the child. She wants to be called Mrs. The man may take a job as a fireman, the woman as an elementary school teacher. They may use words like chairman, he, and lady. They must be stopped. Holy Mother the State must tell them what to do, what to think, what to say. Or else.

More ink has been spilled and more passsion has been expended, more epithets have been hurled and more righteous anti-sexist fury has been unleashed, over the use of gender-neutral pronouns than over any other aspect of the English language.

Christina Hoff Sommers reports that when the subject of what to do about students who pig-headedly insist on using gender-neutral pronouns came up at a feminist academic conference in Austin, Texas, "Most agreed that the instructor should grade them down."[29] When all else fails, whip out the red marking pen.

Margaret L. Andersen's Women's Studies textbook, *Thinking About Women*, states that "the practice of using the word man to refer generically to all people makes women invisible."[30] The evidence is to the contrary—not that Andersen is much concerned about evidence, much less contrary opinions.

In fact, man in Old English was a gender-neutral term to which male and female qualifying words were attached. Over time, the female qualifier (wif) endured but the male qualifier disappeared, which meant that man did double duty as both gender-specific and gender-neutral word. This was well understood by all. Until feminism.

To say that a word cannot have two meanings is to betray oneself as an arrant ignoramus. Look in *Webster's*, for heaven's sake! Nevertheless, even the relatively moderate *Handbook of Nonsexist Writing*, while acknowledging the inclusive origins of man in Old English, declares that "What standard English usage says about males . . . is that they are the species. What it says about females is that they are a subspecies."[31]

No word looms larger or more menacing or more penis-like in its repugnance to the feminist imagination than He in its usage as a generic pronoun.

In traditional usage, "he" is a versatile pronoun, referring both to specifically male subjects and also as a generic term meaning "he or she." It contains, admittedly, a degree of ambiguity, as critics charge, since the word has more than one meaning, but then the majority of words in the dictionary have multiple meanings, and one does not find shrill campaigns being waged against them.

Among the claims made by feminist academics against he are that it "can lead to lower self-esteem"[32] among shes, and that in its "assumed equivalence of maleness with humanness"[33] it excludes one-half of the human race from beingness.

The nub of the question would seem to be this: does the use of he as a generic pronoun lead listeners to believe that only men are being referred to? Does it "evok[e] a disproportionate number of male images,"[34] as John Gastil of the University of Wisconsin-Madison asserts in *Sex Roles* (1990)?

Or were William Strunk, Jr., and E.B. White correct in their timeless *The Elements of Style* (1979; third edition) when they wrote,

> The use of he as pronoun for nouns embracing both genders is a simple, practical convention rooted in the beginnings of the English language. He has lost all suggestion of maleness in these circumstances. The word was unquestionably biased to begin with (the dominant male), but after hundreds of years it has become seemingly indispensable. It has no pejorative connotations; it is never incorrect. Substituting he or she in its place is the logical thing to do if it works. But it often doesn't work, if only because repetition makes it sound boring or silly. . . . No one need fear to use he if common sense supports it. The furor recently raised about he would be more impressive if there were a handy substi-

tute for the word. Unfortunately, there isn't—or, at least, no one has come up with one yet. If you think she is a handy substitute for he, try it and see what happens. Alternatively, put all controversial nouns in the plural and avoid the choice of sex altogether, and you may find your prose sounding general and diffuse as a result.[35]

General and diffuse would be a vast improvement on most feminist prose. Professor Gastil boasts that Strunk and White are now in "the minority position,"[36] as the legendarily clumsy "he or she" or the ungrammatical "they" push he into the nether regions of political incorrectness, just as men may find themselves cast into the darkness at an appropriate time. But don't count out old Strunk and White yet. They've exhibited greater staying power than has the estimable Gastil.

But oh, the academic sweat that has been shed over this matter!

In a routine dog-bites-man (or dog-bites-human) story, Marsha B. Jacobson and William R. Insko, Jr., writing in *Sex Roles* (1985), found that subjects who scored highly on a scale of feminism were likelier to use "nonsexist" pronouns than were the unenlightened dolts in their survey. The authors fret, however, that their subjects were more willing "to accept women in traditional male positions than to accept men in traditional female positions."[37] In other words, while they might designate a hypothetical truck driver as a she, they would not refer to a caring, sensitive midwife as he. Sexism is awfully hard to root out.

Janet Shibley Hyde of Denison University, writing in *Developmental Psychology* (1984), describes her testing of 310 first, third, and fifth graders and college students for impermissible sexist thoughts.

Professor Hyde, no exemplar of pure disinterested scholarship and fearless pursuit of the Truth wherever it may lead, puts her cards on the table upfront, writing that "although 'his' may be gender-neutral in a grammatical sense, it is not gender neutral in a psychological sense. Even when the rest of the sentence explicitly provides a gender-neutral context, subjects more often think of a male when the pronoun is 'his.'"[38]

One example will suffice to reveal the slipshod nature of Hyde's work. Elementary school children were asked if a series of sentences were "right or wrong." For instance, "The average kid likes to play football with—friends." When "his" was inserted, six percent of the children judged the sentence to be wrong, whereas 39 percent thought the sentence was wrong when "her" was inserted.[39]

Far from being evidence that children misunderstand the use of he or its possessive form, his, as generic, it suggests that little boys and girls have eyes with which to see and ears with which to hear. They understand football as a sex-specific sport which most girls do not play. This is the single example that receives the most attention in Hyde's study, and it is obviously an atypical case.

The most widely cited study containing evidence that he leads to a sort of sexist bias was done by J. Moulton, G.M. Robinson, and C. Elias in the *American Psychologist* (1978).

The Moulton-Robinson-Elias study was blasted to empirical bits in the seminal and essential work of C. Maureen Cole, Frances A. Hill, and Leland J. Daley in *Sex Roles*. In "Do Masculine Pronouns Used Generically Lead to Thoughts of Men?" Cole, Hill, and Daley virtually vivisect the hamfisted and tendentious work of the earlier trio, as well as the other biased research that has put he in such bad odor. The Moulton-Robinson-Ellis study, as well as several others frequently cited in feminist literature, suffer from "extreme obviousness."[40] The pro-feminist researchers have designed their studies to elicit certain responses, and the subjects, in best Pavlovian fashion, respond accordingly. Indeed, the subjects in some studies "may well have been aware of the general issue being studied," a basic mistake that might be made by a fairly dimwitted first-year social sciences student but that should never be committed by a professor or professional social scientist.

Noting that while "there is an abundance of statements emphatically stating the effects of the male pronoun used generically, there is a paucity of empirical research on the effect,"[41] Cole, Hill, and Daley conducted six experiments to see whether the use of he in a generic context led subjects (the usual Intro to Psych guinea pigs) to believe that men were the referent. In other words, does "the generic use of male pronouns giv[e] rise to mental images of maleness"?

The answer, across the board, was a resounding "no." Subjects—that is to say, English speakers—are perfectly aware that the use of he as a generic pronoun encompasses women as well as men. Use of the generic pronoun did not lead the students to put male faces on non-gender-specific hypothetical persons.

Cole, Hill, and Daley concluded, "We found no empirical evidence to support the claim that, in and of itself, the generic pronoun gives rise to thoughts of men. . . . As researchers, one of our motives in pursuing this question was a dissatisfaction with the lack of solid evidence for such widely expressed beliefs. Our hunch was that the belief was true and the evidence would be easily obtained. Now we must conclude the opposite. Perhaps a misinterpretation of the sex of the person referred to by the generic pronoun does not occur as readily as is believed."[42]

One might think that this finding would rock the semantic world. The lazy assumptions of the He-baiters had been exposed as false. But as anyone acquainted with standards of androphobic scholarship might guess, the study was cursorily acknowledged and then ignored, rather as dinner guests might ignore a 1,000 pound gorilla on the sofa in the belief that ignoring him might make the unwelcome ape just go away.

Well, the truth never really goes away. He is not going to disappear without a fight.

But a fight is what we have on our hands. One 1984 study of American newspapers found that the incidence of man and he as generics had declined by two-thirds between 1971 and 1979. The years since have seen a steady erosion in these two respectable terms. Yet they have not seen any reasonably say-able substitute for he and man.

Suggestions—or perhaps we should say demands, since the imperative voice comes through loud and shrill in most writing on the subject—for replacements for the despised he range from the wimpy moderate he/she to the in-your-face she/he to a proposal to "simply use she as a generic."[43] (This last idea comes from a putative male. It "re-genders" the pronoun, to use feminist argot.)

It has been proposed, if not accepted. They seems to have been used until "prescriptive grammarians, acting out of androcentrism,"[44] declared it incorrect usage in the eighteenth century. Those damned androcentrists: always spoiling it for the rest of us.

One sage advises students at the Purdue Online Writing Lab to consider "eliminating pronouns"[45] altogether. After all, there are so many words already in the English language: we could easily do without he and she, couldn't we?

A truly wacky attorney named Charles Crozat Converse proposed "A New Pronoun" in an 1884 article. It was "thon," a contraction of "that one," and it was to replace "he."[46] Believe it or not, thon never caught on. Language is like that: words enter the lexicon because people use them, find them useful symbols of things, or perhaps just enjoy the sounds they make. Geek and groovy made the cut, not because a language dictator decreed their inclusion in our dictionaries and their utterance by our tongues, but because countless individuals chose to employ these terms to convey meaning. Thon . . . well, just try using it in a sentence and you'll realize why no one outside Mr. Converse could bear to spit out the unlovely syllable.

Thon is not the only neologism to have been proposed by the enemies of he. Others include co, E, ter, tey, tem, hesh, and hir. Not a one has ever caught on, though pronoun trivia specialists can cite books that tried to make do without "he." In *The Cook and the Carpenter* (1973), novelist June Arnold substituted na, and in Ray A. Killian's *Managers Must Lead* (1979), hir was the gender-neutral pronoun. Neither started a trend.

But the He-terminators are not content to let the language evolve. As Wilma Scott Heide of the National Organization for Women boasted, "In any social movement, when changes are effected, the language sooner or later reflects the change. Our approach is different. Instead of passively noting the change, we are changing language patterns to actively effect the change."[47]

Were Ms. Heide the sort who let facts intrude on her ideology, she might wonder why it is that, as more than one observer has pointed out, those countries whose languages (English, French, German) contain gender distinctions are also the cradles of the modern movements for sexual equality. By contrast, the Persian language is blessedly gender neutral: "There are not even different words for 'he' and 'she,' just the unisex un."[48] And yet, the last we checked, Iran, home of gender-free language, is not exactly a hotbed of women's rights. Might it be possible, just possible, that pronouns do not determine public policy, let alone attitudes?

If pronouns lead to patriarchy, as the language feminists believe, the options are to abolish pronouns or seize them for their own reconstructive purposes. Writing in *Linguistik*, Anne Pauwels of Australia's University of Wollongong reminds us that "mere equality"[49] of the sexes is not necessarily the goal of feminism. She lauds "linguistic disruptions,"[50] which is just a self-dramatizing way of saying neologisms. Feminists such as the incoherent Mary Daly like to make up words and alter spellings: a harmless enough hobby, were not their ultimate goal the coercion of the rest of mankind into using these silly terms. Womyn, wimmin, the endless and tedious stream of words now stuck with the unlovely suffix: person; the claiming of such invidious terms as hag and witch as badges of honor; even entirely new languages for women only, such as "Laadan," which was birthed, if she will excuse the expression, by a science-fiction feminist writer named Suzette Haden Elgin: such is the strange and bitter fruit that feminism has borne.

Universities are the hive from which so many of these anti-language campaigns are run.

The Purdue Online Writing Lab, after excoriating such words as "mailman," advises that "the generic use of MAN and other words with masculine markers should be avoided."[51] Purdue's language maven helpfully informs us that "English evolved through most of its history in a male-centered, patriarchal society," and that the word man is no longer regarded as a generic word by any sentient human; rather, it has "narrowed in meaning to become a word that refers to adult male human beings."[52] That this assertion is just that—a hotly contested assertion rather than a statement of fact—is nowhere admitted. It is best that Purdue students not be presented with too much information.

There is a sense in which the jihad against sexist language is really an effort to control thought, to define non-feminist thinking and political views as illegitimate, dangerous, and eventually, perhaps, illegal. Philosopher Kelly L. Ross sees a "dehumanizing and totalitarian"[53] principle at work, as the preferences and beliefs of individual persons are to be ignored, and their conformity with feminist ideology is to be enforced by political authorities in the realms of behavior and, presumably, thought.

Consider the revealing survey conducted by Janet Swim and Robyn Mallett of the Psychology Department at the Pennsylvania State University and Charles Stangor of the Psychology Department at the University of Maryland. Under the auspices of the National Science Foundation (your tax dollars at work!), the trio of researchers sought to detect "subtle sexism" in a sample of 326 females and 145 males who were captive subjects in introductory psych classes.

Writing in the compulsively unreadable journal *Sex Roles* (which is not, *contra* the title, about dominatrices and submissive men), Swim, Mallett, and Stangor declared their intention to ferret out or hunt down "Modern (or Neo) Sexists, who, [u]nlike old-fashioned sexists who explicitly support gender inequality and endorse traditional gender roles,"[54] express their poisonous inner selves in more indirect ways. For instance, in their politics.

The intrepid researchers devised a Modern Sexism Scale by which hate thought might be detected in those whose bland smiles and courtesy conceal the ugliness within. One's score on the Modern Sexism Scale is determined by one's agreement or disagreement with such statements as "Discrimination against women is no longer a problem in the United States" or "It is easy to understand the anger of women's groups in America." Sexism is thus defined as the failure to mimic the views of Gloria Steinem, NOW, and the Lesbian Avengers.

Modern Sexists, the trio told the breathless readers of *Sex Roles*, were especially prone to committing everyday acts of disrespect, even contempt, toward women. No, they—and in this "they" are included many women—do not insult women using the usual crude maledictions, nor do they beat or pummel or rape women. Their crimes are much harder to detect, which is why your National Science Foundation is writing grant checks to hardy anti-sexist researchers. You see, the Modern Sexist in this study failed to object to the sentence, "The post office advertises that their mailmen aren't never late, no matter how bad the weather." Well, certain of them objected to the obvious grammatical errors in the sentence. But they did not highlight the real flaw in the sentence: the use of "mailmen."[55]

This notion that "sexist" language, which sometimes goes under the phrase "the English language," is linked to sexist attitudes, which are also known as "the way most people behave and believe," and that both the language and the attitudes ought to be repressed, discouraged, or even banned outright runs through feminist academic scholarship. Researchers have found, among other things, that "students who reported strong adherence to the tenets of Christian fundamentalism were more likely to use sexist language" and, even more astonishingly, that there is "a positive relationship between membership in the National Organization for Women and concern about eliminating sexist language."[56] This last conclusion is shocking: next thing you know they'll find a relationship between membership in NOW and the ability to detect humor in the inanities of Ellen DeGeneres.

Other studies in this arid field have suggested that older people are more likely to use non-sexist language in job applications or everyday usage than are young people. But then as the Who once sang, the kids are alright.

Janet B. Parks and Mary Ann Roberton of Bowling Green State University, writing in the indispensable *Psychology of Women Quarterly*, convey their numbingly routine findings that language usage reflects one's cultural attitudes. But it is the gloss that they put on their findings that tells the reader more about the authors than it does about the subjects.

Those subjects, as is so often the case, were 278 18–20 year-old college students in English composition classes. (Do parents realize that in sending their kids off to school to sit in introductory classes they are producing a generation of unpaid lab rats?)

Parks and Roberton begin their paper by informing us that the words "he," "mankind," and "man and wife" serve to "exclude, trivialize, or diminish"[57] women. To their disgust, students in previous samples not only saw nothing wrong with such words, many of them actively defended their usage. Parks and Roberton were bombarded with critical remarks from the guinea pigs, who showed "hostility and rage" at their captors. Even more dispiriting to the dauntless duo of authors was "the uncritical acquiescence to male hegemony" exhibited by those were silent. This was "alarming,"[58] they reported. Disagreement has no place in a university!

Parks and Roberton fared no better in this study. They grimly concluded that "in North American culture, sexist language may be symbolically important to young people who either consciously or unconsciously still believe in the superiority of men." These chauvinist pigs and their female collaborators freely use such hateful memes as "he" and "mankind," and if you try to set them straight with a cogent lecture on feminist semiotics they respond by "disparag[ing] women."[59]

Somewhat more optimistic about their ability to reshape the language patterns of young people were Christopher Cronin and Sawsan Jreisat of Transylvania University. Vampiric in their search for the fresh blood of sexist ephebes, the authors give their *Sex Roles* paper a classic title: "Effect of Modeling on the Use of Nonsexist Language Among High School Freshpersons and Seniors."

Yes, "freshpersons." Don't tell the authors that the final syllable in freshperson is just as testesterone-charged as the last syllable in freshman.

Cronin and Jreisat interrogated, via questionnaire, 144 high-school students. The unsuspecting twelve dozen completed a test on "ethical dilemmas"; their responses were graded by a Sexist Language Detector, or SLD, as the authors helpfully acronymize. The term Sexist Language Detector reeks of the phraseology of the police state, of sweaty, beady-eyed sexists wilting under hot light bulbs under the harsh questioning of Anti-Sexist cops. But maybe this is the point.

About one-third of the students received instructions containing sexist examples, another third received instructions using non-sexist examples, and the final third received no instructions.

The results? "Participants with nonsexist instructions used significantly more nonsexist langauge than the other two groups."[60] In other words, hectoring and badgering can work, at least in the short term. You can imagine the lessons the authors drew from this not terribly enlightening study.

Acknowledging "the difficulty of changing university students' use of sexist language,"[61] Cronin and Jreisat realize that the long march to a non-sexist utopia will be, well, long. While those students who were harassed to use non-sexist language did so to a greater degree than did the others, not a single participant used "anti-sexist" language, e.g., referring to a long-haul trucker as "she," or a kindly kindergarten teacher as "he."

Still, the propaganda had worked, to an extent. Perhaps a more proactive, to use the management buzzword, approach might work. The authors recommend just that. It's time to put the hammer down: "[W]e should also specifically discourage the use of sexist language."[62] In a school setting, this may be done in one of two ways. First, punish those who use "he" as a gender-neutral pronoun. Send to the principal's office a miscreant who says "man and wife," lock in the coatroom closet some wayward slip who utters "mankind." Second, the enforcer may reduce a student's grade for the use of "he"—that is, for assuming that an NHL goalie is a male, or for making a reference to "housewives" or "waitresses."

Either way, the world becomes a little less free. And a little less honest.

Matters in Canada, that sensitive socialist utopia to our north, are at a further stage of decay than they are in the erstwhile land of the free. One illustrative example of the campaign to create the New Improved Canadian Person is provided by Professor Deborah Kennedy, who as a confessedly feminist professor of composition at Mount Saint Vincent University became concerned that many of her students exhibited "no awareness of gender-inclusive language,"[63] even though her Nova Scotia school was overwhelmingly (85 percent) female. (Ms. Vincent made a dubious teacher of composition; she does not know the meaning of the word "reticence," as evidenced by this sentence: "Thus more women than men expressed reticence about finding a substitute for the word mankind."[64] But this is a matter for the parents of Mount Saint Vincent students to take up with the cowed administration.)

Contrary to the sassy boast of the Virginia Slims cigarette ads of those ancient days when such advertisements were permitted on television, "we have not come a long way,"[65] baby, says Kennedy, and I probably don't have to note that she did not use the word "baby."

The bright, eager, apple-cheeked young Nova Scotians who filled her classes appalled Professor Kennedy. Surveying her classes, she made the shocking discovery that "sexist language is a problem of the patriarchy and that its victims are, for the most part, women."[66] She cannot believe that barely one-third of her female students have ever used the word "Ms." to identify themselves. Indeed, "my students have shown little interest in the 'Ms.' form,"[67] she laments. (That may be because Ms. is an undignified little squib which came into view in secretarial handbooks of the 1940s. It has no history, no fund of meaning, no purpose, really, except to stand for a phony equality beside Mr.)

The comments that women wrote on Kennedy's questionnaires filled her with dismay. "I don't think this is sexist,"[68] one wrote about the word "mankind." Another had the temerity to write, "I do not find words such as mankind offensive because it is well understood that the human race is meant here."

Well of all the nerve! These ignorant youths do not understand, Ms. Kennedy, that mankind is an "exclusionary, and even detrimental"[69] word.

The fact that these are women belittling the feminist language Gestapo drives Kennedy up a wall. One coed offers that "Women have become so liberated and picky about the language we use," which provokes Kennedy into a "blaming the victims" tirade. She detects "an attitude of resentment toward other women, who are viewed as troublemakers for bothering about masculine generics." Whether or not she is a troublemaker seems not to occur to the author.

Kennedy repeats other remarks by female students, which she regards as revealing of their intellectual peonage but which sound cogent and sensible to this reader:

- "People go overboard on this topic. It's ridiculous. It doesn't mean anything."
- "I don't think of the language as sexist. Only people can be sexist."
- "I personally have never encountered a sexist situation."
- "I am a very independent woman and feel if you are secure about your femininity these terms would not bother you."
- "I am comfortable with the language I was taught—why change now?"[70]

Wise young ladies, and none misuses the word "reticent." Yet Kennedy adduces them as exhibits in the case for turning Canadian schools into re-education camps.

The state must "break down . . . resistance"[71] in students to using feminist language, declares Kennedy. She urges a massive program of non-sexist language instruction in elementary schools.

As Ray Bradbury wrote in *Fahrenheit 451*, you've got to get people when they're young, and I mean really young, in order to do an effective job of brainwashing. Canadian youth "should receive instruction in inclusive language usage before they get to university,"[72] Kennedy insists. The nursery, we may be sure, is not too early to start.

To those who object to "prescriptive teaching methods—namely, telling others what to do," Professor Kennedy offers the back of her hand. Bourgeois liberal fools! Reactionaries! "I believe," states Kennedy, the reflective gleam of jackboots and prison bars in her steely eyes, "the example of non-sexist language instruction demonstrates an instance when prescription is necessary."[73]

To which an American can only say to those Canadian youth who are to be told what to do: Resist! Arise ye brave sons and daughters of the Great White North and Resist!

Which many do. College students, being naturally refractory and disobedient to authority, have not behaved in a sheeplike enough fashion to satisfy the language police.

Writing in the *Journal of Experimental Education*, Mark R. McMinn, Pamela K. Troyer, Laurel E. Hannum, and James D. Foster of Canada's George Fox College boasted that they and other psychologists "feel an ethical and didactic responsibility to emphasize the importance of using nonsexist language to introductory students."[74] The students, to their great credit, feel an ethical responsibility to totally ignore their hectoring profs.

The four George Fox pedagogues found that inflicting a 20-minute lecture on non-sexist language on undergraduates had no beneficial effect. Thirteen George Fox students received the lecture; the other 13 in the study did not. The finding? "There were no significant changes in sexist language use by giving a 20-minute oral presentation on the topic." In fact, the "presenters noted that some participants in the study were vocal in their resistance to using nonsexist language, complaining that it would be too cumbersome to write 'his or her' as an alternative to generic male pronouns."[75]

All hail the rebels of George Fox!

The professors drew the suitably gloomy conclusion "that changing sexist language among college students is not easily done."[76] Behaviors learned over the course of a lifetime, even a young lifetime, are not easily changed. But that doesn't mean that the Foxes are giving up. No, they propose that a "more power [*sic*] intervention," whatever that is, "might have a stronger effect."[77] Just what degree of "power" the instructors are willing to use—or willing to let the state use—they do not specify. Let your imagination run wild. Imagine the inside of a prison cell.

Resistance even shows its lovely head in middle school. Canadian eighth-grader Emilie Muto asked her local newspaper why the word manhole is being changed to "sewer access hole."[78] When men are denied even the honor of having their gender denote portals to sewers, things have gone much too far.

The reaction to this madness can go off in wrongheaded directions, too. In what one wishes were a tongue-in-cheek proposal but which appears to be, alas, all too serious, the New Zealand Men's Rights Association has proposed that the "media and Government should be just as careful to avoid sexist language that belittles men (e.g., 'gunman' instead of 'gunperson,' 'hatchet-man' instead of 'hatchet-person') as they are to avoid language that belittles women."[79]

Come on, guys, one wishes to shout, grow a pair, will you?

The censorious impulse is said by feminists to run only one way. If girls wear t-shirts bearing obnoxious slogans such as "Boys are stupid, throw rocks at them," they are expressing themselves in a fresh and provocative way, but when a Canadian store displayed poor taste by selling a shirt featuring a bloody hammer and the nitwit message "She was asking for it," feminists picketed—as is their right—and the store removed the item from its shelves. But the protest against this and other moronic shirts (such as one declaring "I f**king HATE [slurs for numerous ethnic groups]—But I love niggers!") went far beyond the venerable act of picketing. "These shirts validate racist feelings and validate violence against women. It's ugly. I think it can be harmful," said one female member of Parliament. Feminists and professional anti-racist crusaders criticized the Canadian Border Services Agency for permitting these t-shirts into the country. They are perfectly willing to overlook Canada's notoriously lax policy for permitting persons with a predilection for terrorism into the country, but allow a sleazy t-shirt to cross the border and the nanny statists roar with righteous rage. (The maker of these t-shirts says that his best-seller depicts a pole dancer with the message "I support single moms." It's a favorite of strippers.)[80]

In Canada, where the feminists need not worry about such American punctilios as the First Amendment, columnists and newspaper reporters are monitored by Press Councils, which are quick to act when a newspaperperson types a verboten word (such as "newspaperman") but which reject out of hand complaints such as that filed by William Levy of the Council for the Status of Men that *Montreal Gazette* columnist Jack Todd harmed his reputation when Todd called Levy a "sexist pig"[81] in a December 2003 e-mail exchange. Censorship, again, runs only one way.

In Belgium, host of the noxiously nitpicking European Parliament, joking about sex and sex roles can become a matter for the police. Consider the case of

Godfrey Bloom, a European Parliament member from the maverick United Kingdom Independence Party. The irrepressible Bloom had gotten himself in hot water in June 2004 when he announced that he had a special interest in women's issues because "I just don't think they clean behind the fridge enough."

Maybe that's funny, maybe it's boorish. The members of the Cambridge University Women's Rugby Club think that Bloom, who sponsors the team, is funny. They accompanied him to Brussels as a show of support; according to the *Independent of London*, they concur in his "views that anti-discrimination laws ended up deterring businesses from employing young women."

Bloom and the rugby gals went out to dinner, and as anyone who has ever partied with a rugby team could predict, the party took a turn for the wild. Lots of bawdy humor, sexual innuendo, booze, fellowship, and sorority. A good time had by all. Well, almost all. You see, a frowning bureaucratess from Cambridge, one Rebecca Bowtell, was along for the ride. And she made a formal complaint to the president of the European Parliament, with a threat to drag the Brussels police into the matter.

According to Ms. Bowtell's letter, "Mr. Bloom asked a colleague, 'Isn't she the most delicious bimbette? Absolutely thick, but good tits.' Of the businesswoman who he had invited to share the platform at the next day's press conference, Mr. Bloom had only four words: 'big tits, very feisty.'"

Rachel Shaw, director of the Cambridge rugby club, leapt to Bloom's defense, saying that "Godfrey says some risque things, he is off-the-wall, but he has huge respect for women."

Ms. Bowtell, however, whined that she felt "intimidated."[82] Like the classic squealer, she went about collecting evidence of Bloom's sexist remarks, and while the colorful member of parliament was not arrested, her threat to press charges illuminates a very real danger of the feminist language cops: they simply do not believe in freedom of speech, or even in the freedom to tell jokes, and they will not shy from seeking to have the state use its police power against those who say things they do not like. The implied threat is there for all to see: get out of line in Belgium, make a crack that the Ms. Bowtells of the world find offensive, and it's into the hoosegow with you, thought criminal.

The French, too, have outlawed "sexist" or "homophobic" speech, with offenders subject to fines and imprisonment for up to a year. Jean-Marcel Bouguereau in *Le Nouvel Observateur* writes that "freedom of expression is being sacrificed in the name of political correctness." Incredibly, the legislation "prevents people from mocking another category of citizen,"[83] which effectively outlaws humor, much of which is based on mockery, broad stereotypes, and outrageous generalizations. Not that the French are funny in any event, but still . . . Mockery illegal? *Sacre bleu!*

The Big-Government feminists have seen the future—and there is nothing funny about it.

NOTES

1. Daly, *Beyond God the Father*, 8.
2. Daly, *Beyond God the Father*, 22.
3. Daly, *Beyond God the Father*, 9.
4. Alice L. Chang, "Speaker Explores Causes of Abuse," *Milwaukee Journal Sentinel*, December 16, 2004, B5.
5. Nilsen, "Linguistic Sexism as a Social Issue," *Sexism and Language*, 6.
6. Casey Miller and Kate Swift, *The Handbook of Nonsexist Writing* (New York: Harper & Row, 1980), 32.
7. Stolba, *Lying in a Room of One's Own*, 24.
8. Miller and Swift, *The Handbook of Nonsexist Writing*, 24–25.
9. Marsha B. Jacobson and William R. Insko, Jr., "Use of Nonsexist Pronouns as a Function of One's Feminist Orientation," *Sex Roles* 13, nos. 1/2 (1985): 1.
10. "Non-Sexist Language: A Guide," University College Cork Committee on Equality of Opportunity, 1994, 7–8.
11. Nilsen, "Linguistic Sexism as a Social Issue," *Sexism and Language*, 4.
12. Daly, *Outercourse*, 292.
13. Nilsen, "Sexism as Shown through the English Vocabulary," *Sexism and Language*, 40.
14. "Non-Sexist Language: A Guide," 4.
15. Virginia L. Warren, "Guidelines for Non-Sexist Use of Language," American Philosophical Association, 2000, 1.
16. Warren, "Guidelines for Non-Sexist Use of Language," 2.
17. Warren, "Guidelines for Non-Sexist Use of Language," 4.
18. Warren, "Guidelines for Non-Sexist Use of Language," 5.
19. Warren, "Guidelines for Non-Sexist Use of Language," 6.
20. Warren, "Guidelines for Non-Sexist Use of Language," 9.
21. Warren, "Guidelines for Non-Sexist Use of Language," 11, 13.
22. Warren, "Guidelines for Non-Sexist Use of Language," 7.
23. Nilsen, "Linguistic Sexism as a Social Issue," *Sexism and Language*, 17.
24. Julia Stanley, "Gender-Marking in American English: Usage and Reference," *Sexism and Language*, 51.
25. Rosa Monckton, "I Will Talk of My Daughter in English, Not Newspeak," (London) *Sunday Telegraph*, May 16, 2004, 23.
26. Anthony Burgess, "Dirty Words," *New York Times Magazine*, August 8, 1976, 150.
27. Kelly L. Ross, "Against the Theory of 'Sexist Language,'" <http://faculty.ed.umuc.edu> (1999).
28. Anne Pauwels, "Feminist Language Planning: Has It Been Worthwhile?" Linguistik online, <www.linguistik-online> (January 1998), 8.

29. Sommers, *Who Stole Feminism?*, 91.
30. Stolba, *Lying in a Room of One's Own*, 24.
31. Miller and Swift, *The Handbook of Nonsexist Writing*, 3.
32. Mykol C. Hamilton, "Using Masculine Generics: Does Generic He Increase Male Bias in the User's Imagery?" *Sex Roles* 19, nos. 11/12 (1988): 786.
33. Wendy Martyna, "What Does 'He' Mean?" *Journal of Communication* 28, no. 1 (Winter 1978): 132.
34. John Gastil, "Generic Pronouns and Sexist Language: The Oxymoronic Character of Masculine Generics," *Sex Roles* 23, nos. 11/12 (1990): 629.
35. William Strunk, Jr. and E.B. White, *The Elements of Style*, Third Edition (New York: Macmillan, 1979), 60–61.
36. Gastil, "Generic Pronouns and Sexist Language," 629.
37. Jacobson and Insko, "Use of Nonsexist Pronouns," 6.
38. Janet Shibley Hyde, "Children's Understanding of Sexist Language," *Developmental Psychology* 20, no. 4 (July 1984): 698.
39. Hyde, "Children's Understanding of Sexist Language," 700.
40. C. Maureen Cole, Frances A. Hill, and Leland J. Dayley, "Do Masculine Pronouns Used Generically Lead to Thoughts of Men?" *Sex Roles* 9, no. 6 (1983): 746.
41. Cole, Hill, and Dayley, "Do Masculine Pronouns Used Generically," 739.
42. Cole, Hill, and Dayley, "Do Masculine Pronouns Used Generically," 747, 749.
43. Gastil, "Generic Pronouns and Sexist Language," 640.
44. Jacobson and Insko, "Use of Nonsexist Pronouns," 2.
45. Carolyn Jacobson, "Some Notes on Gender-Neutral Language," <www.stetson.edu/artsci/history/nongenderlang.html>.
46. Martyna, "What Does 'He' Mean?" 131.
47. Cole, Hill, and Dayley, "Do Masculine Pronouns Used Generically," 738.
48. Ross, "Against the Theory of 'Sexist Language.'"
49. Pauwels, "Feminist Language Planning," 1.
50. Pauwels, "Feminist Language Planning," 2.
51. "Non-Sexist Language," <http://owl.english.purdue.edu/ handouts/general/gl_nonsex.html>.
52. Jacobson, "Some Notes on Gender-Neutral Language."
53. Ross, "Against the Theory of 'Sexist Language.'"
54. Janet K. Swim, Robyn Mallett, and Charles Stangor, "Understanding Subtle Sexism: Detection and Use of Sexist Language," *Sex Roles* 51, nos. 3/4 (August 2004): 117.
55. Swim, Mallett, and Stangor, "Understanding Subtle Sexism," 119.
56. Janet B. Parks and Mary Ann Roberton, "Attitudes Toward Women Mediate the Gender Effect on Attitudes Toward Sexist Language," *Psychology of Women Quarterly* 28 no. 3 (September 2004): 234.
57. Parks and Roberton, "Attitudes Toward Women," 233.
58. Parks and Roberton, "Attitudes Toward Women," 234.
59. Parks and Roberton, "Attitudes Toward Women," 238.
60. Christopher Cronin and Sawsan Jreisat, "Effects of Modeling on the Use of Nonsexist Language Among High School Freshpersons and Seniors," *Sex Roles* 33, nos. 11/12 (December 1995): 819.

61. Cronin and Jreisat, "Effects of Modeling," 821.

62. Cronin and Jreisat, "Effects of Modeling," 828.

63. Deborah Kennedy, "Nonsexist Language: A Progress Report," *Canadian Journal of Education* 18, no. 3 (1993): 223.

64. Kennedy, "Nonsexist Language," 227.

65. Kennedy, "Nonsexist Language," 223.

66. Kennedy, "Nonsexist Language," 224–25.

67. Kennedy, "Nonsexist Language," 227.

68. Kennedy, "Nonsexist Language," 227.

69. Kennedy, "Nonsexist Language," 232.

70. Kennedy, "Nonsexist Language," 230–34, *passim*.

71. Kennedy, "Nonsexist Language," 233.

72. Kennedy, "Nonsexist Language," 223.

73. Kennedy, "Nonsexist Language," 235.

74. Mark R. McMinn, Pamela K. Troyer, Laurel E. Hannum, and James D. Foster, "Teaching Nonsexist Language to College Students," *Journal of Experimental Education* 59 (1991): 154.

75. McMinn, Troyer, Hannum, and Foster, "Teaching Nonsexist Language," 155.

76. McMinn, Troyer, Hannum, and Foster, "Teaching Nonsexist Language," 160.

77. McMinn, Troyer, Hannum, and Foster, "Teaching Nonsexist Language," 159.

78. Emilie Muto, "Non-sexist Language Can Be Ridiculous,"< www.snn-rdr.ca/snn/old/june98> (June 1998).

79. "NZMRA Manifesto," <www.emf.net/-estephen/manifesto>.

80. Trish Crawford, "Shock Value of Profane T-Shirts," *Toronto Star*, January 24, 2005, E1.

81. "Complaint Rejected," (Montreal) *Gazette*, September 25, 2004, A7.

82. Stephen Castle, "UKIP Man in Brussels Faces Harassment Claim After Trying to Quash His Sexist Reputation," (London) *Independent*, October 16, 2004, 3.

83. William Cederwell, "France's Proposed Ban on Anti-Gay Speech," (London) *Guardian*, December 10, 2004, 30.

Chapter Six

Stealing Our Wallets (and Making Us Apologize for It)

It is one of the most venerable myths in American politics: the pay gap between men and women. In the 1970s, buttons starting appearing on lapels proclaiming the gap with all the certitude of a flat-earther in full dudgeon. Canny politicians seeking a nonthreatening issue with which to appease feminists and appeal to ordinary Americans' sense of fair play seized on it.

For years, feminists wore buttons reading simply "59¢." This denoted the alleged wage gap. That is, women were said to earn only 59 cents for each dollar a man made—even though they were doing the same work! Oh, the iniquity! *Ms.* magazine whined, "The average woman is cheated out of about $250,000 in wages over a lifetime,"[1] and the cheaters, we may be sure, are those dastardly MEN who plot day and night ways to keep the sisterhood in chains.

"It isn't right that women should get paid 59 cents on the dollar for the same work as men,"[2] whined Geraldine Ferraro in accepting the Democratic nomination for vice president in 1984. Twenty-plus years later, while the number has been bumped up (2004 Democratic presidential candidate John Kerry said that women make 76 cents for every dollar men make doing the same work), the myth is as strong as ever. Women who do the same work as men make less money. A lot less. The reason? Sexism, pure and simple. Employers don't value women in the way they value men who perform precisely the same jobs. So they disrespect women, they underpay women, they disparage women.

This is nonsense, as decades of research has established. But let us accept the feminists' claims. Let us say that capitalists are greedy pigs. They place profit above all else. Let us further say that I am a capitalist pig. My business employs 1,000 persons—all men, because I am also a sexist pig. My payroll is $50 million annually. But wait. As I toss and turn at night, subordinating the demands of sleep to my unending greed, a light goes on in my head: women make only 70 cents for each dollar a male makes. Assuming they are, as the feminists assert, every bit as good as male employees, if not better, what if I fire my 1,000 males and replace them with 1,000 females, thus reducing my labor costs to $35 million? I then cut my prices and drive my competitors out of business.

The feminist listening to this story wrinkles her brow. "Hmm," she mumbles. She brightens. "Wait! I see the flaw! Your sexism overpowers your greed. So you won't hire those 1,000 women, and the patriarchy remains in place, albeit inefficiently."

Okay, I concede: I am a sexist as well as a greedy pig. I won't hire the women and strike it rich, all based on my misogynistic principles. So then why doesn't a female competitor do so? Why doesn't she hire an all-woman workforce, undercut my labor costs, cut her prices, put me out of business, and vault to the golden fields?

Why not?

I expect I would have to wait a good long time for an answer to that one.

Feminists find it far easier to simply smear those who point out the phantom nature of the wage gap. Consider the case of *Equal Employment Opportunity Commission (EEOC) v. Sears, Roebuck, and Co.*, the largest corporate sex discrimination case ever to go to trial.

The EEOC had collected evidence against Sears for eleven years before the trial began, yet the commission and its feminist allies were unable to produce a single living plaintiff who alleged sex discrimination against Sears. Rather, the EEOC relied wholly on statistics to "prove" its case. For instance, women were not represented in the Sears hardware sales staff to the same degree that they were in the ladies' clothing department. *Ipso facto*, discrimination!

Alas for the EEOC, not a single victim of Sears' alleged sexist bias was found. Nevertheless, the EEOC pressed on, insisting that Sears, which had for decades been regarded as a model employer of women, was in fact just another Chicago chauvinist pig.

Bravely, Barnard College Professor Rosalind Rosenberg testified for Sears in the trial, unleashing on herself a hailstorm of criticism as a traitor to her gender. Never mind that what she said was indubitably true; truth is no defense against such charges.

Rosenberg pointed out to the EEOC that "men and women have had different interests, goals and aspirations regarding work. . . . [H]ousework and child care continue to affect the women's labor force participation even today."

The EEOC threw a bureaucratic fit. It produced its own court historian, Alice Kessler Harris, who sneered that Rosenberg's fact-based argument fit "squarely within a long tradition of employer excuses for and manipulations of women's work experience."³ Harris denied that women turned down non-traditional jobs for reasons as measly as child-raising responsibilities.

Real-life situations were not allowed to impinge on ideology. In the real world, a hardware manager's position requires (1) knowledge of hardware; and (2) a willingness to work evening hours. Men, empirically, are likelier than women to possess the former and to accept the latter. That is how people are, and that is why Sears won its case in 1986 in what was widely regarded as a crushing blow on behalf of common sense and against ahistorical ideology-laden feminist analysis.

And yet Rosenberg is still reviled, as are those economists, male and female, who break with stale orthodoxy. Economist June O'Neill's research led her to conclude that "differences in earnings attributable solely to gender bias are likely to be much smaller than is commonly believed, probably less than 10 percent."[4] The many other factors that account for the mythical "wage gap" include experience, consecutive years in the workforce, age, education, and the type of job one holds.

One factor in the gap may be the greater willingness of men to engage in risks, to take a shot, to go for the moon, even in a job interview. In *Women Don't Ask: Negotiation and the Gender Divide* (2003), economists Linda Babcock and Sara Laschever found that among those earning master's degrees in business from Carnegie-Mellon University, seven percent of women and 57 percent of men asked for a higher starting salary during job interviews. The entire gender gap between male and female Carnegie-Mellon grads could be traced to men's willingness to ask for what they think they are worth.

A groundbreaking, "beyond left and right"-ish work on the subject, *Why Men Earn More: The Startling Truth Behind the Pay Gap—And What Women Can Do About It* (2005), is the product of Warren Farrell, who can hardly be written off as a club-bearing Neanderthal. Farrell boasts that he is the only man ever to have been elected three times to the board of directors of the New York City branch of NOW. He used to clothe himself in a t-shirt, purchased in 1991 from the inerrantly errant American Association of University Women, that read, "For a woman to make as much in a day as a man, she'd have to work until 10:30 at night . . . then who'd make dinner?"[5]

Yet now Farrell insists that "Men have not stacked the decks against women." As evidence he adduces his former and current wives, both of whom outearn him. He disparages those women who seek the false spur of "victim power" and he wonders just what all the whining is about glass ceilings and suchlike in the corporate world. After all, he says, "Companies like I.B.M. have offered women scholarships to study engineering for years, and women engineers routinely get higher starting salaries than men."[6]

Farrell is not some vengeful men's rights crusader out to inflict a rough measure of justice on his erstwhile feminist allies. For some of those allies are anything but erstwhile. Karen DeCrow, the employment discrimination lawyer who served as the national NOW president from 1974–1977, wrote the foreword to *Why Men Earn More*, wherein she concedes that "men are not involved in a nefarious plot to keep the female wage down."[7] This nugget of insight alone elicits a gasp of surprise from the reader and is probably enough to ensure that DeCrow's picture will be ripped down from the wall of NOW headquarters, but the real treasure is in Farrell's carefully documented, mathematically competent account of the non-sexist cause of the pay gap.

He comes up with 25 differences in workplace behavior that, cumulatively, lead to men outearning women. Farrell's work is pathbreaking; because he emerges from a feminist background and addresses the issue from an earnestly feminist perspective, his work is likely to stick. (In some people's craw, too.)

Paraphrased and annotated, his 25 reasons why men earn more than women are:

(1) Men go into technology and hard sciences, which pay more than arts and social sciences. (This is likely to remain true for the foreseeable future. As Farrell notes, "In a 2003 Gallup poll of teenagers, careers in computers were the number one choice of boys, but not even among the top 10 choices of girls.")[8]

(2) Men take hazardous jobs, which pay more. (The single most hazardous job in America is timber-cutter, which is virtually all male. The safest job is secretary, which is 99 percent female. Guess which is more lucrative?)

(3) Men are more willing to expose themselves to the inclement elements. (And shouldn't a UPS courier, braving wind, snow, ice, and rain, earn more than a UPS clerk in a climate-controlled office?)

(4) Men take stressful jobs that one can't simply "leave at the office." (The example Farrell gives is corporate attorney vs. librarian. Of course men who marry their careers are likely to divorce their spouses: they pay a personal cost for their professional gain.)

(5) Women prefer fulfillment (say, as a child care professional) to higher pay (as a tax accountant).

(6) Higher risks yield higher rewards, and men are likelier to take those risks. ("Ninety-one percent of venture capitalists are men.")[9]

(7) The worst shifts and worst hours usually pay more. (This is true not only on assembly lines but among, for instance, doctors, too: a private practice doctor whose "off-hours" are not always his own makes more than an HMO doctor.)

(8) Jobs with unpleasant surroundings (say, a coal mine) may pay to attract employees.
(9) Men "update"; that is, they select fields in which one has to work and study to remain current, such as computer software engineer. Women are much more likely to choose fields, e.g., French language scholar, in which one's skills need no updating.
(10) Subfields—which require updating—often pay more than the general field. As Farrell notes, "A nurse anesthetist can make twice the pay of a general nurse."[10]
(11) Men work longer hours, and the pay gap widens for every hour past 40 per week. As Farrell notes, "[w]omen today are less than half as likely as men to work in excess of 50 hours per week."[11]
(12) More experience means higher pay. Women are far more likely to have gaps in their résumés, stretches of time during which they left full-time work to raise children. Women in the workforce, notes Farrell, "are eight times as likely to spend 4 or more years out of the labor force than are men." For instance, fully 94 percent of female attorneys who in 1987 were working at the top law firms in the country "left their jobs between one and eight years later."[12] Given that, on average, an additional year of experience is worth a 3–4 percent increase in pay, why wouldn't there be a gender gap in pay for attorneys?
(13) Uninterrupted experience with the same employer pays off. Those with seniority earn more. Men, who are nine times less likely than women to drop out of a workplace for "family reasons,"[13] typically achieve seniority at greater rates than do women.
(14) Men work more weeks of the year.
(15) Men have half the rate of absenteeism as do women.
(16) Men are more willing to commute, which greatly broadens their job market.
(17) Men are more willing to relocate to undesirable locations.
(18) Men are more willing to take jobs that require extensive travel. (Women make up only 16 percent of frequent flyers.)[14]
(19) When men and women have the same job titles, men often take on different—and more remunerative—responsibilities. For instance, male corporate vice presidents tend to be in finance or sales, while women aspire to—dare we say softer?—roles in human resources and public relations. Finance pays more than p.r., and why shouldn't it?
(20) When men and women have the same job title, the male's responsibilities are often bigger. For instance, a sales manager for the Northeast will make more than a sales manager for southwestern Connecticut.

(21) Men, as risk takers, require less job security. Men are far more likely than women to work on commission, which is a route to riches or penury, depending on one's aptitude. In addition, women are represented disproportionately in the public sector, where salaries are lower than in the private sector.
(22) Higher paid persons have more training that is of greater relevance to their field. For instance, 59 percent of male surgeons but only 30 percent of female surgeons are board certified.[15]
(23) Men have higher career goals. This is no indictment of women: indeed, one can argue that flexibility, a humane work environment, and making plenty of time for one's family and avocations, as many women do, make for a better human being than does working 70 hours a week in pursuit of higher pay.
(24) Men cast wider nets in searching for a job; they are more likely to engage in national searches, while women tend to the local.
(25) People who make more are more productive. This is a touchy subject, but Farrell plunges right in, adducing as evidence studies that show men to be more productive in fields ranging from ob-gyn to academic research and from publishing to court reporting.

Farrell notes the media's reluctance—refusal, really—to cover the wage gap issue honestly. "[A]s long ago as the 1980s," he writes, the U.S. Bureau of Labor Statistics found that "companies paid men and women equal money when their titles were the same, their responsibilities the same, and their responsibilities were of equal size—for example, both regional buyers for Nordstrom's, not one a local and one a regional buyer. But although this was published in the official publication of the U.S. Bureau of Labor Statistics, I had never read of the study in a single paper or heard of it in the media. To my surprise (in those years of my innocence), once gender equality was found, the gender comparison was not only ignored but never updated."[16]

Way back in the dark ages of the 1950s, which predated considerably the Equal Pay Act of 1963, the Census Bureau found that never-married women made only two percent less than never-married men, and in fact never-married white women between the ages of 45–54 actually outearned their male counterparts! By the late 1960s, never-married and unpublished female professors earned 145 percent of what their male counterparts earned. (A feminist explained to Farrell, "Never-married women are winners; never-married men are losers."[17] So much for that vaunted compassion gap.)

This was hardly a shocking finding: many researchers have confirmed Farrell's general argument. For instance, Jennifer Roback Morse pointed to the "fact that never-married women earn much more than women who have been married—essentially the same amount as never-married men. This pattern has been observed at least since the 1960s. Controlling for married status alone closes nearly all of the earnings gap."[18] (The earnings gap is far wider within the male gender, and also inverted: men who have never married make an average of 62 cents for every dollar a married man makes. Without families to support, many single men may be unwilling to make the trade-offs—travel, education, unpleasant working conditions—that married men make.)

Using 2004 Census data, Farrell found that the sexual wage gap remained: never-married educated men working full time make just 85 percent of what their female counterparts earn. Responding to his colleagues' protests that the real sex discrimination is found among part-time workers, Farrell discovered that the truth is quite the opposite: "A part-time working woman makes $1.10 for every dollar made by her male counterpart."[19]

In fact, women actually make more than men in 39 fields, from sales engineering to modeling. In the latter, women outearn men by a factor of five. But do you hear Fabio bitching?

In medicine, female doctors earn pay equal to that of male doctors—if, that is, one considers such variables as hours, specialty, and experience. That the annual income of male doctors is 141 percent that of female doctors is a reflection of the tendency of women to choose shorter hours and more family and "life-friendly" specialties (family practice versus thoracic surgery).[20]

Certain careers remain, in effect, closed to men. Hospitals, in act if not in policy, often discourage male nurses from caring for female patients, while female nurses work with both sexes. This has the effect of boosting salaries for nurses, who are disproportionately female. Farrell remarks that while five percent of those who earn degrees in dental hygiene are men, fewer than one percent of dental hygienists are male. "Oh yes," one dentist told him, "when a man calls to apply to be a dental hygienist, I just say, 'Sorry.'"[21] Don't hold your breath waiting for the EEOC to investigate that one.

Of the *Jobs Rated Almanac*'s list of the 25 worst jobs—their rottenness determined by income, stress, job security, work environment, and other factors—all but one (dancer) are dominated by men. In fact, 92 percent of those toiling at these undesirable posts (dishwasher, garbage collector, roofer, lumberjack, sheet metal worker, and meter reader, inter alia) are men. Some of these jobs—dishwasher, for instance—also appear on lists of the lowest-paying jobs. But others pay well, in part for their very undesirability. Yet as Farrell notes, "women tend to be drawn" to jobs whose characteristics include "physical safety, little financial risk, no exposure to inclement weather, pleasant working conditions, short commutes, and no midnight–8 a.m. shifts."[22]

Consider what happened when in 1973 the EEOC ordered Bell Telephone to end sex segregation by job within the company. "Male jobs," noted Mary

Ann Mason, "were largely outdoor jobs with higher pay scales than female indoor jobs." Yet the "number of women who went outdoors to take male jobs was less than half the number of men who came in from the cold to take female jobs."[23]

Perhaps there is a reason why climbing telephone poles in snow, cold, and driving rain carries higher pay than entering data on a computer in a well-lit and comfortable office. At the very least, climbing poles can be a cold, snowy, rainy proposition, not to mention dangerous—according to the "Census of Fatal Occupational Injuries" compiled by the U.S. Department of Labor, job-related deaths are consistently over 90 percent male.[24]

This is not to say that, little by little, women are not assuming more of these jobs. By the dawn of the twenty-first century, as Richard T. Hise points out, 2.6 percent of workers in the construction trades were women, as were 4.7 percent of truck drivers, 14.4 percent of U.S. armed services personnel, and—significantly?—over half (51.8 percent) of bartenders.[25] But, contrary to the illustrations used in elementary school textbooks, most long-haul truckers are still men, most kindergarten teachers are still women, and the assistant manager who is taking a couple of years off to stay home with the kids is almost certainly a woman. No matter how loudly the grimalkins of NOW screech over the fact, women love their children. And usually their husbands, too.

Warren Farrell's basic explanation for the wage gap is simple: "It's marriage and children, stupid!"[26]

Women leave the paid workforce to bear and care for children, a biological responsibility—a blessing, most mothers would say—for which feminism has yet to find an antidote. "This absence from the labor force," says economist Jennifer Roback Morse, "has important economic consequences that have nothing to do with discrimination."[27]

Women, as a rule, do not pile up the continuous years in the labor market that men do. Far from being evidence of sexist bias, the checkered pattern of many women's careers is exactly what they want. As Mary Ann Mason wrote in a new (2002) introduction to her book, *The Equality Trap*, "Unofficial 'mommy tracks' have crept into law offices and up corporate ladders, allowing women to work at a slower pace without dropping out of the race."[28] These "mommy tracks," as feminists never point out, are a response to demands by women for options that permit a middle ground between leaving the workforce and subordinating one's family to it.

Ah, but this behavior does not comport with feminist dogma. Elizabeth Cady Stanton may have said, "Let us remember that womanhood is the great fact, wifehood and motherhood its incidents,"[29] but for most women, wifehood and motherhood are far more than incidental. They carry great meaning, and certainly far greater responsibilities and rewards, than mere womanhood.

The wisest of our scholars understand this. Elizabeth Fox-Genovese notes that "Children, not men, restrict women's independence; children, not men, tend to make and keep women poor. Few but the most radical feminists have been willing to state openly that women's freedom requires their freedom from children. Yet the covert determination to free women from children shapes much feminist thought and most feminist policies even, and especially, those policies aimed at having the government assume a large part of the responsibility."[30]

Fox-Genovese points out that the failure of the federal income tax child deduction to keep pace with the child-care deduction means that we "have a tax policy that favors working mothers over mothers who stay home."[31] Thus "[o]ur public policies . . . [discourage] . . . private arrangements that most Americans prefer and most closely resemble what parents would do themselves if they were not working, or if they were only working part-time." The form of child care that is most preferred by working mothers is care by aunts, neighbors, and friends, but small informal day-care providers have to do everything off the books, for they "could not meet federal day care standards."[32] Government standards, as is usually the case, seek to standardize even so private a choice as arranging care for one's child.

In *The Equality Trap*, Mary Ann Mason argues that feminism slighted and made life worse for working-class women, those far from the boardroom and the classroom, those who had no rungs to grab on the career ladder. They were service workers, in the main, waitresses and clerks and single moms and minimum-wage-earning wives who saw less and less of their children. Yet "it was the relatively small class of women who were trying to push into the high-stake male professions . . . which drove the feminists movement."

These women scorned child-bearing (unless the child could be raised, fed, nursed, cared for, and taught by others and produced on a moment's notice for a two-minute game of patty-cake with Mother the Career Monster) and "were not greatly concerned with secretaries or poor single parents."[33]

"The modern women's movement has put almost all its effort into creating and promoting women who live to work," charged Mason. "It has romanticized the male status jobs and taken the position that systematic discrimination is the only reason that men rather than women hold these status jobs."[34]

Mason's prescriptions amounted to a reworking of the "social feminism" of the 1930s. She called for special treatment for mothers in the workforce, subsidies for daycare and maternal leave, and the repeal of no-fault divorce laws, which make it easy for men or women to put asunder their unions, whether holy or not. Her proposals recall the protective legislation for women that were in force throughout nineteenth and first half of the twentieth century and were based on regnant beliefs ranging from the supposed interference of industrialism with menstrual cycles to a woman's inability to lift heavy weights.

Mason wrote, "I now understand the adamant opposition of most feminists of the 1920s and 1930s, like Jane Addams and Florence Howe, to the Equal Rights Amendment. They grasped the fundamental truth that modern women have lost, that women need special consideration in their role as mothers."[35]

"Equality is a trap for women,"[36] concludes Mason. Instead, they deserve privileges and arrangements that acknowledge the biological differences between the sexes. Such policies as maternity/paternity leave are specious, she argues, because no matter how strenuously feminists might object to the fact, it is women who carry and deliver babies, not men. It is women at whose breasts these infants suckle. It is women who act as mothers. To wish otherwise is to deny all the evidence of our sense and our history.

The choice of motherhood, of making a home for a family, of choosing to stay home with one's child rather than enter the rat race, profoundly offends some feminists. Simone de Beauvoir once told Betty Friedan, "we don't believe that any woman should have this choice. No woman should be authorized to stay at home to raise her children. Society should be totally different. Women should not have that choice, precisely because if there is such a choice, too many women will make that one."[37]

The language has the metallic clang of a jail door slamming shut; the ideas it expresses are as repulsive as the sounds of whips cracking on gulag prisoners' backs.

Still, despite the overwhelming evidence that the society desired by the de Beauvoirs is harsh and inhuman, the would-be totalitarians hatch their fetid plans. Wendy McElroy notes that Heidi Hartmann, in "Capitalism, Patriarchy, and Job Segregation by Sex," locates "the roots of women's present social status . . . in this sex-ordered division of labor." With all the certitude of Stalin announcing a new five-year plan she declares, "Not only must the hierarchical nature of the division of labor between the sexes be eliminated, but the very division of labor between the sexes itself must be eliminated."[38]

Men, we must assume, will be ordered to develop uteruses and breasts under a Hartmann regime. Until that time, fetuses will gestate within antiseptic labs, mothered and fathered by technicians in white coats. What a brave new world awaits.

Equal pay for equal work may have been a catchy slogan of the 1960s, but by the 1980s feminists had replaced it with a more, well, expansive view of the matter. As Michigan Women's Commission member Myra K. Wolfgang explained, "We, who want equal opportunities, equal pay for equal work and equal status for women, know that frequently we obtain real equality through a difference in treatment, rather than identity in treatment."[39]

In other words, all this guff about equality was so much rubbish to be swept away with yesterday's fads. What the women's movement wanted now was legislated superiority to men, and one of the most astonishing and egregious instruments of that superiority was to be comparable worth, a scheme by which a centralized bureaucracy would set the pay scales of every person in America.

A snobbishness usually intrudes in such discussions. How dare people without advanced degrees make more money/join clubs/enjoy privileges that I, the credentialed aspirant to the upper middle class, may not, huffs the affronted feminist. To use a religious, or anti-religious, parallel, Mary Daly was astonished that "Women were able to accept the fact that any boy was allowed to serve Mass, whereas a woman with a Ph.D. was absolutely excluded from such a function."[40]

Why the Ph.D. makes any difference in the preceding example is a puzzle. The rituals and rules of Catholicism are a matter for Catholics to sort out, but it would seem that post-graduate education ought not to be a factor in determining just who may become an altar boy. Or altar server, as the phrase now goes, since in many parishes girls assist the priest in the Mass.

But the point is this: feminists chafe at the "unfairness" of the free market, which often rewards men who are willing to do unpleasant or dangerous jobs more than it rewards women with softer jobs. That these men have not endured 18 years of schooling and taken out a lifetime's worth of student loans makes it all the more galling. The grunts and proles, it seems, are on top!

Warren Farrell observes that female librarians, garlanded with master's degrees, may make only slightly more than uneducated male garbage collectors. "But a person wishing to be a librarian finds herself competing with more people, since more people enjoy reading books than smelling garbage." The same principle explains why a coal miner may earn as much as an art historian. Farrell calls it the "death professions bonus"[41]: those jobs fraught with health hazards, up to and including the risking of one's life, must pay more to attract employees. (Yet as Farrell points out, "the more men, the less we care about making the job safer."[42] Ninety-two percent of those who die as a result of workplace accidents are men. And on the subject of men dying young, let us not forget another government program, this one not a pie-in-the-sky dream but a concrete reality for over seven decades, and one that systematically shortchanges the male of the species: Social Security. Men have lifespans more than five years shorter than women. We are much likelier than women to die before reaching the age at which we can receive benefits, which for workers born after 1960 is 67. Cries for a reduction in the payroll tax for men—in the interest of fairness and equity—have been muted, to say the least.)

Under comparable worth, the federal government would effectively set wages. It would be illegal for employers to pay women less than men who work in "comparable" jobs—and the comparability is to be determined by a federal bureaucracy. The scheme promised to be a nightmare of Rube Goldberg proportions. And it was deeply offensive to blue-collar workers as well.

Comparable worth would be one of the most blunderbuss interventions in the history of state regulation of the economy. By fixing the pay of an art historian above that of a coal miner, it would amount to a subsidy of middle- and upper-middle-class feminists at the expense of working men; it would also mandate "higher pay for higher fulfillment positions that everyone wants and lower pay for lower fulfillment positions that are hard to fill unless we pay more."[43] We will end up with a superabundance of art historians and a shortage of trash collectors.

Comparable worth is a classic feminist proposal, motivated by equal parts hatred of working-class men, idolatry of big government, and crass self-aggrandizement, all gussied up in the language of "fairness." It disparages the hard work of construction workers, truckers, loggers, and carpenters whilst privileging the favored activities of Women's Studies majors. No wonder Brigette Berger, a feminist, called comparable worth "one of the more aggressively elitist visions of modern life that has surfaced in recent decades."[44]

Based in contempt for blue-collar work and resentment toward men, comparable worth is a scheme that only a Women's Studies professor could love.

The issue had a bit of traction in the early 1980s, despite the opposition of the Reagan administration. "The momentum toward eliminating sex-based wage discimination is now irreversible," claimed Gerald W. McEntee, president of the American Federation of State, County and Municipal Employees (AFSCME), which stood to gain from the overthrow of market principles. "There is a growing movement all over the country to adopt pay equity and to eliminate pay discrimination," screeched Claudia Wayne, executive director of the National Committee for Pay Equity, who added that "the Reagan administration . . . is not going to be able to stop that momentum."[45]

Guess again, Claudia. In 1985, led by the sensible Clarence Thomas, then chairman of the Equal Employment Opportunity Commission, the EEOC unanimously affirmed Chairman Thomas's statement that "Congress never authorized the government to take on wholesale restructuring of wages that were set by nonsex-based decisions of employers—by collective bargaining or by the marketplace."[46]

So died the insidious effort of McEntee and others to slide comparable worth in through the bureaucratic backdoor. The obvious solution to the supposed problem that comparable worth addresses—the tendency of women to study subjects that ultimately pay less than do those subjects studied by men—is no solution at all, according to comparable worthies. Because engineering and math and computer science are just too . . . well, hard. It's so much easier and more fun to major in Art History. And if, on graduating from college, one finds that an Art History major is worth considerably less in the marketplace than is an engineer, then let's condemn the marketplace and let the politicians set salaries. That's only fair, after all, and if fairness requires coercion on a scale unknown outside the most rigid command economies, then that's an ethical sacrifice the Art History majors are ready to make.

If comparable worth has slipped from its position in the vanguard of "progressive" policies, other schemes of dubious intent and disastrous effect have taken its place. Ironically, the unintended consequences of feminist-inspired economic regulation often redounds to the disadvantage of women. Take the sexual harassment laws that send corporate America into such a tizzy of self-abasement and nervous monitoring of relations between men and women. Sure, they provide jobs to "sexual-harassment counselors" and those therapeutic busybodies who always seem to profit when government sticks its nose into private affairs, but in the main, the laws hurt women.

Individualist feminist Wendy McElroy complains that such laws, and the corporate policies adopted to follow those laws, return women "to the status of victims." The woman envisioned by sexual-harassment law and policy is not a strong, confident, competent actor in the business world; rather, she is a cringing, whining little crybaby. "Like small children or the mentally disabled," writes McElroy, "they need a paternalistic state."

Moreover, women on the early rungs of the corporate or academic ladders are finding it harder to attract the helping hand of a mentor. As McElroy puts it, "A mentor naturally comes into close and friendly contact with the person being nurtured. As the charge of sexual harassment rears its litigious head, fewer and fewer men are willing to put their careers at risk by helping young women up the ladder."[47] Would-be male mentors must be careful not to socialize with female underlings; even a closed-door meeting is verboten, or at least strongly frowned on. By treating men as the enemy, sexual harassment laws and policies force men to remove themselves from the lives of younger women—to the detriment of both parties.

If older men are not able to serve as mentors to younger women, Uncle Sam is more than happy to step in. Women in business receive special help that no bureaucrat would dream of giving men *qua* men. For instance, the U.S. government publication, *Federal Programs Benefitting Women*, runs over 100 pages, but no such list exists for men. The feds sponsor everything from networking teas for women at NASA to a Women's Networking Roundtable at the notoriously inefficient Small Business Administration. "The buddy-boy network is called discrimination," writes Warren Farrell; "the buddy-girl network is called the law."[48]

Affirmative action is working within the Fortune 500. Or at least it is working demographically. While 21.4 percent of the female executives at the largest U.S. companies are under 40 years of age, a mere 1.4 percent of their male counterparts are under two score years. Yet, according to Warren Farrell, studies of CEOs indicate that "male executives work more hours, travel more, move more, earn more MBAs, have more job continuity, and make more of almost all of the sacrifices" associated with higher pay. Women, contrary to the "glass ceiling" myth, rise faster in corporate settings than do the supposedly advantaged men. "[A]t this point in history," Farrell informs men, "there are female tollbooths and male tollbooths, and the toll charged to women is lower."[49]

There is, running throughout the literature of feminist corporate empowerment, an assumption that women are, and will be, better bosses than men. They will be more empathetic, more caring, better able to delegate, better listeners, more humane in their treatment of subordinates, better able to elicit from employers their maximum effort: superior in every way, it seems. They'll even be likelier to pick up the check at lunch. (A fantasy if ever there was one. Women, bless their parsimonious hearts, are famous for splitting checks seven ways, getting out their mini-calculators—men could do the math in their heads—and assigning each diner her share of the meal. A man would just pick up the whole check.)

There is only one problem with the Woman as Sensitive Boss scenario: no one, not even women, believe it.

Opinion polls in the former Soviet bloc, where decades of communist propaganda (if not practice) preached complete equality in the workplace, find that in overwhelming numbers—from six to ten times greater—both men and women prefer male bosses. An international Gallup poll of 22 countries in 1996 discovered that 47 percent of men and 47 percent of women preferred male bosses, while only 14 percent of men and 21 percent of women preferred female bosses.[50] Either women around the globe are victims of an epidemic of false consciousness, or there is something about a female boss—about many individual female bosses, I should say—that rankles.

One supposes that if it were possible, the ideological wardens of feminism would herd that unenlightened 47 percent into one huge diversity education camp.

In his eye-opening work of investigative reporting, *The Diversity Machine: The Drive to Change the "White Male Workplace"* (1997), sociologist Frederick R. Lynch catalogues the thought-control, the ideological hectoring, and the simple shake-downs and scams that go by the name "diversity training."

White men—or at least those with an ounce of gumption and moxie—protest the manifest idiocies inherent in this training (or "re-education," as the phrase applies to such brainwashing when it happens in communist countries). One session described by Lynch degenerates into a stony period of sullen and resentful silence, broken by complaints about quotas and affirmative action, as the exasperated diversity facilitator lectures, "Diversity and affirmative action are not the same thing. Diversity goes beyond race. It goes to who you hire and why. Don't point the finger at quotas and have quotas be at fault. Don't scapegoat."[51]

Saying a thing does not make it so. Diversity, a fine word in and of itself, has become a mushy euphemism for quotas, for affirmative action, for passing over those oppressors of the human race known as white males.

Lynch argues that affirmative action, the policy manifestation of "diversity," was "a redistributionist policy implemented by white corporate and government elites against younger, working- and middle-class white males."[52] The men whose fat white heads were in the center of the diversity bull's-eye never knew what hit them—until it was too late.

Most diversity trainers are former teachers, as Lynch discovered, who found that subjecting captive employees of major corporations and government bureaucracies to politically correct preachments and forcing them to play silly games which reveal the evil nature of white maleness pays much more than managing a classroom full of squalling nine-year-olds. Single-day diversity workshops net their conductors thousands of dollars, and full-scale diversity overhauls (designed to root the whiteness and maleness out of a corporate culture) run easily into the hundreds of thousands. Nice work if you can get it.

The diversity racket boomed in the 1980s and 1990s; by 1995, "70 percent [of Fortune 500 corporations] had formal diversity management programs in place," and most of the stragglers were catching up—this despite the fact that "there is still no systematic proof that diversity management programs decrease ethnic and gender tensions while increasing profits, productivity, and creativity."[53] There was a small fortune to be made in peddling videos, seminars, and consulting services, and a well-tailored army of charlatans, hucksters, and true believers fanned out across corporate America to ram diversity down the recalcitrant throats of every last wicked white male in the Land of the Free. "A good many [diversity trainers] harbor covert or overt hostility toward white males,"[54] wrote Lynch after years of observing the species.

In an egregious if not really atypical example, Lynch describes *You Make a Difference* (1991), among the most popular films shown in diversity seminars:

"The worst stereotypes were reserved for whites. In one scene, a nerdy-looking white male wanders through his office building repeatedly offending minority and female coworkers. He asks a black security guard, 'Hey, my man! How about that game last night?' The reply: 'Hey, my man! I went to the symphony last night!' To a Chinese woman, 'Hey, Rose—so what do you think is the best Chinese restaurant in town?' He sees black men exchanging money in the men's restroom and assumes it's a drug deal; it is actually a football pool payoff."[55]

Subsuming all males of Caucasian racial background under the monochromatic rubric "whites" is the grossest of insults, implying as it does that there is no real difference between, say, an Italian-American cop in Brooklyn, a Jewish-American shopkeeper in Greenville, Mississippi, a Norwegian-American farmer in North Dakota, a Basque-American shepherd in Nevada, and an Estonian-American jewelry-maker in New Mexico. White is white, to the commissars of diversity, and white is never right.

One trainer whom Lynch witnessed told a room of 150 Southern California middle managers to use the "three-year-old rule" before telling a joke. That is, "consider whether a three-year-old child should hear such a joke or whether the child could tell it without being reprimanded."[56] In other words, these grown men and women were being ordered to effectively infantilize themselves, to reduce the level of their daily discourse, the give-and-take and water-cooler discussion that is the social lifeblood of any office, to a pre-nursery-school level.

The achievements of "white males," that most despised of all classes, are systematically denigrated by diversity trainers. Sure, we've produced Isaac Newton, Leonardo da Vinci, George Washington, Thomas Jefferson, Thomas Edison, Ernest Hemingway, John Ford, Babe Ruth, and Stephen Hawking, but that's only because the game is rigged, the rules are fixed, and everything is set up on a silver platter for your average white male—even, presumably, those who grew up in orphanages, who begged for bread, who lived in garrets or hovels whilst composing their masterworks. It all comes so easily to white men.

The success of white males on tests, standardized or not, is ascribed to the cultural bias of the testers. The questions are unfair. Algebra, geometry, calculus, grammar, chemistry, physics: these are the silly little fiefdoms of white men, and women and persons of color are barred entry by . . . well, it is never quite clear just who or what is barring the entry. Adding to the confusion is the claim by some of the more adventurous Afrocentrists that math was invented in Africa centuries before the first doltish European could add two plus two.

A mantra of the diversity crowd has it that "equal treatment is not fair treatment." Women and nonwhites ought to be held to different standards than white males; after all, as diversity-crats lecture in their most oleaginous manner, we don't treat every flower in the garden equally, do we? Some need more sunlight, some need more water to bloom. The white male flowers, alas, seem to get the bulk of the manure.

As Lynch notes, an ideology has grown up around Diversity. Whereas in the not so distant past the stated goal of civil rights and feminist lobbyists was to ensure equal opportunity for those they claimed to represent, "diversity" is now "hailed as an end in itself. Ethnic and gender diversity was morally good. It qualitatively changed and enriched an institution."[57] The ideology of diversity, with its concomitant devaluing of white men, was conceived and born in the sociology departments of American universities and in the civil-rights lobbies of Washington, DC, and New York City. It was picked up by the Fortune 500, particularly its self-consciously liberal CEOs, and imposed on the American workplace in the last three decades of the twentieth century.

Oddly, the one thing that advocates of Diversity most loathe is diversity of opinion. For instance, the Balanced Workforce Plan of Xerox, which subjected the copy-making giant's workforce to strict departmental quotas, was described this way by one admiring affirmative-action advocate: "Xerox senior management used an interesting approach. It did not attempt to change attitudes; it changed behavior by saying, 'You will have a certain number of women managers by next year.' Managers who were unable to comply were held accountable."[58]

If, indeed, Diversity were good for business, businesses would not need to be forced to adopt it. Yet the Fortune 500 firms that were among affirmative action's earliest and most energetic supporters in turn lobbied the federal government to impose and enforce strict anti-discrimination rules on smaller businesses. David Kearns, then-CEO of Xerox, might say, "The company that gets out in front of managing diversity will have a competitive edge,"[59] but that edge has yet to take on visible form. To the contrary: in a major 1993 study, Peter Brimelow and Leslie Spencer of *Forbes* estimated the cost of quotas and affirmative action at $236 billion—or approximately four percent of the gross national product.

Ultimately, the decision on whether to give a leg up to females in the business world rests—or should rest—entirely with the companies involved. It goes without saying, though I will say it anyway in order to avoid any misunderstanding, that many, many women excel in business and its related pursuits, from accounting to marketing to personnel management. And these women, like the rest of us, are being done no favors by the purveyors of marketophobic myths and the wearers of 70 cents or 59 cents buttons. No matter how sedulously many unscrupulous or clueless politicians flog the pay gap horse, it remains a phantom and a fairy story. And as usual, it is the truth that will set us free.

NOTES

1. Farrell, *Why Men Earn More*, 144.
2. Farrell, *Why Men Earn More*, 143.
3. Mason, *The Equality Trap*, 27.
4. Sommers, *Who Stole Feminism?*, 241.
5. Farrell, *Why Men Earn More*, 144.
6. Claudia H. Deutsch, "Are Women Responsible for Their Own Low Pay?" *New York Times*, February 27, 2005, Section 3, 7.
7. Farrell, *Why Men Earn More*, xii.
8. Farrell, *Why Men Earn More*, 20.
9. Farrell, *Why Men Earn More*, 61.
10. Farrell, *Why Men Earn More*, 74.
11. Farrell, *Why Men Earn More*, 82.
12. Farrell, *Why Men Earn More*, 85.
13. Farrell, *Why Men Earn More*, 88.
14. Farrell, *Why Men Earn More*, 100.
15. Farrell, *Why Men Earn More*, 109.
16. Farrell, *Why Men Earn More*, xxi.
17. Farrell, *Why Men Earn More*, xxii.
18. McElroy, *Sexual Correctness*, 91.
19. Farrell, *Why Men Earn More*, xxii.
20. Farrell, *Why Men Earn More*, 76.
21. Farrell, *Why Men Earn More*, 181.
22. Farrell, *Why Men Earn More*, 10.
23. Mason, *The Equality Trap*, 128.
24. Stolba, *Lying in a Room of One's Own*, 29.
25. Hise, *The War Against Men*, 45.
26. Farrell, *Why Men Earn More*, xxii.
27. McElroy, *Sexual Correctness*, 91.
28. Mason, *The Equality Trap*, 4.
29. Mason, *The Equality Trap*, 36.
30. Fox-Genovese, *"Feminism Is Not the Story of My Life,"* 228.
31. Fox-Genovese, *"Feminism Is Not the Story of My Life,"* 239.
32. Fox-Genovese, *"Feminism Is Not the Story of My Life,"* 246.
33. Mason, *The Equality Trap*, 3.
34. Mason, *The Equality Trap*, 110.
35. Mason, *The Equality Trap*, 16.
36. Mason, *The Equality Trap*, 48.
37. Sommers, *Who Stole Feminism?*, 256–57.
38. McElroy, *Sexual Correctness*, 94.
39. McElroy, *Sexual Correctness*, 65.
40. Daly, *Beyond God the Father*, 133.
41. Farrell, *Why Men Earn More*, xxv.
42. Farrell, *Why Men Earn More*, 27.

43. Farrell, *Why Men Earn More*, 211.
44. McElroy, *Sexual Correctness*, 96.
45. Warren Richey, "New Fury Over Pay Scales for Women," *Washington Post*, June 19, 1985, A3.
46. "Comparable Worth and the EEOC," *Washington Post*, June 24, 1985, A12.
47. McElroy, *Sexual Correctness*, 59.
48. Farrell, *Why Men Earn More*, 176.
49. Farrell, *Why Men Earn More*, 86.
50. Farrell, *Why Men Earn More*, 164.
51. Frederick R. Lynch, *The Diversity Machine: The Drive to Change the "White Male Workplace"* (New York: Free Press, 1997), xv.
52. Lynch, *The Diversity Machine*, 32.
53. Lynch, *The Diversity Machine*, 7.
54. Lynch, *The Diversity Machine*, 68.
55. Lynch, *The Diversity Machine*, 55.
56. Lynch, *The Diversity Machine*, xiii.
57. Lynch, *The Diversity Machine*, 12.
58. Lynch, *The Diversity Machine*, 42.
59. Lynch, *The Diversity Machine*, 53.

Chapter Seven

Guilty Pleasures—or Guilty of Pleasure? Balls, Guns, and the Recreational Tyranny of the Male

Girls outpace boys in high school, in college, in classrooms and in honor societies and everywhere else people are judged and graded, or so it seems. Surely the sporting field remains a hallowed ground of male achievement. Michael Jordan was male, Babe Ruth was male, Wayne Gretzy was male, Jim Brown was male: the finest athletes in the most popular sports have had to shave everyday, and by this I do not mean to include the East German women's track team.

But even here, boys and men are under the gun. We are not being outplayed on a level field, however. No, feminists, unable to come within 50 points of men on the playing field, are using the brutal cudgel of state coercion to punish men for the supreme effrontery of being superior to women in pretty much every sport this side of chess. Or should I say including chess, since few activities are as dominated by a single sex as is the game of kings and queens and grandmasters. (Even though, ironically, the most powerful piece on the chessboard is the queen, and the weakest, least powerful piece is the king.)

The highest-profile piece of anti-male legislation was directed at college athletes. The infamous Title IX of the Education Amendments of 1972 barred discrimination by sex in any school that receives federal monies. This amendment to the Civil Rights Act of 1964 has become one of those sacred cows which is worshipped in public discourse but which in fact, in dirty messy fact, has mired many college and university athletic departments in cow dung.

In order to prevent lawsuits alleging them to be favoring male athletics, schools of higher learning have been dropping men's sports (approximately 400 in the last decade and a half alone) like raindrops in a monsoon. The big money sports—football and basketball—are of course untouched, but the classical sports, many of them dating to the ancient Greeks, are thrown overboard to propitiate the harpies of Title IX. Wrestling, men's gymnastics, swimming, diving: sports with honorable histories are tossed aside like so many beer cans at a fraternity party. Even the UCLA swimming and diving team, which has produced 10 Olympic gold medalists, is gone.[1]

Title IX and the explosion of girls' sports presents a chicken-and-egg problem, though there is no gainsaying the rapid growth of women playing games. "In 1971," the year before the passage of Title IX, "only 294,015 girls participated in high school sports, compared with 3,666,917 boys. By the 1989–1990 academic year, there were 1,858,659 girls participating in high school sports, compared with 3,398,192 boys."[2] In the 2004–2005 school year, 2,908,390 girls participated, as did 4,200,319 boys.

As mentioned earlier, in a kind of elementary school warmup for Title IX, dodge ball has been effectively banned in most schools for rewarding accurate throwing, quickness of foot, and an aggressive attitude. In other words, for rewarding male attributes.

Even the timeless game of tag has come under fire. Consider *Quit It!*, a curriculum guide funded by the U.S. Department of Education and published in 1998 by the Women's Educational Equity Act Publishing Center (remember its director, Katherine Hanson, who claimed that four million women are beaten to death each year in America?); the Wellesley College Center for Research on Women, led by the equally unreliable spouter of anti-male bigotry Nan Stein; and the National Education Association. According to Christina Hoff Sommers, *Quit It!* contained this gem: "Before going outside to play, talk about how students feel when playing a game of tag. Do they like to be chased? Do they like to do the chasing? How does it feel to be tagged out? Get their ideas about other ways the game might be played."[3]

Quit It! goes on to describe a wussed-up version of tag called "Circle of Friends," in which no one is tagged out. It will bore and frustrate boys, and many girls as well, but perhaps this is the point: since males are subhuman, the best that schools can do for them is to stifle their impulses, suffocate their natures, try to extract that poison called "maleness" from them. And that's where pseudo-games like *Quit It!* come in.

Not that we don't already have more than a handful of potential *Quit It!* players in positions of influence. There will always be self-hating men, castratoes basking in the fluorescent glow of political correctness. Take Bob Ryan, columnist for the *Boston Globe*. He hailed the April 2004 Boston Marathon as "brilliant" for its adoption of "an idea whose time had come, and come, and come."

And what was this long-overdue idea, this refreshing proof that at long last, "Common sense has prevailed"?

Women started the race 29 minutes before the men. So when Catherine Ndereba of Kenya broke the tape at 2:24:27, she was declared the "winner" and her picture went out over the wire services as the first-place finisher of the most prestigious and venerable marathon in the world—even though the runner with the fastest time, Timothy Cherigat of Kenya, finished in 2:10:37, or 14 minutes less than it took Ms. Ndereba to run the race.

To the epicene Mr. Ryan, whose effusions were headlined with "New rule engenders equal footing" (letting women start half an hour earlier is "equality"?), this condescending arrangement was the feel-good story of the spring. To the retired marathon runner Joan Benoit Samuelson, April 20, 2004 was "a great day. With the new start, the women were able to put on a show. That was a great race. We've proven our abilities. I think, relatively speaking, that the women's times were more impressive than the men's."[4]

Well, yes, one supposes that "relatively speaking," a time of 2:24:27 is "more impressive" than 2:10:37. But would you want to speak to such a relative?

Feminist proselytizers argue that the "muscle gap," or the "degree of difference between male and female athletic performance in measurable sports like swimming and track and field,"[5] is closing. And recall that the gap closed fastest in the late 1980s, when theretofore unthinkable times were being posted by Eastern bloc athletes who were female in name only, so altered were their bodies by the daily doping regimen of the Soviet bloc sports bureaucracies. (Girls seem to be using anabolic steroids at a greater rate than ever before—in 2005, one survey found that five percent of high-school girls had used steroids at least once[6]—though the purpose seems to be to enhance physical attractiveness rather than to increase the number of feet Staci can throw the shotput. American girls use steroids to look like Jennifer Garner, not like an East German discus hurler.)

The percentage of female athletes in the Olympics has shot from 14.8 in the summer Munich games of 1972 to 44 percent in the 2004 summer games at Athens. (No women participated in the first games of the modern era, the 1896 Athens Olympics.)

Although women (or girls, in the case of pubescent golfer Michelle Wie in 2005) are permitted to compete in many men's sporting events, the reverse is not true and probably never will be permitted. In every major and even minor sport that attracts spectators, men play at a considerably higher level then do women.

And still, despite the massive propaganda campaign, the vast majority of Americans will not pay to watch women's sports. In fact, they wouldn't even take money to watch them. Norman Chad, the sports columnist, writes, "I realize this is somewhat politically incorrect to say, but I'd watch a seven-on-seven Arena Football scrimmage from a 7-Eleven parking lot before I'd watch a WNBA game from my couch."[7]

Studies have consistently shown that less than 10 percent of the column inches on newspaper sports pages or the screen time on televised sporting events is devoted to women's sports, though that number has likely increased in recent years due to the proliferation of low-rent cable sports channels scrounging for something to show between poker contests and dog shows.

Most network coverage of women's sports is now scrupulously p.c. Yes, the cameras may linger on Maria Sharapova longer than they do on some less comely tennis player, and the reason Jennie Finch is the only softball player with a name recognition factor higher than that of your typical assistant undersecretary of Commerce is not due solely to her talent, but to offset the camera's lovingly lingering on the Finches and Sharapovas, we are lectured by the announcers, ad nauseam, that the women's game is just as exciting and skill-filled as the men's. If we turn it off, as almost all of us do, it is because we are boors, not because they are bores.

Nevertheless, feminist academics have a field day picking apart the vocabularies of the announcers of women's sports. Mary Jo Kane and Janet B. Parks, hyperventilating on "The Social Construction of Gender Difference and Hierarchy in Sport Journalism—Few New Twists on Very Old Themes" in the august pages of *Women in Sport and Physical Activity Journal*, kvetch that in *Sports Illustrated*'s coverage of the French Open and Wimbledon, "the majority of the descriptors for female athletes focused on their emotions— [Steffi] Graff 'fled the court in tears' after her victory, and Sanchez 'hurried, crying into Graf's arms.'"[8]

One may hold no brief for the quality of sports journalism in our age, but surely when a competitor cries during or after a match that fact will make it into the subsequent story. Human (hu-persyn?) interest and all that.

The indomitable Ms. Parks was at it again, so to speak, this time with Mary Ann Roberton, her colleague at Bowling Green State University, in the pages of *Sex Roles*. Their article, which bore the un-tantalizing title "Influence of Age, Gender, and Context on Attitudes Toward Sexist/Nonsexist Language: Is Sport a Special Case?" inflicted a sexist language test on a sample of 292 students, faculty members, and others, including coaches. One's sexist-ness, if not sexiness, was determined by one's reaction to such burning questions as "how willing are you to use the term 'letter winners'. . . rather than 'lettermen'?" and does "calling the men's team 'Wildcats' and the women's team 'Wildkittens' reinforc[e] the idea of male superiority"?[9]

Threateningly, Parks and Roberton view sport as "an agent of social change." Yes, it is "a traditionally masculine domain that has a particularly strong emphasis on maintaining its traditions,"[10] but hey, traditions are made to be broken, and as for masculinity, well, just give the remakers time.

The language of sport vexes the authors. It "trivializes and diminishes female athletes, renders them invisible, denies their adulthood, and treats them as interlopers in a traditionally masculine domain." Despite their hectoring of students, Parks and Roberton reported that disturbingly few were willing to call the basketball defense "player-to-player" instead of man-to-man or to call the person who holds down Lou Gehrig's spot on the baseball diamond a "first-base player"[11] instead of a first baseman. That such changes would involve throwing out more than a century of tradition, of daily usage, of historically honored memories, means nothing to Parks and Roberton.

Sport, the authors found, was not a "special case." Those who play or coach athletics were no more or less likely to have a favorable attitude toward non-sexist language than were the nonathletic. Age, it turns out, did cleave the sample, though perhaps in an unexpected way: "Participants 23 years old and above were more favorable toward nonsexist language than were younger participants."[12] Hope, as always, resides in youth.

Michael A. Messner, Margaret Carlisle Duncan, and Kerry Jensen—notice how they list the male first, thus unconsciously ratifying the phallocracy?—preen and strut their feminist analysis of sports journalism for all to see in "Separating the Men from the Girls: The Gendered Language of Televised Sports," in the always entertaining *Gender and Society*.

Their opening sentence is a classic of the gender genre: "Feminist scholars have argued that in the twentieth century the institution of sport has provided men with a homosocial sphere of life through which they have bolstered the ideology of male superiority."

Plus they're fun to play!

Sport, the trio of authors asserts, "has provided a basis through which men have sought to reconstitute an otherwise challenged masculine hegemony." Well, yes, there's that, as well as dominating the Nobel Prize for Physics.

Working under a grant from the Amateur Athletic Foundation of Los Angeles, the intrepid team of "Mr." Messner and Ms. Duncan and Ms. Jensen did the sort of academic heavy-lifting that would put your typical Shakespearean scholar or research biochemist to shame: they watched TV. Like narcotized drones from sea to shining sea, they sat on their couches and watched the 1989 men's and women's NCAA basketball tournament Final Four and the 1989 men's and women's U.S. Open tournament.

Much as they might wish to cook the books, they admittedly "found less overtly sexist commentary than has been observed in past research."[13] Aw, shucks! But they did find, to their tut-tutting dismay, that announcers acknowledged that men and women are different.

For instance, the brutes at CBS Sports had the unmitigated temerity to refer to the tournament as the "Women's final four." They even called Tennessee coach Pat Summit "a legend in women's basketball." And although the men's tournament was referred to as "the men's championship," it was called simply The Final Four, not The Men's Final Four.[14] Be still my fainting heart.

CBS referred to the U.S. Open men's and women's singles and doubles tournaments in "a roughly equitable manner," conceded the TV-watching scholars, but—and this is a huge but—they used "a pink on-screen graphic for the women's matches and a blue on-screen graphic for the men's matches."[15]

The horror of it all!

But the crimes against women were just beginning. Both the tennis and the basketball announcers sometimes referred to the female athletes as "girls" or, even more offensively, "young ladies." Not a single male was referred to as a "boy." The fact that "boy" has unpleasant racial connotations when directed at black men was not a factor for our fearless scholars, nor was the generally younger age of female tennis pros.

The authors were also driven up the walls of their smoke-free apartments by the announcers' habit of using "the first name only of the women far more commonly than for the men."[16] This is a puzzler. Isn't the use of the first name a sign of familiarity, of affection, of respect? Isn't calling a player "Steffi" a friendlier ID than calling her "Graff"? After all, the men were not called "Mr." or referred to with an honorific before their names; the commentators simply used their last names.

Ever on the *qui vive*, the scholars also noted the tendency of the basketball announcers to refer to black players by their first names. This proves that at "the top of the linguistic hierarchy sit the always last-named white 'men.'"[17] We can't jump, it seems, but we can be called by our surnames. Not that that makes up for sitting at the end of the bench for the entire 40 minutes of a college basketball game.

One last offense against humanity: Tennessee coach Pat Summit was twice said to be "screaming" at her players, which, as anyone who has ever watched University of Tennessee women's basketball can tell you, Pat Summit—an excellent coach—is wont to do. "Screaming," the authors complain, "implies lack of control, powerlessness, even hysteria."[18] They note that the male coaches in the Final Four—excuse me, the Men's Final Four—were not described as screamers. Well, perhaps. But if one had a dollar for every time that Bobby Knight has been said to have "screamed" in his career, one might buy the state of Indiana and have enough left for Lubbock, too.

In the end, the 1989 NCAA basketball tournaments and the U.S. Open tennis tournament did one thing. No, they didn't offer an opportunity to watch some of the best male and female athletes ply their trades. Nor did they offer entertainment to the couch-sitting masses. Rather, they "construct[ed] and legitimiz[ed] heterosexual, white, middle-class men's power and privilege over subordinated and marginalized groups."[19] Bet you didn't know that.

The ways in which heterosexual, white, middle-class men assert their privilege and dominance over supine women, especially but not limited to lesbians of color, are various, *mani*fold, and oh so insidious. To the dismay of the people who speak in such gibberishese, and despite their insistence that women and blacks share victimhood in America, a common front never developed. Possibilities for an alliance of radical feminists and black radicals were aborted, if you will excuse the phrase, when black power radical Stokely Carmichael said in 1967, "The position of women in our movement should be prone."[20] Witty, perhaps, but hardly enlightened.

Carmichael's bad manners were matched by the feminists he abhorred, however. A year later, on September 7, 1968, a gaggle of feminists crowned a sheep Miss America whilst protesting the Bert Parks-emceed spectacle in Atlantic City. They tossed "old bras, girdles, high-heeled shoes, women's magazines, curlers, and other instruments of torture to women" into what they didactically called a "freedom ashcan."[21] They did not, contrary to legend, burn any bras—not that Stokely would have objected.

For a trip to what they call "the dark side" of intercollegiate athletics, we could have no more hysterical if unintentionally entertaining guides than the sober duo of D. Stanley Eitzen of Colorado State University and Maxine Baca Zinn of the University of Michigan-Flint. What do we find on the "dark side"? Not steroid-pumped thugs, or lads with a Stokely Carmichael-esque understanding of women, or "student-athletes" on scholarship who never bother attending class, or football players menacing coeds in their dorm rooms, or even the occasional under-the-table, $50-an-hour, no-show job that a money-bags alumnus arranges for the star halfback. No, these are mere peccadilloes; they barely register as foibles on the meter of sin carried by Professors Eitzen and Zinn. The real scandal of intercollegiate sports, they say, is in the sexist nicknames, logos, colors, and mascots that represent and cheer on these teams.

For as Eitzen and Zinn revealed in a 1989 paper published in *Sociology of Sport Journal*, more than half of the 1,185 four-year colleges and universities that field men's and women's athletic teams "employ names, mascots, and/or logos that demean and derogate women's teams." The reason? To maintain "male dominance within college athletics by defining women athletes and women's athletic programs as second class and trivial," of course.[22]

These nicknames have been shaped by patriarchal forces across time, we are informed by the learned, if no doubt unathletic, professors. The problem is much, much bigger than the fact that the University of Tennessee's storied basketball team is called the Lady Vols. For you see, men are christened with short, abrupt, upper-cut-to-the-jaw names (they instance Bret, Lance, and Bruce, which sound like a trio of hair stylists, but be that as it may). Women, on the other hand, are cursed with "melodic" and "softer"[23] names such as Deborah, Caroline, and Jessica. So you see, the patriarchy really has it in for women. They get the felicitous names and men get the one-syllable spurts.

The authors, suitably disgusted by such practices, turn their furrowed brows to team nicknames. They found that of the 1,185 schools in their sample, a shocking 451 employed sexist nicknames for their women's teams. (They also examined logos for 903 of the schools and found that 45.1 percent were sexist, which they seem to define as being identifiably female. Just why using a female image to identify a female team is sexist is a matter best taken up in Misogyny 201.)

The 451 sexist names fell into eight categories, though the first two categories contain only three nicknames: Belles, Rambelles, and Green Gals. Another 29 schools use feminine suffixes: the Duchesses, the Tigerettes. One hundred fourteen schools use the word lady (Lady Jets, Lady Eagles), which we are informed is a word that is intended to "demean" women because it "carries overtones recalling the age of chivalry."[24] Far and away the most common offensive nickname is the "male false generic": that is, a masculine name such as Rams or Stags or Cowboys or Hokies that is applied both to the men's and women's teams. A whopping 248 schools are guilty of this offense, though grant them a measure of pity: they really can't win. For you see, the next offensive category, with 21 miscreants, is "male name with female modifier." This would include, say, Lady Rams or Lady Stags or Lady Cowboys or Lady Hokies, if such things existed. So the teams are damned if they do and damned if they don't. Cowboys is sexist. Cowgirls is sexist. Cowbelles is sexist. Lady Cowboys is sexist. Heads the anti-Cowboys win, tails the Cowboys lose.

The nadir of nickname wickedness is reached by those schools that commit "double gender marking": that is, they modify the masculine name and then add a gratuitous "Lady" in front of it. The Lady Jags are one of the 10 examples of this hideous crime against half the human population. The eighth and final category, consisting of 26 institutions, is "male/female polarity": that is, a school that calls its male teams the Blue Hawks and its female teams the Blue Chicks. One might think that such a compromise is Solomonic in its wisdom, but these names, Eitzen and Zinn solemnly inform us, are often "playful and cuddly"[25] instead of, well, bitchy and dykish.

Predictably, "Southern schools [were] more likely to use sexist names than schools elsewhere." (Remember, they owned slaves.) They also promote "traditional notions of femininity,"[26] which apparently include dominating the

152   Chapter Seven

Top 20 in NCAA Women's Basketball, which schools from the Southeastern Conference (SEC) routinely do. In a ladylike manner, of course.

Eitzen and Zinn emerge from the study discouraged but with a grim resolution. "Institutional sexism is deeply entrenched in college sports,"[27] they sigh. Sexist nicknames "contribute to the maintenance of male dominance within college athletics."[28] Well, that and the fact that the Duke male basketball team could beat the Duke female basketball team by 100 points any day of the week.

But they have a plan. Change the names. Whether students, alumni, fans, or faculty want to or not, change the names. "Because language is intimately intertwined with the distribution of power in society," they conclude, "the principle of renaming can be an important way of changing reality."[29]

Big Brother—or Big Brotherette—couldn't have said it any better.

Eitzen and Zinn weren't done. Not by a long shot. Professor Eitzen next campaigned to change the nicknames of the teams at Colorado State University, the school where he was paid handsomely by the taxpayers of Colorado to propagandize—er, teach—impressionable young minds. His campaign was a spectacular failure, but it did yield another piece coauthored with the estimable Maxine Baca Zinn, this one bearing the oppressive title "The Sexist Naming of Collegiate Athletic Teams and Resistance to Change."

Resistance, in this case, was not futile.

Eitzen and Zinn, having studied the matter to death, or at least in much more detail than such a trivial subject deserves, therein decided to do something about it. These "blatantly sexist names"[30] cannot be permitted. And as it happens, Eitzen had the great misfortune to draw a salary from Colorado State, whose sports teams have been known, since 1946, as the Rams.

Colorado State began fielding women's intercollegiate athletic teams in 1976. They bore the nickname "Lady Rams," which, if you will recall, is an example of the dreaded "double gender marking." The nickname Ram is masculine, and therefore sexist, and the modifier "Lady" is demeaning, deprecating, offensive, slanderous, and virtually a libel on any woman saddled with the term.

Perhaps anticipating Eitzen's tantrum, CSU dropped "Lady" in 1987. The teams, both male and female, were thereafter known as "Rams."

The first sign that the Rams might run afoul of foul-tempered feminists and their male helpmeets came in 1981, when History Professor David McComb began a lonely letter-writing campaign complaining that Rams was insensitive and insulting. To women, that is, and not the sheep. Professor McComb took to the editorial pages of the student newspaper in 1988 and 1989 but he received "little support inside and outside the university." The Professor had found his Big Issue—something to make life worth living—but the benighted dolts in and around CSU could not have cared less. Cretins!

What's worse, female athletes at Colorado State—the very people on whose behalf Professor McComb allegedly was campaigning—not only did not support McComb, they opposed him. As Eitzen and Zinn report with long faces, the coaches of female athletic teams polled their players and found that the "women, regardless of their sport, overwhelmingly said that the name 'Ram' was a non-issue for them."[31] This was true of the coaches as well. The female coach of the women's softball team said that the use of Ram "doesn't bother me," and it didn't bother any other coach, either.

A female athlete turned the tables on McComb, writing in the school newspaper: "We feel that having a different mascot than the male athletic teams is sexist; the fact that the mascot happens to be a ram is not. . . . Real supporters concentrate on our efforts and accomplishments instead of our name."[32]

You can almost hear the good professor protest his innocence: But I'm doing it for you!

The professors attribute the overwhelming female support for Rams to "false consciousness." Women athletes, they write, "do not see the sexism inherent in the name."[33] They're too damned stupid!

Professor Eitzen rode to the rescue of the valiant anti-sexist crusader Professor McComb, but to no avail. He gave his "Sport and Society" class a questionnaire including the statement "The use of a ram (a male sheep) as the symbol for female teams at CSU is sexist and should be changed." We can expect that the good professor, shall we say, urged his students to take a certain view of the matter, but the bullheaded Rams did not: on a scale of one to five, with one being "strongly agree" and five "strongly disagree," Eitzen's 94 students averaged a 4.32, which he concedes was "a very strong rejection of the statement."[34] There was no real difference between males and females or athletes and nonathletes: everyone rejected the imputation of sexism.

The Faculty Senate—in most universities a bastion of political correctness—assigned this burning question to its Committee on Intercollegiate Athletics, which gathered data from various sources and issued an all-but-unanimous report affirming its support of the "Rams." Only one member objected: Professor Eitzen, who produced a minority report which gathered only his lone signature. Can't you just see him strike his pose? The valorous martyr, the non-sexist Gary Cooper standing up to the dark forces of McCarthyism. Be still your beating hearts, Lady Rams!

Eitzen emerged from the battle hardened in his contempt for students and democratic procedures. He views the anti-Rams crusade as a study in "how a school name is accepted by most without question even when it is sexist." The women of CSU were sadly unenlightened. Rumor has it that many even like men. But Eitzen was not content to accept the verdict of all of his neighbors and colleagues. "Since a sexist team name reinforces and socializes sexist thinking and practices, it must be changed."[35] To the gas chambers, Ram-lovers! This sentence carries a strong whiff of totalitarianism.

What to do? First comes propaganda: the university must "strive to educate the public about the moral correctness" of rejecting the nickname Rams. But what if the public disagrees, as it so manifestly does in this case? Then it's time to bulldoze the public: "To await a mandate from the public, as the case study . . . has shown, insures that sexism will continue just as racism would have surely continued in the South if the federal government had not forced the issue on the white majority in the 1950s and 1960s."[36] In other words, people who like or do not object to calling the Colorado State teams the Rams, including pretty much every female athlete on the Rams, have the moral status of Klansmen. They must be bulldozed; their opinions must be disregarded; they must be forcibly re-educated by their moral superiors, for instance Professors Eitzen and McComb. Though the case of the Colorado State Rams may seem trivial, totalitarian feminism doesn't get much more obvious, or much uglier, than this.

If you think the theory class throws a collective conniption fit when a hapless TV talking head calls a 15-year-old female tennis player a "girl" or a female college basketball player a "Lady Vol," you should hear what they say about that violent collision of masculinity and commerce known as football.

Peter Carlson of the *Washington Post* decided to interview a gaggle of (mostly male) anthropologists and other assessors of the human condition about the Super Bowl. You remember the Super Bowl: that occasion for the orgy of wife-beating that NOW claims happens every bleak midwinter. Well, it's even worse than you, me, or NOW thought. Keith Strudler, a professor of communications at Marist College, sneered, "The Super Bowl is the reinforcement of everything American. It serves a functionalist purpose, reinforcing ideas of military strength, cultural supremacy, and gender norms."

Where others see superb athletes running, throwing, blocking, and tackling, Professor Strudler sees . . . well, let him tell you what he sees. "Other sports are about scoring points," he says, perhaps forgetting that the object of a football game is to score more points than one's opponent. "Football," Strudler insists, "is about taking territory. And you have the generals running the show—either the coach or the quarterback—and before the game you have the flyover by the military jets." Adding sexist insult to militaristic injury, "Men do the fighting and women do the cheering."

According to University of California at Berkeley anthropology Professor Alan Dundes, those quarterbacks and coaches are interested less in the cheerleaders than in the tight end.

"The lingo is so sexual—to score, to go all the way, deep penetration, jocks," says Dundes. "You have all this sexual imagery. Plus the military language—the blitz, the bomb, the sack, down in the trenches. It's all this stuff about pillage and rape." (Rape? Which of those phrases are redolent of rape?)

Then Dundes opens the closet door. "The way the linemen line up is kind of an odd position, don't you think?" he asked Peter Carlson. "You're basically presenting yourself to your own quarterback . . . It all has to do with primates. When primates want to show dominance, they don't just snarl and growl. One male will mount the other male. You assert your domination by putting your opponents in a feminine position. And when the team is losing at halftime, the coach says, 'Get into the locker room, ladies.'"[37]

There is one sport, one male activity, one traditional pasttime engaged in largely by men that makes football seem by comparison as p.c. as a Melissa Etheridge concert. And that is shooting. With guns. And again, the feminist response is to ban the sport. Ban the gun.

"Ban" is such a harsh, ugly, male-sounding word, though. The milder, less confrontational gun prohibitionists shy from it. They like nice words, words that don't sound so forceful. So masculine.

In fact, corrupting language is essential to the gun controllers. When the Million Moms March of 2000 descended on Washington, DC—several hundred thousand moms short of its title—they claimed to be jackbooting their way through the Imperial City in the cause of stopping "gun violence." Or, in the ridiculous euphemism of gun-prohibitionist Senator Frank Lautenburg (D-NJ), "They were pleading for child safety."[38]

And what sort of monster can possibly be against child safety? The implication, of course, is that those who disagree with the Million Moms are against child safety. They are furtive, disreputable, creepy: they hang out on street corners and whisper to impressionable tykes, "Hey, kid, take off that bike helmet," or "Say there, sweetie, can I interest you in a high-tar starter cigarette?"

Liberal gun-control groups have reorganized under such vanilla monikers as Americans for Gun Safety. But—wink, wink, nudge, nudge—we all know what safety is a euphemism for. Carrie Nation, after all, was for saloon safety.

Although nowhere near a million human beings, let alone a million moms, marched in that overhyped demonstration of 2000, subsequent demonstrators have patterned themselves after the Million Moms. A Washington, DC March for Women's Lives in April 2004 paired the causes of abortion and gun control. Curiously, and without regard for that consistency which Ralph Waldo Emerson—a man, admittedly—said was the hobgoblin of small minds, the marchers were "pro-choice" on the former and anti-choice on the latter. In the pages of *USA Today*, editorialist Mary Zeiss Stange, the token independent mind in the Women's Studies department at Skidmore College, noted that it "is odd when it comes to gun control, feminists welcome the same sorts of government intrusion on individual rights that they rightly abhor when it comes to reproductive freedom." Stange, drawing on the work of Professor Nicholas Johnson, a constitutional law scholar at Fordham Law School, argued for a common philosophical base in the defense of gun rights and abortion rights. Each, she claimed, is based on the rights to self-defense; to the protection of "one's own physical integrity"; to personal autonomy; and to the "right to make private choices regarding life decisions."[39]

But somehow, the concept of "choice" never does seem to be extended to gun ownership, even though our gun laws remain considerably less tyrannical than those of Europe. Foreigners sneer, as does *The Economist* of England, that the U.S. is "the only rich nation in the world where mothers find it easier to procure a gun than a welfare cheque."[40] This is an odd put-down from a publication that has more than a passing familiarity with free-market principles. For you see, women buy guns with their own money, while the welfare "cheque" comes from the taxpayer.

The Economist should keep its sneer to itself. British women have been among the most adept users of firearms. As Mary A. Procida writes in her study of women and firearms in the British colony of India, "many British women in India were competent markswomen who employed their skills in a wide variety of ways, including target practice and recreational hunting. They used their knowledge of firearms, as well, to protect themselves, their families, and their empire from the threat posed by the wild animals of the Indian subcontinent and, during the nationalist disturbances of the 1920s and 1930s, from the even more insidious dangers of Indian terrorists."[41] Far from representing a revolt against the patriarchy or an uprising against British male tyranny, these women simply viewed the gun as a necessary and perhaps enjoyable tool. Their husbands encouraged their hunting and shooting and even took delight in displays of their marksmanship.

No trace of these spunky British women was in evidence in May 2004, when a scraggly remnant of Million Moms milled around the west lawn of the Capitol in their "Mother's Day March to Halt the Assault."

What assault? you ask. Why, the assault on the assault weapons ban, that phony Clinton-era gun control measure that effectively banned certain hunting rifles for no good reason other than to make liberals feel good about themselves. The founder of the Million Moms, Donna Dees-Thomases, a Hollywood crony who posed as the mom-next-door and was assisted in this deception by a compliant puppy-dog media, told the credulous that if the ban expired, "terrorists, drug lords and the mentally unstable will be able to stock up on assault weapons that can wipe out a schoolyard full of kids in a matter of minutes."[42]

Now that's dispassionate and closely reasoned discourse! In any event, the ban did expire, and psychotic nuts and al Qaeda agents did not rush out to buy their weapons of mass destruction at the local K-Mart. The fact that long guns are virtually never used in rapes and sexual assaults—and in fact guns of any kind are used in only 4 percent of these crimes—somehow escaped mention in the collected speeches of Ms. Dees-Thomases.

Mother's Day may come nine months after Father's Day, as the wag says, but for the organizers of these marches fathers don't deserve five minutes of honor, never mind an entire Sunday. For although the gun is the object of execration whenever the Million (give or take 975,000) Moms march, the real enemy, lurking darkly in the background, is the American male.

For instance, Lolis Eric Elie of the *Times-Picayune* of New Orleans went so far as to claim, based on statistics from a rabid gun-control group misnamed the Violence Policy Center, that "Louisiana is a particularly dangerous place for women."[43] Now, this is true if you're a woman and you run into a drunken politician during Mardi Gras, and it was certainly true during Hurricane Katrina in 2005, but that is not what Lolis Eric Elie meant. No, the learned Elie was quoting a Violence Policy Center study that claimed that men killed an average of 2.91 women per 100,000 in the Bayou State. Yes, of course, even one murder is too many, but to say to the 99,997 women out of every 100,000 who are not killed that their state is dangerous, their very life parlous and lived on the edge of the precipice, is idiotic.

If anything, the women of Louisiana could increase their safety by buying a gun. As a quartet of Canadian women argued vainly when their nation tightened its already stringent gun regulations, "gun controls are detrimental primarily to the people who are most vulnerable to violence and the least able to defend themselves in a physical struggle, namely women and the elderly."[44] (The situation in Canada has reached such a state of absurdity that citizens are forbidden from carrying pepper spray to deter attackers.)

According to criminologist Gary Kleck, women were involved in over 50 percent of the two-and-a-half million incidents from 1988–1993 in which a gun was used defensively in the United States. (The gun was fired in only eight percent of those cases.) So Louisiana Governor Mike Foster had a point when he told the women of Baton Rouge, who in 2002 were terrorized by a serial killer, "if you know how [to use a gun] and you have a situation with some fruitcake running around, like they've got right now, it sure can save you a lot of grief."[45]

Gun owners and gun rights groups have tried to make this point to the women of America, with varying degrees of success. The vast majority (85 percent) of the National Rifle Association's almost four million members are men, though its nearly half a million female members dwarf the female membership of, for instance, the National Organization for Women, whose membership claims—like those of most direct-mail political groups—cannot be taken seriously. (Such organizations typically count anyone on their mailing list as a member, which leads to absurdly inflated membership claims that are passed on by a helpful press.)

The NRA has established an Office on Women's Issues and has promoted the notion of gun-ownership as an act of self-defense for women. Groups promoting and defending gun ownership for women have sprung up under such fetching monikers as the Liberty Belles and the Second Amendment Sisters. Smith and Wesson introduced a LadySmith revolver to the approval of feminine shootists.

In the wake of 9/11, gun dealers and firearms safety instructors reported far more women than ever before exercising their rights to gun ownership. Still, Florida, to take one example, reports that only 15 percent of its concealed carry permits are held by women. Annie Oakleys remain the exception.

It would be heartening to report that women are as strongly committed to Second Amendment liberties as are men. It would certainly be in their interest to be so. Nevertheless, two facts are incontrovertible. First, that firearms ownership is far more common among men. And second, that women are significantly more likely than men to favor government control over or even confiscation of firearms.

On the first point, there is evidence, as scholars Tom W. Smith and Robert J. Smith write in "Changes in Firearms Ownership Among Women, 1980–1994," published in the *Journal of Criminal Law and Criminology*, that "pro-gun groups and the media have exaggerated the rate of gun ownership among women."

One of the most commonly referenced findings was a survey by Smith and Wesson claiming that the rate of gun ownership by American women increased an astounding 53 percent between 1983 and 1986. According to the Smiths, who, it must be pointed out, appear to write from a pro-gun regulation point of view, the Smith and Wesson claim resulted from confusion over a Gallup poll in which women were asked not if they were gun owners but if they were potential buyers. In any case, optimistic estimates of the rate of female gun ownership usually rely on affirmative answers to such questions as "Is there a gun in your house?"

The Smiths' more conservative—which is to say politically liberal—judgement is that perhaps 11–12 percent of women own a gun and between five and eight percent own a handgun.[46]

The pro-gun Wendy McElroy estimates that about 40 percent of men and 10 percent of women own guns, though the percentage of women who live in a gun-owning household may approach 30 percent. Mary Zeiss Stange and

Carol K. Oyster, coauthors of the "unabashedly feminist"[47] but unashamedly pro-gun *Gun Women: Firearms and Feminism in Contemporary America* (2000), estimate that from 11–17 million American women are firearms owners. They also assert that the percentage of the U.S. hunting population that is female has zoomed from perhaps three percent to upwards of ten percent.

This is all to the good, from the viewpoint of those who cherish traditional American liberties. Yet the most visible and emotional advocates of gun prohibition have been women, from Sarah Brady, whose husband Jim was crippled in the 1981 shooting of Ronald Reagan; to Carolyn McCarthy, who parlayed her husband's tragic 1993 death aboard a Long Island Railroad commuter train at the hands of an anti-white maniac named Colin Ferguson into a seat in the U.S. House of Representatives as a liberal Democrat and gun prohibitionist.

These women use language imprecisely, as their ideological ilk are wont to do. For instance, Mrs. Brady heads the Brady Campaign to Prevent Gun Violence, which might be more accurately denominated the Brady Campaign to Repeal the Second Amendment.

Brady and McCarthy stand arm in arm with such gun-control zealots as Senator Barbara Boxer (D-CA), the former cheerleader from Brooklyn who moved to the Golden State and brought Big Apple statism with her.

Boxer's senior senator is California Democrat Dianne Feinstein, the woman who had the distinction of being nosed out by Geraldine Ferraro in the 1984 Democratic vice-presidential sweepstakes because Walter Mondale's background checkers judged Feinstein's husband to be even less reputable than Ferraro's hubbie, the notorious John Zaccaro. Senator Feinstein has said, "Banning guns addresses a fundamental right of Americans to feel safe."[48] This is a "fundamental right" of the sort enjoyed, perhaps, by a prisoner, or an inmate in a lunatic asylum, but not by a freeborn American. One has a right to life, to liberty, to property, but not to "safety," under which word any manner of government intervention may be excused.

Senator Feinstein would seem to confirm anti-suffragist Emma Goldman's fear that women politicians would elevate busybodyism to a fine art. Unfortunately, she is more typical than not. Feinsteins flourish not only in Washington but in the 50 state capitals as well.

Studying those laboratories of democracy from Augusta to Honolulu, a trio of political scientists—Geralyn M. Miller, Linda Murphy, and Thomas D. Stucky—used the 2000 National Political Awareness Test to establish that "net of relevant factors such as party, region, and education, gender strongly impacts the policy preferences of state legislators on gun control issues. Specifically . . . female legislators indicate much higher preferences for gun control policies than male legislators."[49]

Their constituents evince similar attitudes. Public opinion polls consistently show that women are significantly more likely than men to favor gun control or prohibition. If the notoriously anti-gun Louis Harris Poll's optimistic 1993 prediction that banning guns would be "the next great women's issue in the country"[50] has not come true, neither have women politicos distinguished themselves as brave and steely defenders of the Second Amendment.

At the time of the paper's presentation to the 2003 Annual Meeting of the Midwest Political Science Association, almost one-quarter (23 percent) of state legislature seats were held by women. Washington was tops at 37 percent, while Neanderthalic—and freer?—South Carolina lagged with but 9.4 percent of its seats filled by female bottoms.

The triune authors note political scientist Sue Thomas's prediction—or is it a threat?—that "bringing women into politics has the potential to usher in new ways of doing things or new things to do."[51] These "new things" are uniformly statist: they cost taxpayers money, they require greater regimentation and a more powerful state, they lead to more folks being thrown into jail or thrown onto the gravy train. They often use as rhetorical cover such unassailable goals as "safety" or—always the trump card—protecting the children. The National Foundation for Women Legislators found that in the first three years of the twenty-first century, women sponsored three-quarters of legislation involving domestic violence, sexual harassment, and teen pregnancy.[52] If a single bill called for less government intervention in these matters, it would be a shocker.

Female state legislators also support stricter, more onerous gun controls across every individual manifestation of the issue, from mandatory child-safety locks to licensing laws to background checks. Liberty and privacy are nonstarters when it comes to lady legislators: safety and statism are their beau ideals.

"Men supported easing or repealing restrictions and conceal and carry laws, whereas women were more likely to support banning the sale of semi-automatic weapons, enforcing existing gun restrictions, and background checks or licensing gun owners,"[53] concluded the authors. And if nine out of ten of these legislators couldn't tell a semi-automatic weapon from a Pez dispenser . . . well, it's for the safety of the children. Please check your liberties at the door, gentlemen.

Canadian lawyer Marilou McPhedran, who sits on a federal gun control panel, sees the issue as a battle, sometimes bloody, between the sexes. "Part of my role here is to ask repeatedly for gender-based analysis,"[54] McPhedran bleats. One rather doubts that her analysis incorporates research showing that men and women commit acts of violence against each other in roughly equal numbers.

Underlying the position of McPhedran, Senators Boxer and Feinstein, and the phalanx of lady gun controllers is a worldview summarized by Alana Bassin in the *Hasting Women's Law Review*: "Firearms are a source of male domination—a symbol of male power and aggression. . . . First, the gun is phallic. Just as sex is the ultimate weapon of patriarchy used to penetrate and possess women, the gun's sole purpose is to intrude and wound its victim. Historically, men have used guns to conquer and dominate other people."

"Packing a Pistol Perpetuates Patriarchy," says Bassin in an alliterative mood. Gun control is therefore a way to "curb the perpetuation of patriarchy"[55]—to control men.

Even kind and helpful men must be controlled and put under constant surveillance. Among the more astonishingly bigoted pieces of social comment to appear in recent years was an essay in the December 1989 *Yale Law Journal* by one Wendy Brown, who teaches—what else?—Women's Studies at the University of California at Santa Cruz. It seems that Professor Brown and some sisterly comrades had gone backpacking in the High Sierras. They returned to a car that would not start.

What to do?

Now, the sorts of feminists who populate Women's Studies texts would have rolled up their sleeves, pumped their glistening muscles, and fixed the car. But these women were quite helpless. Brown, the damsel in distress, flagged another motorist, a man wearing an "NRA freedom" hat. She called him, sneeringly—from the safe remove of the *Yale Law Journal*—"a California sportsman making his way through a case of beer, flipping through the pages of a porn magazine and preparing to survey the area for his hunting club in anticipation of the opening of deer season."[56]

In the words of Mary Zeiss Stange and Carol K. Oyster, who were appalled by Professor Brown's snobbery, "After two hours of concentrated labor, the man managed to get Brown's auto running, and she and her friends were on their way."

Was Professor Brown grateful? Surely you jest! No, she was relieved that this encounter with Primitive Man had not resulted in a violent act, even death: "It occurred to me then, and now, that if I had run into him in those woods without my friends or a common project for us to work on, I would have been seized with one great and appropriate fear: rape. During the hours I spent with him, I had no reason to conclude that his respect for women's personhood ran any deeper than his respect for the lives of Sierra deer, and his gun could well have made the difference between an assault that my hard-won skills in self-defense could have fended off and one against which they were useless."[57]

If only Brown had "hard-won skills" in car repair!

This is about as ugly an example of middle-class feminist disrespect for working-class men as one is likely to find. The poor guy plays the Good Samaritan, spending two hours helping some snotty feminists and fixing their car, and off Wendy Brown drives, back to the comfort of her affluence to write an arrogant paper ridiculing as a potential rapist the man who rescued her!

Douglas Laycock noted that the fact that the man was white permitted Brown to spew her venom. Imagining that the same encounter had taken place between Brown and a black man who was equipped with gun, beer, and porno mags, Laycock writes: "Either her fear of rape would not have appeared in a respectable journal, or it would have appeared in a confessional tone and emphasized a very different moral. The point would have been: 'He came only to help me, and I was afraid to let him; see how fear and racism distorts our whole society.' The point would not have been: 'I was forced to ask him for help, and it is a good thing I was not alone or he might have raped me.'"[58]

The potency, if you will excuse the word, of the image of The Gun throws feminists into a veritable tizzy. Guns perpetuate patriarchy, guns make men feel manly, guns keep women in their place—which is six feet under, or so men are said to believe. Misandry—misogyny's just as unattractive twin—raises its castrating hand on both sides of the gun debate. Stange and Oyster report that pro-gunners Tara Baxter and Nikki Craft market buttons bearing such slogans as "So Many Men, So Little Ammunition," "Men and Women Were Created Equal, and Smith and Wesson Make Damn Sure It Stays That Way," "The Best Way to a Man's Heart Is Through His Chest," "Feminine Protection" (a gun, naturally), and "How Dare You Assume I'm Non-Violent."[59] Baxter and Craft have tongues in cheek—I hope.

Sociologist H. Taylor Buckner of Concordia University in Montreal has framed the matter of gun control in a way that is joltingly honest and refreshingly unconventional. After conducting three surveys of Concordia students and their attitudes toward gun ownership and control in 1993–1994, he concluded that "gun control is, symbolically, male control."[60]

That deserves to be repeated. Gun control is, symbolically, male control.

Buckner undertook his research after noticing the gap between women and men in their opinions of gun control. Trying, vainly, to discern the rational basis for these opinions, he wondered if perhaps the question had become purely "an emotional and symbolic issue."[61]

Buckner, puzzled by the ferocity of feminist hostility toward guns and their owners, was admittedly stunned by the responses of pro-gun control Concordia students to sentence-completion questionnaires. Asked to finish the sentence "When I think of Gun Clubs, I think . . ." pro-control women conjured up "Violent men," "heartless men," "uneducated" men displaying their "ignorance," "Boys trying to prove their value," and other spiteful, often condescendingly class-ist remarks.

Pro-control males, asked to complete the sentence "When I think about Hunters, I think . . ." filled in the blank with "Idiots," people who are "sadistic" or have an "inferiority complex," and, most humanely, "I'd rather they shoot each other."[62] The pro-control students, we may be sure, love Bambi—in the abstract, that is; most have never seen a deer in their lives and would flee at the first sight of antlers—but they hate Bubba.

Using regression analysis on a 1994 representative sample of 780 students, Buckner concluded that "men and women have different patterns of motivation for being pro gun control. The men who favor gun control are those who reject traditional male roles and behavior. They are opposed to hunting, are pro homosexual, do not have any experience with or knowledge of guns and tend to have 'politically correct' attitudes. The women who support gun control do so in the context of controlling male violence and sexuality. Gun control is thus symbolic of a realignment between the sexes."[63]

That realignment is well underway in Buckner's home to our north. Canada, whose firearms regulations are among the most oppressive in the world, became Ground Zero in the debate on December 6, 1989, after a psychotic nut named Marc Lepine, agitated by his rejection from the L'Ecole Polytechnique in Montreal, burst into a classroom, shouted "you are all feminists," and, in a rampage that took him through three floors of the building, massacred 14 women (and killed himself) with a semi-automatic hunting rifle. (One of the women he stabbed to death with a knife.) Twenty-seven women were injured.

Feminists and gun prohibitionists exploited the L'Ecole Polytechnique tragedy as shamelessly as Bill Clinton milked the Oklahoma City bombing for political gain. It demonstrated, in the words of federal Women's Minister Mary Collins, that "Men often have a feeling of omnipotence . . . that they have to control women and control can also be exercised through violence."

Coalition for Gun Control Executive Director Heidi Rathjen asked the Status of Women Committee, "How is this murderer different . . . from a man who is unhappy and blames, denigrates and regards with contempt everything female around him?"[64] Well, for one thing, that imaginary man does not go around slaughtering women at will. . . .

And for another, "Marc Lepine" was not born Marc Lepine but rather Gamil Gharbi. Son of an Algerian father and French Canadian mother, he grew up in a broken home allegedly wracked by violence. Young Gamil was rejected by the Canadian Armed Forces for anti-social tendencies; he was such a sociopath that even an organization ostensibly committed to violent acts against strangers would not accept him. By the time he enrolled as a long-shot candidate for admission to L'Ecole Polytechnique, he was penniless and had been unemployed for some time.

Gharbi/Lepine left a demented suicide note blaming feminism for his troubles. Unlike most death-dispatches of crazed psychopaths, Lepine's was treated with great gravity after his death. His communique was not the mad scribbling of a wicked man but an archetypal document by yet another man committed to "shutting up women."[65] Lepine was no nut, according to the feminist press: he was just a man with the courage of his evil masculine convictions.

Had Marc Lepine been a rural man without formal education, he'd have been the apotheosis of how H. Taylor Buckner's students imagine a gun owner. Better yet if he had been an American male. For even in an unarmed state we are the personification of patriarchal tyranny. Give us a gun and the weak of heart faint, the cowards take cover, and feminists pound furiously at their keyboards, trying to efface us on paper—for starters.

Just how successful the campaign against the American male will be remains an open question. Large shards of feminist orthodoxy are deeply embedded in the U.S. education and political systems; in other areas, a common-sense resistance has blunted the deadlier shafts of male-hatred. Ultimately, the would-be tyrants of Big Sister feminism cannot overcome liberty-loving Americans if we act with a combination of vigilance, passion, reason, good humor, and courage. Contrary to Women's Studies 101 textbooks, men and women are not enemies. We are, instead, spouses, lovers, complements, friends. It's the busybodies, the remolders, the anti-male propagandists who are the enemy. In denying our humanity, they make themselves all that much less human. And it doesn't take an English teacher to tell us which way the pronouns are pointing.

NOTES

1. Hise, *The War Against Men*, 110.
2. Michael A. Messner, Margaret Carlisle Duncan, and Kerry Jensen, "Separating the Men from the Girls: The Gendered Language of Televised Sports," *Gender and Society* 7, no. 1 (March 1993): 122.
3. Sommers, *The War Against Boys*, 52.
4. Bob Ryan, "New Rule Engenders Equal Footing," *Boston Globe*, April 20, 2004, C4.
5. Messner, Duncan, and Jensen, "Separating the Men from the Girls," 122.
6. "Girls Use Steroids, Too," *Omaha World-Herald*, May 2, 2005, B6.
7. "Comfort Zone," *Rochester Democrat & Chronicle*, July 31, 2005, D1.
8. Mary Jo Kane and Janet B. Parks, "The Social Construction of Gender Difference and Hierarchy in Sport Journalism—Few New Twists on Very Old Themes," *Women in Sport & Physical Activity Journal* 1, no. 1 (1992): 49.

9. Janet B. Parks and Mary Ann Roberton, "Influence of Age, Gender, and Context on Attitudes Toward Sexist/Nonsexist Language: Is Sport a Special Case?" *Sex Roles* 38, nos. 5/6 (March 1998): 479.

10. Parks and Roberton, "Influence of Age, Gender, and Context," 480.
11. Parks and Roberton, "Influence of Age, Gender, and Context," 481.
12. Parks and Roberton, "Influence of Age, Gender, and Context," 477.
13. Messner, Duncan, and Jensen, "Separating the Men from the Girls," 121.
14. Messner, Duncan, and Jensen, "Separating the Men from the Girls," 125.
15. Messner, Duncan, and Jensen, "Separating the Men from the Girls," 126.
16. Messner, Duncan, and Jensen, "Separating the Men from the Girls," 127–28.
17. Messner, Duncan, and Jensen, "Separating the Men from the Girls," 131.
18. Messner, Duncan, and Jensen, "Separating the Men from the Girls," 130.
19. Messner, Duncan, and Jensen, "Separating the Men from the Girls," 132.
20. Mason, *The Equality Trap*, 39.
21. O'Neill, *Feminism in America*, ix.
22. D. Stanley Eitzen and Maxine Baca Zinn, "The De-Athleticization of Women: The Naming and Gender Marking of Collegiate Sport Teams," *Sociology of Sport Journal* 6 (1989): 362.

23. Eitzen and Zinn, "The De-Athleticization of Women," 364.
24. Eitzen and Zinn, "The De-Athleticization of Women," 365.
25. Eitzen and Zinn, "The De-Athleticization of Women," 366.
26. Eitzen and Zinn, "The De-Athleticization of Women," 368.
27. Eitzen and Zinn, "The De-Athleticization of Women," 369.
28. Eitzen and Zinn, "The De-Athleticization of Women," 362.
29. Eitzen and Zinn, "The De-Athleticization of Women," 369.
30. D. Stanley Eitzen and Maxine Baca Zinn, "The Sexist Naming of Collegiate Athletic Teams and Resistance to Change," *Journal of Sport and Social Issues* 17 (1993): 35.

31. Eitzen and Zinn, "The Sexist Naming," 36.
32. Eitzen and Zinn, "The Sexist Naming," 36–37.
33. Eitzen and Zinn, "The Sexist Naming," 40.
34. Eitzen and Zinn, "The Sexist Naming," 37.
35. Eitzen and Zinn, "The Sexist Naming," 39.
36. Eitzen and Zinn, "The Sexist Naming," 40.
37. Peter Carlson, "Everything You Wanted To Know About Football But Were Afraid To Ask," *Washington Post*, February 6, 2005, D1.
38. Elizabeth Williamson and Cameron W. Barr, "March Leaders Not Settling for High Turnout," *Washington Post*, April 27, 2004, B1.
39. Mary Zeiss Stange, "Guns, Like Abortion, Are a Matter of Choice," *USA Today*, May 6, 2004, 13A.
40. "Lexington: Freedom, Guns, and Women," *The Economist*, June 14, 1997, 30.
41. Mary A. Procida, "Good Sports and Right Sorts: Guns, Gender, and Imperialism in British India," *Journal of British Studies* 40, no. 4 (October 2001): 455.
42. Stange, "Guns, Like Abortion, are a Matter of Choice."

43. Lolis Eric Elie, "Putting a Black Face on Violence," (New Orleans) *Times-Picayune*, November 12, 2004, 1.

44. Claire Joly, Marie Latourelle, Maryse Martin, and Karen Selick, "Testosterone and Gun Control," (Montreal) *Le Devoir*, February 19, 1999, A11.

45. Wendy McElroy, "War May Redefine Gun Control," <www.gunowners.org> (April 2003).

46. Tom W. Smith and Robert J. Smith, "Changes in Firearm Ownership among Women, 1980–1994," *Journal of Criminal Law and Criminology* 86, no. 1 (Autumn 1995): 145.

47. Mary Zeiss Stange and Carol K. Oyster, *Gun Women: Firearms and Feminism in Contemporary America* (New York: New York University Press, 2000), 2.

48. Rachel Jurado, "Gun Control Victims: Women Receive Little Encouragment for Self-Defense from Mainstream Feminists," *The American Enterprise*, January-February 2004, 44.

49. Geralyn M. Miller, Linda Murphy, and Thomas D. Stucky, "Gender, Guns and Legislating: An Analysis of State Legislative Policy Preferences," presented at the 2003 Annual Meetings of the Midwest Political Science Association, 2.

50. Stange and Oyster, *Gun Women*, 24.

51. Miller, Murphy, and Stucky, "Gender, Guns and Legislating," 3.

52. Miller, Murphy, and Stucky, "Gender, Guns and Legislating," 5.

53. Miller, Murphy, and Stucky, "Gender, Guns and Legislating," 16.

54. Crawford, "25 Years of Women Making Progress," *Toronto Star*.

55. Quoted in Richard Poe, "Guns and Feminism," <www.lewrockwell.com> (6 November 2003).

56. Stange and Oyster, *Gun Women*, 36.

57. Stange and Oyster, *Gun Women*, 37.

58. Stange and Oyster, *Gun Women*, 38.

59. Stange and Oyster, *Gun Women*, 44.

60. H. Taylor Buckner, "Sex and Guns: Is Gun Control Male Control?" presented to the American Sociological Association Annual Meeting, August 5, 1994, <www.tbuckner.com/SEXGUN>, 14.

61. Buckner, "Sex and Guns," 1.

62. Buckner, "Sex and Guns," 9.

63. Buckner, "Sex and Guns," 1.

64. Buckner, "Sex and Guns," 2.

65. Rebecca MacDonald, Siobhan Taylor, Sara Reardon, Michael Coughlan, and Carl Dalton, "Masculinism, Feminism, and a Gun: A Look Behind the Belief Structure of the Ecole Polytechnique Murders," *Truth & Society*, March 27, 2003, 5.